C000048415

Rethinking Rural

Series Editors
Philomena de Lima
Centre for Remote and Rural Studies
University of the Highlands and Islands
Inverness, UK

Belinda Leach
Guelph, ON, Canada

This series will foreground rural places and communities as diverse, mutually constitutive and intrinsic to contemporary Sociology scholarship, deeply imbricated in globalisation and colonisation processes stretched across national spaces. This is in contrast to an urban focus which is the implicit norm where (urban) place often can appear as the sole backdrop to social life.

Rather than rural places being marginal to Sociology, this series emphasises these places as embodying plural visions, voices and experiences which are fundamental to making sense of places as sites of solidarity, contestation and disruption in different national contexts.

Colin Turbett • Jane Pye
Editors

Rural Social Work in the UK

Themes and Challenges for the Future

Editors
Colin Turbett
Shiskine, Isle of Arran, UK

Jane Pye
Bowland North
Lancaster University
Bailrigg, Lancaster, Lancashire, UK

ISSN 2730-7123   ISSN 2730-7131   (electronic)
Rethinking Rural
ISBN 978-3-031-52439-4   ISBN 978-3-031-52440-0   (eBook)
https://doi.org/10.1007/978-3-031-52440-0

Cover illustration: Mr Doomits / Alamy Stock Photo

This Palgrave Macmillan imprint is published by the registered company Springer Nature Switzerland AG. The registered company address is: Gewerbestrasse 11, 6330 Cham, Switzerland

Paper in this product is recyclable.

Foreword

Although the UK was one of the first industrialised countries, with rapid urbanisation taking place in the nineteenth and early twentieth centuries, significant numbers of people still live in rural areas and many of them are poorly served by social services. The problems they endure are often exacerbated by social isolation, sparse service provision, and poor transport networks. Furthermore, concerns about confidentiality, stigmatisation, or personal safety may result in a reluctance to engage with social work services. In the UK, rural social work remains an under-recognised and little researched aspect of social work practice. Consequently, prospective service users may have difficulty in accessing and using services, while practitioners may feel isolated and uncertain as to how best to deliver them.

This collection is a welcome addition to the relatively scarce literature. It provides a wide-ranging set of contemporary readings written by practitioners and educators from a variety of standpoints. The contributors recognise that there is considerable diversity in rural settings and do not attempt to establish some general theory of rural practice. Instead, what they share is a common recognition of the importance of understanding context in rural work. While much of the social work literature assumes an implicitly urban context, and rarely develops any discussion of the underlying assumptions about how and where practice takes place, rural social work often necessitates an understanding of how these broader factors shape service users' experiences and how they impinge upon practitioner's efforts to deliver services.

The social dynamics of small communities may be important features in understanding how best to plan and deliver services. For instance, the increased social visibility of both workers and service users in more sparsely populated rural areas may not permit the relative anonymity and privacy of personal life that is possible in larger towns and cities. Indeed, managing dual relationships where workers and clients encounter each other outside of the professional meeting, perhaps at the local garage, playgroup or pub, can be challenging. Similarly, while the social visibility of minority groups and individuals may result in greater vulnerability, the likelihood of discrimination may also depend upon perceptions of deservedness, family ties, or social utility, as well as local concerns about incomers, school closures, and depopulation.

Several chapters consider how workers might engage with contemporary issues—such as masculinity, environment, technology—and develop their practice accordingly. At a time when local authorities are struggling to meet their statutory obligations and many charitable bodies have undergone severe cuts in funding, the authors encourage readers to become more proactive in developing innovations in services, and in anticipating future needs and shaping local plans and priorities. This book, like much of the international literature on rural practice, encourages readers to recognise the merits of more participative community-oriented approaches to practice and several chapters provide stimulating examples of how this might be done.

Refreshingly, this book provides a valuable correction to the assumption that individual casework is, and should be, the dominant model for social services. It argues for an explicit commitment to social justice and contends that rural social work with its necessary focus upon social relations and contexts embodies ideas and principles for all forms of practice. Indeed, the devolution of welfare to the four nations of the UK offers greater opportunities for disseminating innovation and influencing policy and provisions.

Keele University   Richard Pugh
Keele, UK

Contents

Notes on Contributors

Lena Dominelli is an action researcher and is keen to engage social workers in addressing key challenges facing humanity and has devised a unique, innovative MSc in Disaster Innovation and Humanitarian Aid to do this at the University of Stirling.

Karin Eyben was, at the time of writing, Development Lead for the Garvagh People's Forest Project in Northern Ireland; a project focusing on the value of the connections between a town and its forest for wellbeing and community regeneration.

Allison Hulmes is a Welsh Kale Gypsy and is a registered social worker. At the time of writing, she was National Director for Wales at the British Association of Social Workers and is a co-founding member of the Gypsy, Roma and Traveller Social Work Association. Allison is now Senior Lecturer in Social Work at Swansea University, Wales.

Tina Laurie at the time of writing, was a social work practice educator working for Dumfries and Galloway Council in South West Scotland and an associate lecturer for the University of the West of Scotland. Now she is a lecturer and practice learning manager at the University of the West of Scotland, based at their campus in Dumfries.

Carla McLaughlin is a social work practitioner in a Multi-Disciplinary Team in Primary Care in Garvagh, County Derry/Londonderry, Northern

Ireland where the focus is on community, relationships, and preventative approaches. She has recently completed a Postgraduate Diploma in Community Development for Social Workers.

Sarah Nelson OBE CRFR, University of Edinburgh, has written and presented widely for decades on sexual abuse issues. Her research includes the voices of young survivors, critiques of current child protection systems, backlash theories, organised abuse, community prevention, and physical and mental health issues for survivors. She now lives in Newport, Fife, in Scotland.

Jane Pye is Lecturer in Social Work at Lancaster University, England, and a former practitioner at social worker and manager levels. She has research interests in rural social work and social work education.

Gillian Ritch was a practising social worker in the Orkney Islands in Scotland at the time of writing. She was born and raised in Orkney and has spent most of her adult life there. She has an interest in issues around dual relationships and rural social work practice.

Becky Squires is Principal Social Worker for Adults in Cumbria in the North of England. She is especially interested in relationship-based practice, social pedagogical approaches, and rural social work practice. She teaches on the Social Work degree programme at Lancaster University.

Heather Still works in public health in Greenock, Scotland, and has a background in social work and qualitative psychosocial research. She recently completed a commissioned study into drugs and alcohol use in a small Scottish island community.

Colin Turbett practised social work in a remote rural location in Scotland for many years and has written previously on this subject, and on community social work and radical social work themes. He lives on the Isle of Arran.

Peter Unwin is a social worker and principal lecturer at the University of Worcester, England, where his teaching and research interests are in working alongside marginalised groups.

List of Abbreviations

ACE   Adverse Childhood Experiences
AOD   Alcohol and Other Drugs
ASD   Autistic Spectrum Disorder
BASW   British Association of Social Worker
CAMHS   Child and Adolescent Mental Health Service
CSA   Child Sexual Abuse
CSE   Child Sexual Exploitation
CS   Contextual Safeguarding
CSW   Community Social Work
FASD   Foetal Alcohol Spectrum Disorder
GRTSWA Gypsy, Roma and Traveller Social Work Association
IFSW   International Federation of Social Workers
IMD   Indices of Multiple Deprivation
LGBTQ+   Lesbian, Gay, Bisexual, Transsexual, Queer and Others
MASH   Multi-Agency Safeguarding Hub
MDT   Multi-Disciplinary Team
NAS   Neonatal Abstinence Syndrome
NMCS   Neighbourhood Mapping for Child Safety
NRCN   National Rural Crime Network
RGSW   Rural Green Social Work
SCIE   Social Care Institute for Excellence
SENCO   Special Educational Needs Coordinator

List of Figures

1

Introduction: Rurality and Rural Social Work

Colin Turbett and Jane Pye

Why This Book: The Rediscovery of Rural Social Work

It is with a sense of great privilege that as editors of this book, we open this collection with a tale that exemplifies the possibilities of people who are geographically spread connecting over a shared passion. It seems the contributors to this book, people originally unknown to each other, were practising, researching, teaching and thinking about rurality and social work in their respective worlds. Individually, important questions were percolating about how recent events, new technologies and changing understandings could be impacting on the uniqueness and distinctiveness of rural places and rural lives. This group of dispersed people shared

C. Turbett (✉)
Shiskine, Isle of Arran, UK
e-mail: ctur282388@aol.com

J. Pye
Bowland North, Lancaster University, Bailrigg, Lancaster, Lancashire, UK
e-mail: j.pye4@lancaster.ac.uk

1

(and share) a view that 'rural' often seems to be a secondary thought when compared to 'urban' to those in power and associated policy makers. It is fair to say that in the UK, the concept of rural social work has struggled to gain real traction within the mainstream social work profession, and it has been left to a few dedicated scholars to produce work that those of us with a belief that rural practice is different to urban have poured over hungrily. It is perhaps no surprise that eventually a group of those committed to ideas of rural social work formed a network of jointly interested parties and through this network, the idea for this book was born. The role of digital technology should be acknowledged here—in fact this whole book has been organised through the use of technology demonstrating the power of these forms of communication for bringing together communities of people with a shared interest and passion.

The aim of this book is to re-visit and re-consider rural social work through a contemporary lens. It is addressed primarily to a UK audience—all the chapters cover issues that relate to UK legal frameworks and processes in a general sense but will be of interest to an international audience because of the universal commonalities of the profession. Indeed, much of the literature and research on rural social work emanates from the settler-colonial societies of North America and Australasia—and that fact will be reflected in the references throughout the book. Within the UK there is also an underlying issue that with devolved government, each of the four jurisdictions (England, Wales, Northern Ireland and Scotland) set their own policy and legal frameworks. Whilst the welfare benefits (and state pensions) system is largely determined through the reserved powers of the UK Westminster Government, some aspects have been devolved in part, so differences are emerging here also. This is not the place to describe them in detail, but it is worth stating that this has taken all four in different directions which will be reflected in some chapter content. The wider context of social work practice and education within which policies are laid out across the UK (with echoes internationally) are explored later in this chapter.

The book includes contributions from those who do not always have the chance to share their perspectives as social workers practising in rural settings. As such the writing styles are inevitably varied, ranging from authors with a strong academic base to others rooted in day-to-day practice, but whose contribution is no less rigorous in terms of quality and value to the reader. A key concept here is that of 'practice wisdom'—a term that crops up in several chapters of the book; our chosen contributors all exemplify learning based on experience as well as scholarly effort. Their experience grows from the interactions they make daily with all aspects of the rural environment, including those for whom they provide social work services. It is now recognised that this cautiously approached human skill is a highly developed attribute of effective social work (Cheung, 2017). We would join others in contending that practice wisdom forms a core foundation of social work based on warm relationships, empathy and what Samson (2015) describes as a bridge between art and science.

We hope that this collection has resonance with practising social workers; our desire here was to prompt discussion and debates that are relevant to actual practice. As editors of this book, we are keen to state from the outset that there is no intention to criticise or cast negative assertions on anything or anyone associated with 'urban-ness', rather the aim is to reinvigorate discussion and debate about 'rural' in relation to social work.

What Is Rurality?

As editors we must acknowledge at this early stage that much of the literature cited in this and later chapters is Anglo-centric in the sense that it cannot be described as of universal application. We are very conscious that the situations and lives of most people in the world cannot be defined by UK, settler-colonial or northern hemisphere experience. However, as the book is describing social work in rural areas in the UK, we must proceed with our selective references on that basis and in that context.

Even a fleeting review of the vast array of available literature reveals very quickly that defining rural is difficult and contested. Somerville et al. (2015, p. 221, referencing Halfacree, 2006) captures this complex picture:

> Rurality is concept, a category, a discourse, an organising architecture, a location and a material space dependent upon the unit of analysis used.

Clearly, then, the term rural means many things to many people. According to the World Bank, in 2020, 44% of the global population was counted as rural and 16% of the UK's population described as rural (World Bank, n.d.-a, n.d.-b). Whilst this is a reduction from about 21% in 2000, 16% remains a significant amount of people deserving focus and ongoing consideration in what some would describe as an urban-centric or urbanised lens of UK governance and policy making (May et al., 2020). This downward rural population trend in the UK is concerning due to its potential to reduce the influence of rural places in policy formation and creating uncertainties about opportunities and services available to an ever decreasing rural community (Nelson et al., 2021).

Paying attention to rural places and their changing nature has important moral functions in terms of understanding people's experiences and opportunities, and we would argue that considering the role of rurality is worthy and important in the fight for a socially just society. This edited collection is premised on this view and seeks to focus on the role of rurality in social work practice in the UK.

A shared understanding of what rural is, matters for planning, policy, practice and governance, and therefore ultimately how people living rurally experience their lives. However, defining rural is not so simple, and globally, there are clear differences as to how rural is conceptualised and defined (MacGregor-Fors & Vázquez, 2020). There is an argument to be made that in trying to define rural, we create a false binary or dichotomy between rural and urban and in some ways set rural places out as being the 'poor cousins' to default thinking of urban being the standard. Such binaries can fail to adequately consider differences within different types of rural places (Gilbert et al., 2016) and feed into conceptualising rural as homogenous (Nelson et al., 2021). They also fail to acknowledge the increasing 'blurring' of rural and urban (Woods, 2009). Despite the concerns, applied ways of understanding rural and urban have persisted for understandably practical reasons. Attempts to define rural have tended to fall into two approaches, firstly one offering a way of describing rural based on quantitative features of a place. Measures such as settlement size, population density, nearest neighbour, accessibility, land-use and multivariate methods have all been used to try to describe urban and rural areas (Martin et al., 2000, p. 738). The descriptive measurements of rural has changed overtime in line with new thinking, technology and available data. The highly advanced techniques for using detailed data and complex use of many factors have elevated the practice of defining rural into one which seeks to capture the features of rural in its own right, not simply as that which is non-urban (Nelson et al., 2021). Rurality is therefore defined in different ways for determining policy across the UK—reflecting wide-ranging geographical differences ranging from remote Scottish islands to villages within a short commuting distance from Central London. The Scottish Government's classification system looks at drive time from population centres and so at one extreme has a definition of a remote community that would be superfluous in rural England (2016). In England conversely, rurality is officially defined by population size within a defined range of communities (Gov.UK, 2016).

The second method of defining rurality employs a socio-cultural approach valuing qualitative experiences to offer a perspective of what rural is and has been constructed to be (Shucksmith & Brown, 2016). Although descriptive and observable definitions of rurality remain popular, they have been criticised for their lack of nuance and limitations in capturing the experiences of people living rurally (Nelson et al., 2021). Despite socio-cultural approaches seemingly being able to offer a 'real' sense of rural life, the more objective measures have a significant impact on people living rurally. This is because it tends to be these that are used to categorise and assess rural places and their challenges, which in turn influence the opportunities created through policy and practice (Curry & Webber, 2012). The lack of consistent methods for defining rural even within a European context makes it difficult to comparatively analyse rural and/or import learning from one place to another. From the perspective of social services, this is likely to mean introducing policies and practices that have been successfully implemented for good in one rural context into another will be inappropriate (Manthorpe & Livsey, 2009). Using the example of how poverty is understood in a specific rural location, Shortall (2013) explores how different knowledge is used to construct understandings and highlights how subjective knowledge can be used to support particular agendas which do not necessarily support understandings when more objective measures are used. Thus, methodology matters when we are trying to understand contested spaces such as 'rural', and researchers, academics, policy makers, practitioners and people living in rural areas must be open to challenging preconceptions through critical awareness. This demonstrates that perhaps investigations which combine approaches to how we understand rural are what is needed (Shortall & Brown, 2019).

These challenges in defining rural, regardless of how creative we aim to be, arise from a normative view that something that we currently call 'rural' exists. Whether or not it is a definable entity is beyond the scope of this discussion, but regardless, we do seem to be able to instinctively identify areas as rural or urban (Woods, 2009). Some scholars debate the influence of the 'mobilities turn', which recognises the flow and movement of all aspects of society including people, thus raising questions about the perceived bounded nature communities and places and explores the continuing importance of place for identity in light of these increasing mobilities (Savage, 2010, referenced in Shucksmith, 2012). Given the increased levels of movement and connection between societies in the context of ongoing globalisation, can we claim that specific rural places exist at all? (Shucksmith, 2012). As we (hopefully) become better at considering the Earth as a whole, especially as we recognise the damage that humankind reaps on the natural environment (Robinson, 2018), a further question is whether 'rural' is a term that should be reserved to describe only places which involve human activity, or is it correct to continue to include areas of genuine wilderness? (MacGregor-Fors & Vázquez, 2020). Despite some of these conceptual questions beginning to arise, we cannot get away from the fact that we currently do recognise some form of rural-urban split or continuum in the UK. With this in mind, the following section explores some of the features and important aspects of rural places that are particularly important for social work.

Rural Places

As the nature of communities change in line with global events and social influences, rural places will experience these in comparatively different ways to urban areas as well as across different rural places (Kerrigan & de

Lima, 2023). It is essential to remember that rural does not equate to homogenous: communities in rural places, however defined, might be deprived, affluent, changing or stable (Martin et al., 2000). The recently published State of Rural Services Report in England (Rural England, 2021) indicates how differently rural communities responded to and coped with the global pandemic demonstrating the need for careful consideration of the differences and diversities within and between rural places—they are not all the same. Narratives capturing the 'rural idyll' remain, creating representations of all rural places as nostalgic, honourable and desirable, potentially masking the reality of poverty, deprivation, social exclusion and exploitation in some rural communities (Shucksmith, 2018). It is interesting to note that whilst ideas of community and care for others are thought to be the predominant values of rural places, these can be premised on discriminatory views about who can access the beneficial aspects of community—not everyone is likely to be welcomed 'in' (Shucksmith, 2018). The closeness of some communities whilst on one hand being seen as supportive can, on the other, be experienced as harmful and judgemental (Somerville et al., 2015). The enduring images of a romanticised rurality are likely to have been powerful in enabling the denial of a number of uncomfortable realities about rural settings. One of these is the lack of focus on racism in rural places—a theme explored later in this chapter. There is evidence that older people may be disadvantaged in terms of gaining access to required services in rural places (Scharf et al., 2016) and the experiences of disabled people in rural places can be complicated and challenging (Morgan, 2017). There is some evidence that when using objective measures, adults with an intellectual disability are less socially excluded in rural areas than urban. However, as the authors of this research note, these findings could change if more subjective measures were used (Nicholson & Cooper, 2013). Even from this very limited discussion, strong evidence exists to indicate that rural places can be challenging places to live, and many people living there will experience some form of discrimination and oppression.

Deprivation is widely measured in the UK using Indices of Multiple Deprivation (IMD). The use of these area-based measures is devolved, and the measures used are slightly different between the four UK nations meaning that exact comparison is not possible. The IMD involves a ranking process to reveal geographical areas that are experiencing deprivation with the intention then that these areas are prioritised for support. In England, seven domains are used: income, employment, education, health, crime, barriers to housing and living environment (Greig et al., 2010). Such measures are not without criticism, and assumptions about causes of deprivation should not be made from the IMD (Noble et al., 2006). However, the general consensus appears to be that IMD provide a fairly accurate picture of areas deprivation in the UK, but that IMDs, with their urban-centric measures of deprivation, may fail to fully reveal the levels of deprivation in rural areas (Fecht et al., 2018). This is because rural deprivation is unlikely to be accurately revealed by measures that are urban-based (Martin et al., 2000). An example of this might be that rural measures are unlikely to identify levels of deprivation spread across sparsely populated wide areas, whereas poor households in urban locations are often concentrated in pockets. Austerity measures have impacted dramatically on already deprived rural areas in England and Wales (May et al., 2020), exacerbating inequalities following the financial crisis of 2008 (e.g., Black et al., 2019). Poverty continues to receive more attention in urban places than rural for a variety of reasons. These include methodological challenges associated with measuring poverty amongst dispersed people and the relative hidden nature of rural poverty. Further, some continue to have difficulty in associating poverty with rural because of entrenched beliefs about the 'rural idyll' (May et al., 2020, p. 410). It is imperative then that there is appreciation of rural poverty, deprivation and social exclusion to avoid further compounding these issues through lack of awareness.

There are a number of benefits that those living rurally can experience such as a sense of community, access to the environment and lower crime rates. However, these exist alongside structural disadvantages associated with poverty and deprivation such as reduced opportunities for employment, education, access to public transport and health and services (Gilbert et al., 2016). More recent thinking has included the lack of digital infrastructure in the concerns about structural disadvantage (Philip & Williams, 2019). It is important to remember that some of these disadvantages create challenges for services trying to operate in rural areas as well as for those in need of the services (Manthorpe & Livsey, 2009). The concept and practice of rural proofing exists to try to mitigate some of the challenges that policy makers have when trying to construct policy which is designed to benefit all. The approach harnesses the binary of urban-rural and in doing so perceives rural areas as ancillary to urban and in need of being in some way 'protected' or 'supported' via rural proofing (Sherry & Shortall, 2019). Perhaps the urban-rural dichotomy could be used instead to acknowledge that in remote areas, service delivery simply costs more and what we need is a framework that acknowledges diversity and need within rural areas (Sherry & Shortall, 2019). Ideas of communities having agency to manage their own assets and be resilient (Skerratt & Hall, 2011) are relevant and interesting ways to consider how they could and can be inclusive and pro-active. However, ideas of community empowerment should be approached critically and include the recognition that they can serve to confirm the status quo of the already powerful in communities—as some people become more empowered, others can become disempowered (Skerratt & Steiner, 2013).

Rural places have been subject to neoliberalism, and this includes the commodification of the features of rural places (Higgins et al., 2014). Research indicates that it is the physical aspects of rural places, that is, the landscape that appears to have the most value rather than the social aspects for people looking to belong in rural places (Shucksmith, 2012). In some ways, this could be interpreted as opposite to the traditional ideas that the pull of rural communities is about the sense of community and neighbourliness that are said to be found there. Indeed, the literature that describes what migrants and minority ethnic groups are seeking emphasises social and relational aspects of community (Flynn & Kay, 2017), so the research referred to seems true of those who are able to exercise economic choices denied to less privileged groups, and not all incomers to rural areas. These people are described elsewhere as 'amenity migrants' whose aspirations and accompanying economic power threaten the sustainability of rural communities (Moss, 2006). Such people move to the countryside because of a perception of the lifestyle benefits it will bring (Bell & Jayne, 2010), but this appears to be about access to the landscape rather than the sense of community on offer. Rural places have become places to consume the opportunities for leisure and tourism (Bell & Jayne, 2010), and one of the authors is very familiar with an anecdotal local narrative that describes one of the UK's National Parks as a 'playground for the rich' rather than as a place for thriving cohesive communities. Rural areas can be seen as areas that are attractive for a particular kind of lifestyle associated with wellbeing measures.

The services that labour migrants require are predicted to become problematic post-Brexit: after the accession of Eastern European countries to the European Union in 2004, there was an influx of free moving migrants to rural areas who, often over-qualified, took up low-paid employment in tourism-related and social care sectors (de Lima & Wright, 2009; McAreavey, 2012). Brexit has reversed this process and created a labour crisis in rural areas (Scottish Government, 2019). The UK Government announced in 2022 that asylum-seeking migrants crossing the Channel 'illegally' in small boats would be dispersed in greater numbers to rural areas (*Guardian* 16th November 2022). However, as many are prohibited from working in most cases, this may not immediately impact on rural employment deficits even setting aside considerations of social justice regarding compulsion and absence of choice.

Maybe rural districts should be measured in terms of contribution to wellbeing rather than economic productivity (Curry & Webber, 2012), a move that would no doubt stimulate the consumption of rural places beyond what we already see. However, the focus on rural places as places for leisure and tourism has surely fuelled the serious problems with rural housing as only the wealthy can now afford to live in many rural areas because of the price of properties (Gallent et al. 2019). As we observe and experience the changing nature of rural places, the concepts of *gemeinschaft* (community) *and gesellschaft* (society) as suggested by Tönnies (1855–1936) remain relevant and useful (Tilman, 2004). Many rural places are struggling to hold on to their traditional community foundations, instead a more orchestrated functional approach to the creation of societies is taken. Whilst we can feel nostalgic and bemoan the shifting nature of rural places, many would benefit from progression, and many do maintain their unique and distinctive nature. It is this that requires a unique and distinctive approach to practise within them.

Social Justice, Diversity and Difference

Research evidence demonstrates that rural communities can be unwelcoming and indeed hostile to those perceived as 'others' (Shucksmith, 2018). This is a process probably reinforced by political turbulence such as the UK's BREXIT referendum of 2016 (Neal et al., 2021). Vital health and housing services fail to take account of ethnic diversity and can be difficult to access and use (de Lima, 2008). Often attitudes are entrenched and developed from long lines of what are claimed to be traditional cultural values and a concern about 'outsiders' (Chakraborti, 2010). The increased role of migrant workers in the rural food production industry, combined with the 'hostile environment' of UK immigration policy, creates concerns that some of these essential workers may experience intolerance at best and blatant racism at worst (Stevens et al., 2012; Moore, 2013; Jones & Lever, 2014). Writing in an American context, Hoffelmeyer (2021) explores the heteronormativity of rural spaces and highlights the discrimination that those face who do not fit with this stereotype experience, a factor explored in much more detail in Chap. 9 of this book. The UK might be smaller in size and distance, but this reflects the situation here too. Indeed, one of the authors can recall working in a remote community in the 1980s where it was not uncommon to hear that a reason for inward white migration was a wish to get away from the diversity found in cities. Since those times that particular community has barely changed in terms of profile. This reflects the UK generally: in 2020 the UK Government reported that 96.8% of the rural population was 'white ethnic' compared with urban areas; ethnic diversity decreases, the sparser the population of an area—1.5% in those described as 'sparse' (Gov. UK 2021).

One might want to believe that things are changing for the better, but this is not how blackness is experienced in rural communities. Lemn Sissay, the Black Poet with lived experience of the care system as a child, says: 'Growing up, I used to ask myself why everyone had such a big issue with the colour of my skin. Men would shield their women from me, bars would go quiet. The incendiary racism that is in the country is never challenged' (quoted in Cloke, 2011, p. 18). The *boundaries* movement of

2020 that followed the death in police custody of George Floyd in the USA gave some expression to the lives of Black people in the British Countryside. Writing in the *Guardian Newspaper* in October of that year, Black musician VV Brown documented what it feels like to stand out—the constant, innocently meant, but offensive questions about origins:

> The daily micro-aggressions of country life are constant, and the anticipation of negative reactions to my presence has become tiresome. (*Guardian* October 2020)

Such comments should shake any belief that the countryside necessarily offers a haven from the pressures of urban life—clearly that depends on identity—and whiteness. Chapter 4 discussing Gypsies, Romani and Travellers suggests that racism is not reserved for people of colour and that this predates Black migration. Chapter 9 on masculinities looks at how difference is adversely experienced by LGBTQ+ people in what is a homophobic and patriarchal environment. All this suggests an embedded rural culture of heteronormativity, patriarchy and domination by individuals who share a common heritage.

This book stands in the anti-discriminatory tradition of social work, and all the chapters rest on a premise that the first step towards challenging racism, homophobia and cis normativity in rural life is to acknowledge their presence and depth. Efforts to challenge the homogenous notion of rural communities are evident in the general literature of contemporary rurality (Philo, 1992; Neal et al., 2021). In the rural social work literature, this is a point emphasised by Pugh in his discussion on how responses might be organised when determining the shape of rural services (Pugh, 2010). The Department of Health propose a 'Three R's' approach that takes in:

- the *recognition* of black and ethnic minorities and their diverse range of needs, aspirations and experiences;
- *respect* for their right to appropriate and effective services;
- the aim of *relevant services*, to meet specific needs in culturally appropriate and accessible ways.
(Quoted in Pugh, 2010, p. 191)

This approach can be easily extended to LGBTQ+ communities and is in keeping with other themes in this book about understanding rural communities not just in terms of geography and distance, important though they are, but looking behind the scenery to understand how rural life is experienced.

The themes discussed here highlight the tensions of social work's place within the machinery of the state whose functions perpetuate the injustices the profession seeks to challenge and mitigate. This has been discussed in UK social work academic and practice circles since the 1970s (Bailey & Brake, 1975; Turbett, 2014) but has rarely been covered in the international rural social work literature—Collier (2006) being a notable exception. Both editors of this book are strongly aware of such considerations and keen that the book should reflect a social work practice that locates the personal issues that social workers support people to address, within the context of community and society rather than individual pathology. This fits perfectly with the contextual specificity of rural social work, its concerns with the marginalised and disadvantaged of rural society, and with the model of community social work that is discussed in some detail in this and the final chapter.

What Is Rural Social Work?

In offering a brief review of the international literature this section links to previous discussion in this introduction, social work in rural localities is defined by their individual characteristics. Importantly, this includes those strengths and weaknesses which are located in their history, networks and institutions, whether experienced positively or negatively. The literature agrees that social work service, based on values of social justice and delivered through helping relationships, does not differ between urban and rural settings (e.g., Martinez-Brawley, 2000; Pugh, 2000; Lohmann & Lohmann, 2005; Pugh & Cheers, 2010; Turbett, 2010; Ginsberg, 2011). The difference is in the method of delivery. Our view as authors is that good social work is always rooted in community, and we recognise that neoliberal approaches have marginalised social work's potential and forced it downstream to cost-driven attention to severe risk.

This has led to over-specialised and siloed service delivery, especially in the public sector settings that dominate the profession in the UK. We would nail our colours to the mast that this approach is in dire need of reform in all social work settings—we urgently need to return to a community-based and accessible social work based on relationships rather than assessment models; to a practice that seeks to preventatively address the causes of family and personal dysfunction and distress, rather than just their symptoms (Turbett, 2021).

There is a rich international literature of rural social work, but mostly quite dated and, as noted earlier, Anglo-centric. The more recent texts are careful to restrict coverage to a single country (e.g., Daley, 2021; Maidment & Bay, 2021). The reduction in output reflects the neoliberal and restrictive trends already referred to, whereas the rural literature that was abundant in the final twenty years of the twentieth century was international in outlook (if mainly restricted to the English-speaking settler-colonial societies of North America and Australasia). This promoted the idea of *rural generalism*: a community-orientated form that took account also of the need to work across traditional service boundaries to find solutions to issues when there were no other services to refer on to. Martinez-Brawley (1982, 1984, 1990, 2000) was a powerful advocate of such approaches, and although US based, she also wrote about the Western Isles in Scotland (1986), acknowledging that ideas about community social work had emanated from the UK. Martinez-Brawley also made a strong case for consideration of the work of Tönnies on community characteristics (2000). Community social work approaches specific to practice in the USA were also promoted by Scales et al. (2014).

Generalism was also described in successive editions of US texts by Ginsberg (up to the final fifth edition 2011), the Lohmann and Lohmann (2005), and in Australia by Cheers (1998). Generalism goes back to the roots of social work in the USA: in 1933 Josephine Brown wrote about social work practice in the Mid-West of the USA where she describes an interface between effective individual assistance to farming families suffering in the Great Depression, with the community initiatives necessary to alleviate poverty. Whilst her book was not written from a radical standpoint and much of it has dated, there is much that has resonance almost a hundred years later when looking at issues under the surface of the scenery in our own rural communities. *Generalism* as used here must be differentiated from *genericism*: the latter refers to practice, once common in the UK, of working across specialisms: generalism does not exclude such practice but refers to the ability of the practitioner to draw upon a wide range of skills and strategies. This is usefully defined by Collier:

> The generalist considers problem solving on many levels, across a spectrum of conceptual and practical approaches, and pursues any avenue that may be productive. It is not a specific approach, like casework with its theoretical bases. The generalist enters each situation ready to tackle an individual problem, a neighbourhood issue or a political contest.
> (Collier, 2006, pp. 36–37)

The international literature is also strong on its examination of themes about the personal attributes and behaviours of the rural social worker. The detail is striking when compared with most general social work texts. Behaviours, not just in relation to work activity, but including habits in private life, are referred to as significant. Much of this focuses on the notion of 'dual relationships'—the management of situations where an individual can be a neighbour, service provider or even colleague, as well as a service user. Behaviours interpreted as out of keeping with the character of a rural community were discouraged because they will lend themselves to a wider profile than would ever be the case in the anonymity of a city location. They might be shared between community members, and perhaps become barriers to relationship making and help. Some of this might seem unacceptably dated in its intent: we would never tolerate matching social workers to specifications laid down by the service user, as this could foster racist and other discriminatory behaviours. Matters have moved on, certainly in the UK, and most rural communities represent a diversity that might have been rarely encountered twenty or thirty years ago. Where diversity existed, the pressures to conform and deny such differences were arguably stronger (Ageyman & Spooner, 1997). One of the authors can recall a female colleague in the 1980s being advised by a locally born member of staff, on moving to a rural area, to use her husband's surname and not, as had been her choice in the city, her own birth family name. It is unlikely that Ginsberg's advice about integration into the community, in which he advises conventionality in terms of religious observance, dress and personal life, would be seen as acceptable or necessary today (2000). However, his advice about the need to not express polarising opinion or offence to established community 'leaders' until, at least, credibility has been established seems just as relevant today. Here it is worth mentioning again the concept of 'practice wisdom'—an approach learned through the interactions between rural social workers and community members whom they commonly encounter (Cheung, 2017).

The rural literature of the 1980s and 1990s discusses race and racism, and the need to counter discrimination, but not in the terms we might expect today; it is now understood that social justice must be located within post-colonial understanding and practice and an acceptance that white supremacy and hegemony are not simply associated with extreme opinions but rooted in state institutions. That all said, the need to recognise and uphold the rights of indigenous minorities (e.g., Australian Aborigines, or Canadian First Nations People) was championed by the rural social work movement and celebrated and reflected in its literature (Cheers, 1998). However, this has not always led to changes in oppressive practices within the State locations of social work—a factor emphasised by Indigenous scholars within the settler-colonial states (Derosier & Neckoway, 2005). The notion that well-meaning interventions can be unintentionally harmful because of a lack of cultural awareness resonates down the years: this was discussed in the Marxist social worker Collier's Canadian texts (three editions up to 2006). Issues of cultural awareness and its implications for practice apply also to incoming migrants to rural areas. The literature (e.g., Ginsberg, 2000) sees migration through the prism of forced economic migration outwards to cities and rural depopulation. This might still be relevant, but now focus needs to be made on the widespread dispersal of migrants from across the world, some refugees escaping wars and climate change issues. As already discussed, other incomers ('amenity migrants') to some rural areas are at the other end of the economic spectrum—privileged people looking for beauty and quiet, but whose presence lends to housing shortages, population imbalance and rising inequalities. These are all challenges for rural social workers.

Similarly, the literature tackles matters surrounding being Gay and Lesbian in rural communities (Martinez-Brawley, 2000; Lohmann & Lohmann, 2005), still of relevance today where peer pressure for conformity can lead to confusion and distress around identity issues. Discussions focus on isolation, feelings of difference and social work in challenging rural environments where conservative religious belief is predominant. Other issues around challenges to cisnormativity, transgender identity and same-sex parenting are not explored but need to be considered by the anti-discriminatory practitioner today.

Literature on rurally specific social work has been sparse in the UK: Pugh (2000, 2010) echoes themes of rural generalism in his work, and also looks at aspects of personal behaviour and common expectations in rural settings. This includes the aspect of 'placing': the need for users of services to have an idea of where the worker fits into the community they might both share (Pugh, 2000). Pugh argues that this involves the disclosure of some personal information by the worker as an important element of relationship building.

One of this book's editors, Turbett (2010), developed Pugh's work and common themes in the international literature, to look at practice in the Scottish context, making a strong argument for a community orientation. Turbett had earlier (2004) linked a rurally remote, well publicised and controversial incident (the Orkney case mentioned in Chaps. 9 and 11) involving child protection to the need for community-informed services. Coming at a time of managerially inspired and programmatic moves away from community orientation in social work practice in the UK, these arguments and ideas made little impact: practice models were becoming increasingly centralised, specialised and based on procedural models designed in urban settings (as found by Martinez-Brawley, 2012, when she returned to Scotland's Western Isles to re-visit the scene of her 1986 paper). By the end of that decade, this trend was being questioned because of increasing dissatisfaction with universally applied procedural models of service delivery in the UK, and a wish to return to relationship-based social work. This resulted in a better reception for an IRISS Insight paper on rural practice in Scotland (Turbett, 2019). This paper made a case for the rebirth of a rural social work knowledge base, and a celebration of rural practice.

A problematic area for social work generally in the UK in recent decades has been the notion of integration with health services through well-intentioned policy aims such as the improved co-ordination of services to an ageing population, and the better use of resources through avoidance of duplication. This has had consequences that have further marginalised social work and reduced its influence within services dominated by big budget health agendas. The crisis in social care which this policy has failed to successfully address has been a recurring feature of UK politics. In rural areas problems have been exacerbated by recruitment issues for social care staff, and resource scarcity and loss.

In his book *A Fortunate Man—The Story of a Country Doctor*, writer John Berger pens a portrait of Gloucestershire doctor in the 1960s who treats his patients based on his holistic knowledge of their whole lives, and not just their presenting symptoms when they attend his surgery. This is located in a trusting relationship with them as individuals and with the community as a whole entity. Good rural social work practice, as evidenced in the literature quoted, is based on the same premise. 'Landscapes can be deceptive', says Berger, 'Sometimes a landscape seems less a setting for the life of its inhabitants than a curtain behind which their struggles, achievements and accidents take place' (Berger and Moir 1967, p. 19). This reminds us that the 'rural idyll' can mask poverty, isolation and other social ills, but that these will vary from one unique setting to another: 'when you've seen one rural community—you've seen one rural community!' (Lohmann & Lohmann, 2005, p. 316).

Our description of rurality has highlighted the realities of rural life. The commonly experienced challenges these present for social workers occur across the international literature: resource scarcity, distance, isolation, personal safety factors, supervision problems for lone workers, and dual relationship issues. Nonetheless, practice in settings that are scenically inspiring, less hurried, and where networks are more obvious and therefore potentially accessible are attractive and worth celebrating. The challenges open creative possibilities for the worker and team that might be hard to replicate in more complex urban settings. In the words of Lohmann and Lohmann: 'If you can practice effectively in rural America, it is likely you can practice anywhere because you will have learned to be resourceful and creative' (2005, p. 317). This strong statement applies in our view, equally to UK settings, perhaps surprisingly to urban workers who are often led to believe that they are at the cutting edge of the profession. This is no accident considering that UK universities where research and academic papers are created, and where social workers are educated, are almost all in cities. The poor-country-cousin of social work epithet should be consigned to history! Several chapters of the book contain rich rural social work stories, a basis surely for qualitative research that could be more than an equal for the urban-based research upon which universally applied models are often based.

Drawing on the literature, effective rural practice is built on the following:

- Generalist (including community and ecological methods of practice) social work approaches to building capacity and upstream responses to issues that might produce downstream referrals. This might involve groupwork, community work and informal relationship building activity.
- The values of social justice, inclusivity and recognition of pluriversality.
- Strong local networking involving frontline workers in different agencies, e.g., health, education and police, alongside community activists.
- Opportunities to develop practice wisdom through experience gained over time, of a locality, its inhabitants and its networks.
- Opportunity to build understanding and knowledge of social issues affecting rural areas.
- Appreciation of dual relationships and public profile issues.
- Above all, good social work practice is good social work practice, whether found on a remote island or in a major conurbation—the difference is all contextual.

These findings, believed to be highly relevant to the UK, of course reflect their origins in the international literature and so resonate with practice in the settler-colonial states in which they originate. That is why, we believe, this book and its original content will be of interest beyond the UK.

Issues Arising from the Policy Context

In this introductory chapter the editors are keen to place rural social work within the context of social work practice as it has developed across the UK. We believe that a rural model is firmly located within an understanding of community and that this is clear from our brief run through of definitions and descriptions above that principally emerged from the settler-colonial societies of North America and Australasia.

Whilst rural social work in the UK has been characterised generally by an absence of formal recognition, some of the problematic issues that are discussed through the various chapters are reflective of a neoliberal managerial-driven centralisation and emphasise on procedure that has pervaded the profession for more than twenty years. It should be no surprise that in the UK, such trends were bound to be universal—the uniformity that accompanied them ensured that different approaches to social work would be subsumed by ones considered tried and tested, that fitted prevailing agendas. These included the reduction of social work to a prime concern with the assessment of risk, a move away from upstream preventative practice, and growing invisibility within communities (Turbett, 2021).

Some of this, which became embedded in social work education, was welcomed at the time by a beleaguered profession, such as the move towards specialised practice. This turn away from the generic models that were celebrated in the international rural social work literature did not sit well with many rural practitioners (Turbett, 2011). However, that ship has sailed, and specialised practice is now universal, although its application varies, and opportunity for approaches that are closer to communities will always be there, hence the focus throughout this book. Perhaps the tide is now turning: dissatisfaction with social work as practiced within statutory settings seems now to feature in most change agendas: there is a recognition that the profession is quite demoralised with a high turnover of staff, poor public image and a failure to stem the growing weight of intractable caseloads (Miller & Barrie, 2022). Never-ending austerity means that workers and their managers are expected to keep costs as low as possible. These factors are as applicable in rural settings as in urban ones in the UK.

The importance of community and knowledge on the part of the practitioner of the community (or communities) found in a rural area are highlighted throughout the chapters. This offers opportunity to discuss a particular social work approach: *Community Social Work* (CSW). CSW is not about delivering social work along lines usually found within statutory services, but simply located within communities (as opposed to the centralised delivery models that have spread in recent years—often for cost reasons) but constitutes a different approach altogether.

The issues that beset social work described above are promoting some self-reflection on the part of agencies and academics. Jane Fenton contends that many social work students are imbued with neoliberal individualistic ideas that are far from the social justice values assumed within the profession (Fenton, 2019). If this is true, then they will take these values into the workplace and on up the rungs of the career ladder. The abandonment of traditional values of social justice and its promotion might partly explain the poor and misunderstood state that social work finds itself in. The dissonance between what students read about in academic books, and actual practice, is bound to affect morale and confidence. A reversal of such trends requires social workers who recognise their role in challenging injustice and its effects and do not believe that simply trying (often ineffectually) to treat its symptoms is what the job is all about.

CSW was much discussed in the 1980s at a time when social work in the UK saw immense growth as a profession, with generic services based in local offices. It reached its zenith with the Barclay Report (National Institute for Social Work, 1982) and died in the ten years that followed because of an unsympathetic government and the predominance of individualistic ideologies reflected in policies that negated the role and concept of community (Turbett, 2018).

So, what are the components of CSW? Elsewhere one of the authors has written the following which summarises the concept (quoted with permission):

- Community social work challenges the notion that the role of a social worker is to produce assessment and care plans, and gives primacy to work methods based on relationships and partnerships.
- It should not be regarded as a peripheral activity, but as a function of, and located within, mainstream frontline social work teams.
- Community social work recognises that early-intervention approaches can act to prevent the escalation of social problems to the point that statutory interventions become inevitable.
- As a driver of community development, community social work involves working together to tackle disadvantage, and networks that include community members and partner agencies.
- As a collective activity involving creativity and imagination, community social work is rewarding for practitioners and contributes to worker retention strategies and that avoid stress and burnout.
- Community social work is not prescriptive and so, while it can embrace, statutory duties of all types, is flexible and adaptive so that a response can be offered in crisis situations: whether within a family, a locality or in response to global catastrophe.
- Community social work is based on interventions determined through bottom-up rather than top-down initiatives, supported by enabling senior managers, based on local practice knowledge, understanding of strengths and weaknesses, and in partnership with communities. (Turbett, 2020)

Rural social work practice has always lent itself to a community orientation: this is reflected in its literature, and in the chapters in this book that reflect on practice. Some of this has been lost in recent years with the drive to procedurally driven uniformity and centralisation, but the revival of interest in rural social work has opened up considerations of what a practice might involve that was based around the individual characteristics and needs of a locality and the people who live within its boundaries, or who have some claim to feel it is also their community (we refer here to the subjects of Allison Hulme's and Peter Unwin's Chap. 4 of this book rather than privileged second home owners!).

One of the most significant challenges that we have in social work is trying to answer the deceivingly difficult question of 'what is social work?'

There are broadly two ways of conceiving social work; one that involves an individualised casework approach and one that involves a wider community focused approach. This latter broad model includes the consideration of social structures, inequality, values flexibility and is preventative. Relationships and partnership are also considered key. An individualised casework approach depicts working with individuals, families and groups as the narrow focus of practice rather than working within and with communities in the way that CSW is described above. That is not to say that many social work practitioners working within an individualised casework model do not focus on the importance of relationships or want to work flexibly, it is more that the narrow casework approach makes this more difficult to achieve.

Burt (2022) outlines the early developments in social work including tracing a trajectory from its early roots in education to the dominance of individual casework that we see today. It is perhaps the case that the varied and variety of people and community organisations that were involved in the early versions of social work in the UK created a desire to professionalise what this activity was so it had an identity and could be defined. The origins of the move from the community-focused activities towards a more individual casework orientation grew from this desire to professionalise. Education designed to develop social workers naturally fell in line with what social work was thought to be, therefore further consolidating a belief in the casework model (Burt, 2022). The revival of a more community-based focus was seen in the 1970s which reflected the political ideology of the time. However, the political and economic shift towards neoliberalism arose in the 1980s and its influence was felt in social work with social workers being re-branded as case managers rather than people who worked directly alongside people and communities (Dominelli, 2007). It is no surprise that the education of social workers followed this trend with the core areas of social work education being framed around this individualising agenda. Social work education takes place in a political and economic space and is subject to the pressures that the current right learning ideologies bring (McCulloch & Taylor, 2018). We shall discuss social work education in more detail below.

Research highlights how many now conceptualise social work in a narrow form as being about statutory work focused on risk, safeguarding and assessment rather than a wider perception which keeps a firm focus on relationships, ethics and social justice (Higgins, 2015), the core aspects of CSW. As demonstrated throughout the chapters of this collection, this individualised approach does not always fit well within a rural context but is an approach that continues to be imposed on social work practice and practitioners. CSW has a different philosophy which is not only beneficial and appropriate in rural settings but could also be valuable in urban settings too. It has natural affinity with rural social work because of the inevitable need to consider communities when working rurally and we can learn much from our rurally based social work colleagues as a result. In some sense, because working with CSW principles is often the only way to ensure effective practice in rural settings, in rural contexts the view of what contemporary social work is has already had to be widened accordingly. As a result, there is some evidence that a realignment with CSW and the traditional value base of social work is already occurring in some rural settings (Pye et al., 2020).

The questions about what social work is, what it should be and how is it best practised should not be seen as UK based only; these are international challenges too (Muñoz-Guzmán, 2018). As mentioned earlier, some have declared that we are now facing a crisis in social work linked to what social work has become with problems in the recruitment of qualified practitioners, erosion of identity, lack of resources and high turnover of staff. Whilst dramatically framed, this dissatisfaction and serious concerns about social work sits in the context of the individualised casework approach. It seems timely to ask whether we can surface an approach to social work that sees practice as wider than the narrow, statutory function it has become which erodes creativity, imagination and the centring of social justice to practice, approaches that we believe are more likely to be happening under the radar in rural settings already. Given that there are benefits and advantages to a CSW approach, the question that remains is could we fully or at least partly implement a community-based approach to social work in the UK to try to re-establish a different and more fulfilling and effective approach to practice? Statutory work requires to be undertaken wherever and however it arises. However, we would contend that the committal of resources to the type of preventative, relationship-based CSW approach we advocate might pay dividends in the long run. Chapter 8 offers an example from Northern Ireland where such a commitment has been made with the Multi-Disciplinary Team (MDT) initiative, basing social workers in GP Practices.

Regulation grew out of a desire to further professionalise social work. Although social work across the four nations has devolved regulatory regimes, the introduction of the degree in social work as the minimum qualifying standard has resulted in different standards and expectations in relation to the requirements on students, qualified social workers and educators (Parker, 2020). There are similarities across the nations in, for example, what students are expected to demonstrate by the end of their qualifying programmes and what is expected of registered social workers in terms of conduct. Social work qualifying programmes are also required to involve people who use services (Goossen & Austin, 2017) in a positive move, that is, an attempt to work in partnership with community members. However, there is very little evidence of students and qualified registered social workers needing to demonstrate an understanding of the different types of approaches to practice which would include CSW and serve to highlight that individualised casework is an *approach* to practice, it is not the only way to practice.

Social work in Northern Ireland is regulated by the Northern Ireland Social Care Council which sets out expectations about practice and education, as does Social Care Wales in the Welsh context. The social work regulator in Scotland is the Scottish Social Care Council who set the standards required for social work and education known as the Standards in Social Work Education (SiSWE). Social work in England has been regulated by Social Work England (SWE) since late 2019 when the regulation transferred from the generic Health and Social Care Council (HCPC). Since 2012, social work programmes in England have been heavily influenced by the Professional Capabilities Framework (PCF) now hosted by the British Association of Social Workers (BASW, 2018). The PCF outlines capabilities across different domains at different stages of the social work journey and is felt to be a positive model in both academic and practice settings with its acknowledgement of the developmental nature of social work. A review of the regulatory expectations of social workers across the UK indicates that reference is made to the importance of community and communities if not directly to CSW. So, why is it that despite the regulatory and other guidance in place to outline the requirements of social workers to recognise and work with communities in the UK do we continue to see the dominance of the casework or case management model in social work practice? (Smith & Whyte, 2008). Perhaps this is because this aligns with the focus on statutory social work which has increased over recent years and serves to meet the needs of employers (Parker, 2020) rather than communities. Further, statutory social work practice consolidates the current political ideology that individuals are responsible for their own situations in a time of austerity, an attitude much removed from social justice and community-orientated practice (Parker, 2020).

In much of the literature that claims to talk about UK-based social work practice and education generally, very little space is given to any other perspective other than the English context. This of course may well reflect the level of concern that has grown about social work in England fuelled by the media and outspoken politicians in the face of high-profile deaths of children involved with social work services (Grant et al., 2017). There has been what feels like a continuous focus on social work education in the UK with concerns about whether it is appropriately 'training' and educating social workers to be able to fulfil the complex social work which further fuels the undercurrent of blame being laid on social workers when an incident of a child being harmed or worse occurs. In recent times, we have seen the opening up of new ways into social work education in an English context (Hanley, 2022), which many see as a symptom of the belief that traditional university-based programmes were not producing the 'right kind' of social workers. Research carried out across the UK in institutions that provide social work education programmes found that people involved with these programmes have grave concerns about the impact of neoliberal marketisation on social work education (Clearly, 2018) indicating that despite the ongoing inconsistent view of what social work is, there are consistent concerns about the impact of the wider political context on social work education.

The perception of the social work role differs amongst people with an interest in social work education across the UK, and as a consequence, the views about what social work education should be is also disputed. This was highlighted in 2014 with two high-profile reports on social work education, the Croisdale-Appleby (2014) and Narey (2014) reports. These reports had different origins with the Croisdale-Appleby report being commissioned by the Department of Health and the Narey report being commissioned to focus on children's services by the Department for Education. Despite their English origins, both are discussed as having a UK wide focus, and Croisdale-Appleby (2014) explicitly states this intention within his report. Narey (2014) does not and the reports drew different conclusions about social work education. The Narey (2014) report suggested that social work education should develop specialist child-focused social work practitioners which reflected a narrow view of what social work is along the lines of statutory child protection. The Croisdale-Appleby (2014) report made a case for the continuation of generic social work qualifications and drew attention to the requirement for social workers to embrace a wide role encompassing the role of multiple factors in people's lives in recognition of the complex social situations that people find themselves in. This was an interesting set of events in social work education with two government commissioned reports reporting very differently about social work education and indeed, social work as a profession.

We outline all this in detail because we consider it important to locate the following chapters on different aspects of practice within context. If rural social work is to take its place as a focus of education and practice, there are clearly challenges within existing UK structures that must be addressed. Our contention is that the community-based practice required to underpin rural social work approaches needs to be built from the bottom up but requires policy imperative and enabling employers and managers to achieve necessary change. It also needs to be co-produced with the communities it seeks to serve, a process that will only be effective if services are embedded within their networks and places.

The Content of the Book

In broad terms we have chosen the content and arranged the chapters to explore and develop commonalities from the existing literature, but within an evolving UK post-Covid context. We are also introducing new themes that have emerged in the age of digital communication and concerns about climate change and sustainability. Our own networking has been enhanced by a group in Scotland established after the Rural Social Work Conference held under IRISS auspices in Dumfries in March 2020. This for us lends the book strength and applicability for readers engaged in practice, as well as those concerned with the study of rural services—a discipline we are keen to promote in terms of social work.

The book is divided into three thematic sections: *stigma, environment* and *community*. These are inevitably overlapping but suggest a method of viewing issues that we think is helpful to the reader. The first, **stigma**, concerns the impact of rural life on the individual and how this might shape the delivery of personal social work services. Stigma is commonly understood to be a process that underlies and reproduces structural and social inequality, intersecting with concepts such as racism and oppression, especially as it relates to the role of power (Goffman, 1963). Our position is that stigma must be understood to be tackled successfully as a central part of the social work role in the rural setting where visibility is often high for groups affected. We begin by looking at vulnerabilities that might apply to the rural social worker: Gillian Ritch draws on the ample descriptions of dual relationships and their impact, and how these are experienced by her and colleagues in their island setting, and how they work their way through the issues that arise from living and working in the same place. Heather Still, who has research and practice experience in Scotland, will then examine how drug and alcohol issues are located and experienced in rural communities. This section ends with a study by social worker Allison Hulmes, and academic Peter Unwin, on social work with long-standing marginalised communities—Gypsies, Romani and Travellers; by an examination of these groups and their problems of recognition and acceptance in the UK, wider issues of rural racism are touched upon.

The second thematic section concerns **environment.** This starts with Professor Lena Dominelli's contribution connecting environmental concerns with the Covid-19 pandemic and imperatives that support a sustainable future for the planet. Some additional explanation is required about this chapter because it is less about rural social work practice than about the rural environment in a more general sense. It therefore builds on the seminal work of Dominelli (2012) on Green Social Work, that is, social work which is framed through the understanding of the concept of environmental justice and its significance for communities. The editors feel it makes a necessary contribution to critical debates about why green activism might be considered important to community-based practice. Other chapters have mentioned the nature of the rural environment, culture and heritage, and its significance as a source of food, nurturing leisure opportunity and living space. These are all contentious issues, but what the discussions all share is a belief that rural communities must be understood and conserved in a progressive way that serves their populations and which does not further inequality and oppression. Professor Dominelli provides an important analysis of such issues that underpins the objectives of the book.

This theme is continued by rural Scottish practitioner Tina Laurie: farming and agriculture play an important role in rural communities, and changes in the past fifty years have introduced practices that are both wasteful and unhealthy; solutions are of interest to social workers because of their challenge to poverty and associated factors involving health and wellbeing. Geography and environment also affect the physical delivery of rural social work, and the widespread introduction of digital communication methods has changed service delivery—bringing both advantages and disadvantages, matters explored by Jane Pye in her chapter. The final chapter in this section, by Karin Eybin, a community worker, and Carla McLaughlin, a social work practitioner, looks at an example of imaginative and creative use of the rural environment in a community forest project in rural Northern Ireland.

The third thematic section of the book looks at our fundamental premise for rural social work, the notion of **community,** and the challenges that rural characteristics can bring to practitioners across some specific client groups. This starts with a chapter by Colin Turbett on the neglected subject of masculinities and how they impact on the lives of men, women and children across rural communities. This is followed by a chapter by social worker and manager Becky Squires, which concerns issues surrounding the effective community delivery of social work to older people in rural areas. At the other end of the age scale, Dr. Sarah Nelson's chapter examines issues surrounding the protection and safeguarding of the UK's most vulnerable children in rural areas, and how we might ensure that geographic isolation does not equate to disadvantage.

The final chapter of the book examines emergent themes and brings community back to the fore as an overarching current within the book. Conclusions will be drawn from the chapters about a way forward for social work services in rural areas in the UK. A community focus, it is argued, whilst not a method exclusive to rural social work, should be seen as a methodology that can bring social work back to where it should be in all settings: it fits naturally with the characteristics of rural areas in the UK, and a transition to this is an entirely realistic objective.

References

Ageyman, J., & Spooner, R. (1997). Ethnicity and the Rural Environment. In P. Cloke & J. Little (Eds.), *Contested Countryside Cultures - Otherness Marginalisation and Rurality*. Routledge.

Bailey, R., & Brake, M. (Eds.). (1975). *Radical Social Work*. Edward Arnold.

Bell, D., & Jayne, M. (2010). The Creative Countryside: Policy and Practice in the UK Rural Cultural Economy. *Journal of Rural Studies, 26*(5), 209–218.

Berger, J., & Moir, J. (1967). *A Fortunate Man – The Story of a Country Doctor*. Allen Lane.

Black, N., Scott, K., & Shucksmith, M. (2019). Social Inequalities in Rural England: Impacts on Young People Post-2008. *Journal of Rural Studies, 68*, 264–275.

British Association of Social Workers. (2018). *Professional Capabilities Framework [Online]*. Accessed August 18, 2022, from https://www.basw.co.uk/social-work-training/professional-capabilities-framework-pcf

Brown, J. (1933). *The Rural Community and Social Casework*. Family Welfare Association of America.

Burt, M. (2022). Introducing Social Workers: Their Roles and Training. *British Journal of Social Work, 52*, 2166–2182.

Chakraborti, N. (2010). Beyond 'Passive Apartheid'? Developing Policy and Research Agendas on Rural Racism in Britain. *Journal of Ethnic and Migration Studies, 36*(3), 501–517.

Cheers, B. (1998). *Welfare Bushed: social care in rural Australia*. Ashgate.

Cheung, J. (2017). Practice Wisdom in Social Work: An Uncommon Sense in the Intersubjective Encounter. *European Journal of Social Work, 20*(5), 619–629.

Clearly, T. (2018). Social Work Education and the Marketisation of UK Universities. *British Journal of Social Work, 48*, 2253–2271.

Cloke, P. (2011). Rurality and Racialised Others: Out of Place in the Countryside? In N. Chakraborti & J. Garland (Eds.), *Rural Racism*. Routledge.

Collier, K. (1984, 1993, 2006). *Social Work with Rural Peoples*. New Star.

Croisdale-Appleby, D. (2014). *Re-visioning Social Work Education: An Independent Review [Online]*. Accessed August 18, 2022, from https://assets.publishing.service.gov.uk/government/uploads/system/uploads/attachment_data/file/285788/DCA_Accessible.pdf

Curry, N., & Webber, D. J. (2012). Economic Performance in Rural England. *Regional Studies, 46*(3), 279–291.

Daley, M. (2021). *Rural Social Work in the 21ˢᵗ Century: Serving Individuals, Families and Communities in the Countryside*. Oxford University Press.

de Lima, P. (2008). *Rural Minority Ethnic Experiences - Housing and Health*. Race Equality Foundation. Accessed December 2022, from https://raceequality-foundation.org.uk/wp-content/uploads/2022/10/housing-brief7-2.pdf

de Lima, P., & Wright, S. (2009). Welcoming Migrants? Migrant Labour in Rural Scotland. *Social Policy and Society, 8*(3), 391–404.

Derosier, M., & Neckoway, R. (2005). Historical and Social Influences on Violence in Aboriginal Families. In K. Brownlee & J. Graham (Eds.), *Violence in the Family - Social Work Readings from Northern and Rural Canada*. CSPI.

Dominelli, L. (2007). Contemporary Challenges to Social Work Education in the United Kingdom. *Australian Social Work, 60*(1), 29–45.

Dominelli, L. (2012). *Green Social Work: From Environmental Crises to Environmental Justice*. Polity Press.

Fecht, D., Jones, A., Hill, T., Lindfield, T., Thomson, R., Hansell, A. L., & Shukla, R. (2018). Inequalities in Rural Communities: Adapting National Deprivation Indices for Rural Settings. *Journal of Public Health, 40*(2), 419–425.

Fenton, J. (2019). *Social Work for Lazy Radicals*. Bloomsbury.

Flynn, M., & Kay, R. (2017). Migrants' Experiences of Material and Emotional Security in Rural Scotland: Implication for Loner-Term Settlement. *Journal of Rural Studies, 52*, 56–65.

Gallent, N., Hamiduddin, I., Stirling, P., & Kelsey, J. (2019). Prioritising Local Housing Needs Through Land-Use Planning in Rural Areas: Political Theatre or Amenity Protection? *Journal of Rural Studies, 66*, 11–20.

Gilbert, A., Colley, K., & Roberts, D. (2016). Are Rural Residents Happier? A Quantitative Analysis of Subjective Wellbeing in Scotland. *Journal of Rural Studies, 44*, 37–45.

Ginsberg, L. (1976, 1993, 1998, 2005, 2011 – Five Editions). *Social Work in Rural Communities*. CSWE.

Goffman, E. (1963). *Stigma - Notes on the Management of a Spoiled Identity*. Simon & Schuster.

Goossen, C., & Austin, M. J. (2017). Service User Involvement in UK Social Service Agencies and Social Work Education. *Journal of Social Work Education, 53*(1), 37–51.

Gov.UK. (2016) *Rural Urban Classification*. Accessed December 2022, from https://www.gov.uk/government/collections/rural-urban-classification

Gov.UK. (2021). *Rural Population and Migration*. Accessed January 2022, from https://www.gov.uk/government/statistics/rural-population-and-migration/rural-population-and-migration

Grant, S., Sheridan, L., & Webb, S. A. (2017). 'Newly Qualified Social Workers' Readiness for Practice in Scotland. *British Journal of Social Work, 47*, 487–506.

Greig, A., El-Haram, M., & Horner, M. (2010). Using Deprivation Indices in Regeneration: Does the Response Match the Diagnosis? *Cities, 27*(6), 476–482.

Guardian Online 16th November 2022. Accessed from https://www.theguardian.com/uk-news/2022/nov/16/immigration-minister-fears-rural-areas-will-be-asked-to-house-more-asylum-seekers

Guardian Online 20th October 2020. Accessed June 2022, from https://www.theguardian.com/commentisfree/2020/oct/20/black-woman-british-countryside-london-rural-village-stereotypes

Halfacree, K. (2006). Rural Space: Constructing a Three-Fold Architecture. In P. Cloke, T. Marsden, & P. H. Mooney (Eds.), *Handbook of Rural Studies*. Sage.

Hanley, J. (2022). Better Together: Comprehensive Social Work Education in England. *Critical and Radical Social Work, 10*(1), 127–143.

Higgins, M. (2015). The Struggle for the Soul of Social Work in England. *Social Work Education, 34*(1), 4–16.

Higgins, V., Potter, C., Dibden, J., & Cocklin, C. (2014). Neoliberalising Rural Environments. *Journal of Rural Studies, 36*, 386–390.

Hoffelmeyer, M. (2021). "Out" on the Farm: Queer Farmers Maneuvering Heterosexism and Visibility. *Rural Sociology, 86*(4), 752–776.

Jones, L., & Lever, J. (2014). *Migrant Workers in Rural Wales and the South Wales Valleys.* Wales Rural Observatory.

Kerrigan, N., & de Lima, P. (2023). *The Rural-Migration Nexus: Global Problems, Rural Issues.* Palgrave Macmillan.

Lohmann, N., & Lohmann, R. (Eds.). (2005). *Rural Social Work Practice.* Columbia University Press.

MacGregor-Fors, I., & Vázquez, L.-B. (2020). Revisiting 'Rural'. *Science of the Total Environment, 741*, 1–4.

Maidment, J., & Bay, U. (Eds.). (2021). *Social Work in Rural Australia: Enabling Practice.* Routledge.

Manthorpe, J., & Livsey, L. (2009). European Challenges in Delivering Social Services in Rural Regions: A Scoping Review: Les services sociaux des régions rurales de l'Europe: une étude des recherches. *European Journal of Social Work, 12*(1), 5–24.

Martin, D., Brigham, P., Roderick, P., Barnett, S., & Diamond, I. (2000). The (Mis)representation of Rural Deprivation. *Environment and Planning A: Economy and Space, 32*(4), 735–751.

Martinez-Brawley, E. (1982). *Rural Social and Community Work in the US and Britain.* Praeger.

Martinez-Brawley, E. (1984). In Search of Common Principles in Rural Social and Community Work. In J. Lishman (Ed.), *Social Work in Rural and Urban Areas.* Aberdeen University.

Martinez-Brawley, E. (1986). Community-Orientated Social Work in a Rural and Remote Hebridean Patch. *International Social Work, 29*(4), 349–372.

Martinez-Brawley, E. (1990). *Perspectives on the Small Community: Humanistic Views for Practitioners Silver.* NASW Press.

Martinez-Brawley, E. (2000). *Close to Home: Human Services and the Small Community Silver.* NASW Press.

Martinez-Brawley, E. (2012). Revisiting Barra: Changes in the Structure and Delivery of Social Work Services in the outer Hebrides – Are Rural Tenets Still Alive? *British Journal of Social Work, 42*(8), 1608–1625.

May, J., Williams, A., Cloke, P., & Cherry, L. (2020). Still Bleeding: The Variegated Geographies of Austerity and Food Banking in Rural England and Wales. *Journal of Rural Studies, 79*, 409–424.

McAreavey, R. (2012). Resistance or Resilience - Tracking the Pathways of Recent Arrivals to a "New" Rural Destination. *Sociologia Ruralis, 52*, 488–507.

McCulloch, T., & Taylor, S. (2018). Becoming a Social Worker: Realising a Shared Approach to Professional Learning? *British Journal of Social Work, 48,* 2272–2290.

Miller, M. & Barrie, K. (2022) *Setting the Bar.* Social Work Scotland. Accessed August 2012, from https://socialworkscotland.org/reports/settingthebar/

Moore, H. (2013). Shades of Whiteness: English Villagers, Eastern European Migrants and the Intersection of Race and Class in Rural England. *Critical and Whiteness Studies, 9*(1), 1–19.

Morgan, H. (2017). Hiding, Isolation and Solace: Rural Disabled Women and Neoliberal Welfare Reform. In K. Soldatic & K. Johnson (Eds.), *Disability and rurality: Identity.* Gender and Belonging.

Moss, L. (Ed.). (2006). *The Amenity Migrants: Seeking and Sustaining Mountains and Their Cultures.* CABI.

Muñoz-Guzmán, C. (2018). Re-visioning Social Work Education: A Nonexclusive Challenge for the United Kingdom. *International Social Work, 61*(2), 302–307.

Narey, M. (2014). *Making the Education of Social Workers Consistently Effective* [Online]. Accessed August 18, 2022, from https://assets.publishing.service. gov.uk/government/uploads/system/uploads/attachment_data/file/287756/ Making_the_education_of_social_workers_consistently_effective.pdf

National Institute for Social Work. (1982). *Social Workers – Their Role and Tasks.* Bedford Square Press.

Neal, S., Gawlewicz, A., Heley, J., & Dafydd Jones, R. (2021). Rural Brexit? The Ambivalent Politics of Rural Community, Migration and Dependency. *Journal of Rural Studies, 82,* 176–183.

Nelson, K. S., Nguyen, T. D., Brownstein, N. A., Garcia, D., Walker, H. C., Watson, J. T., & Xin, A. (2021). Definitions, Measures, and Uses of Rurality: A Systematic Review of the Empirical and Quantitative Literature. *Journal of Rural Studies, 82,* 351–365.

Nicholson, L., & Cooper, S.-A. (2013). Social Exclusion and People with Intellectual Disabilities: A Rural-Urban Comparison: Rural Social Exclusion. *Journal of Intellectual Disability Research, 57*(4), 333–346.

Noble, M., Wright, G., Smith, G., & Dibben, C. (2006). Measuring Multiple Deprivation at the Small-Area Level. *Environment and Planning A: Economy and Space, 38*(1), 169–185.

Parker, J. (2020). Descent or Dissent? A Future of Social Work Education in the UK Post-Brexit. *European Journal of Social Work, 23*(5), 837–848.

Philip, L., & Williams, F. (2019). Remote Rural Home Based Businesses and Digital Inequalities: understanding Needs and Expectations in a Digitally Underserved Community. *Journal of Rural Studies, 68,* 306–318.

Philo, C. (1992). Neglected Rural Geographies: A Review. *Journal of Rural Studies, 8*(2), 193–207.

Pugh, R. (2000). *Rural Social Work.* Lyme Regis RHP.

Pugh, R. (2010). Responding to Rural Racism – Delivering Local Services. In N. Chakraborti & J. Garland (Eds.), *Rural racism.* Routledge.

Pugh, R., & Cheers, B. (2010). *Rural Social Work: An International Perspective.* Policy Press.

Pye, J., Kaloudis, H., & Devlin, M. (2020). *Rural Social Work in Cumbria: An Exploratory Case Study. [Online].* Accessed August 19, 2022, from https://www.cfj-lancaster.org.uk/projects/rural-social-work-in-cumbria-an-exploratory-study

Robinson, M. (2018). *Climate Justice: A Man-Made Problem with a Feminist Solution.* Bloomsbury.

Rural England. (2021). *State of Rural Service 2021: The Impact of the Pandemic Executive Summary Report.* Accessed February 13, 2022, from https://rural-england.org/wp-content/uploads/2022/01/state-of-rural-services-2021-executive-summary.pdf

Samson, P. (2015). Practice Wisdom: The Art and Science of Social Work. *Journal of Social Work Practice, 29*(2), 119–131.

Savage, M. (2010). *Identities and Social Change in Britain since 1940: The Politics of Method.* Oxford University Press.

Scales, T., Streeter, C., & Cooper, H. (2014). *Rural Social Work - Building and Sustaining Community Capacity* (2nd ed.). Wiley.

Scharf, T., Walsh, K., & O'Shea, E. (2016). Ageing in Rural Places. In M. Shucksmith & D. L. Brown (Eds.), *Routledge International Handbook of Rural Studies.* Routledge.

Scottish Government. (2016). *Urban Rural Classification.* Accessed December 2022, from https://www.gov.scot/publications/scottish-government-urban-rural-classification-2016

Scottish Government. (2019). *Brexit: Unheard Voices - Views from Stakeholders Across Scotland on Leaving the EU.* Accessed December 2022, from https://www.gov.scot/publications/brexit-unheard-voices-views-stakeholders-scotland-leaving-eu/pages/8/

Sherry, E., & Shortall, S. (2019). Methodological Fallacies and Perceptions of Rural Disparity: How Rural Proofing Addresses Real Versus Abstract Needs. *Journal of Rural Studies, 68*, 336–343.

Shortall, S. (2013). The Role of Subjectivity and Knowledge Power Struggles in the Formation of Public Policy. *Sociology, 47*(6), 1088–1103.

Shortall, S., & Brown, D. L. (2019). Guest Editorial for Special Issue on Rural Inequalities: Thinking About Rural Inequalities as a Cross-National Research Project. *Journal of Rural Studies, 68*, 213–218.

Shucksmith, M. (2012). Class, Power and Inequality in Rural Areas: Beyond Social Exclusion? *Sociologia Ruralis, 52*(4), 377–397.

Shucksmith, M. (2018). Re-imagining the Rural: From Rural Idyll to Good Countryside. *Journal of Rural Studies, 59*, 163–172.

Shucksmith, M., & Brown, D. L. (2016). Framing Rural Studies in the Global North. In M. Shucksmith & D. L. Brown (Eds.), *Routledge International Handbook of Rural Studies*. Routledge.

Skerratt, S., & Hall, C. (2011). Community Ownership of Physical Assets: Challenges, Complexities and Implications. *Local Economy: The Journal of the Local Economy Policy Unit, 26*(3), 170–181.

Skerratt, S., & Steiner, A. (2013). Working with Communities-of-Place: Complexities of Empowerment. *Local Economy: The Journal of the Local Economy Policy Unit, 28*(3), 320–338.

Smith, M., & Whyte, B. (2008). Social Education and Social Pedagogy: Reclaiming a Scottish Tradition in Social Work. *European Journal of Social Work, 11*(1), 15–28.

Somerville, P., Smith, R., & McElwee, G. (2015). The Dark Side of the Rural Idyll: Stories of Illegal/Illicit Economic Activity in the UK Countryside. *Journal of Rural Studies, 39*, 219–228.

Stevens, M., Hussein, S., & Manthorpe, J. (2012). Experiences of Racism and Discrimination Among Migrant Care Workers in England: Findings from a Mixed-Methods Research Project. *Ethnic and Racial Studies, 35*(2), 259–280.

Tilman, R. (2004). Ferdinand Tönnies, Thorstein Veblen and Karl Marx: From Community to Society and Back? *The European Journal of the History of Economic Thought, 11*(4), 579–606.

Turbett, C. (2004). A Decade After Orkney: Towards a Practice Model for Social Work in the Remoter Areas of Scotland. *British Journal of Social Work, 34*(7), 981–985.

Turbett, C. (2010). *Rural Social Work Practice in Scotland*. Venture Press.

Turbett, C. (2011). *Rural Social Work Practice in Scotland*. Venture Press.

Turbett, C. (2014). *Doing Radical Social Work*. Palgrave Macmillan.

Turbett, C. (2018). *A Critical History of Community Social Work in Scotland Glasgow*. IRISS.

Turbett, C. (2019). *Rural Social Work in Scotland*. IRISS Insight 47. Accessed January 2022, from https://www.iriss.org.uk/resources/insights/rural-social-work-scotland

Turbett, C. (2020) Rediscovering *and Mainstreaming Community Social Work in Scotland*. IRISS Insights 57. Accessed August 2022, from https://www.iriss.org.uk/sites/default/files/2020-11/insights-57_0.pdf

Turbett, C. (2021). Accessed January 2022, from https://commonweal.scot/policies/struggling-to-care/

Woods, M. (2009). Rural Geography: Blurring Boundaries and Making Connections. *Progress in Human Geography, 33*(6), 849–858.

World Bank. (n.d.-a) *Rural Population (% of Total Population)*. Accessed February 13, 2022, from https://data.worldbank.org/indicator/SP.RUR.TOTL.ZS?end=2020&start=1960&view=chart

World Bank. (n.d.-b). *Rural Population (% of Total Population) – United Kingdom*. Accessed February 13, 2022, from https://data.worldbank.org/indicator/SP.RUR.TOTL.ZS?end=2020&locations=GB&start=1960&view=chart

Part I

Stigma

2

Social Work at Home: Dual Relationships

Gillian Ritch

Introduction

This book will explore many unique features of rural social work. I would argue that whilst relationships define social work, dual relationships define social work in the rural context.

I first became interested in dual relationships whilst completing my social work degree. My fellow students hailed from the four nations of the UK and brought differing perspectives and experiences. One of the students from London reported a site on social media where service users posted the names of social workers. This was seen as both an invasion of privacy and concerning for the worker and their family. Coming from a small island off the north of Scotland, I was instantly aware that the anonymity experienced by urban workers was utterly unknown to me. Within minutes, people in rural areas can find out where people live, work, the vehicles they drive, and where their children go to school. In remote areas, people will know whom you went out with as a teenager

G. Ritch (✉)
Orkney Islands, Scotland, UK

© The Author(s), under exclusive license to Springer Nature Switzerland AG 2024
C. Turbett, J. Pye (eds.), *Rural Social Work in the UK*, Rethinking Rural,
https://doi.org/10.1007/978-3-031-52440-0_2

and if you got into trouble at school. Anonymity, described on a linear scale, may place a worker serving London at one end and a worker serving Yell, Eday, or Barra at the other. As I continued my education and practice learning placements, I became aware of the strategies and skills the social workers around me used to manage their daily lives. I also noted how my community viewed me and how my family was affected by my career choices. This interest led to discussions with social work colleagues from Scotland and further afield. Their experiences of dual relationships are shared later in this chapter.

Much of the dual relationship discussion concerns *confidentiality*—an issue of general interest in social work and regarded as a fundamental principle quoted widely with its appearance as one of Biestik's 'seven principles' of social work (1961). Just what confidentiality means in practice, given the fact that the rights of individual service users are not absolute and under certain circumstances are limited by the rights of others, including that of the social workers, remains contested (Banks, 2020). Rural communities offer particular challenges to notions of confidentiality (Galambos et al., 2005).

Features of Dual Relationships

What do we mean by the term dual relationships? In much of the academic literature, social work guidance, and policy documents, dual relationship appears interchangeable with terms such as professional boundaries, professional barriers, and boundary transgression/violation. However, the negative connotations associated with the language of the latter is not helpful or accurate when applied to the experiences of rural social workers.

Professional guidance presents a theme. The British Association of Social Workers (BASW), Code of Ethics for Social Workers (2021) 3, *Maintaining professional boundaries state*:

> Social workers should not abuse their position for personal benefit or gratification, financial gain, or for any reason. This applies to people who use their services, colleagues and employers.

Scottish Social Services Council's *Codes of Practice* states:

> As a social service worker, I must uphold public trust and confidence in social services. I will not form inappropriate relationships with people who use services or carers.
> (Scottish Social Services Council, 2016)

BASW *Social Media Guidance* states:

> It is not appropriate to 'accept' service users and their carers as online 'friends' (…) or in any other way to create an online personal relationship. It could also be used as evidence in conduct hearings.

And,

> workers should maintain appropriate personal and professional boundaries (…), recognising that not to do so could be detrimental to themselves, their careers, service users, other individuals and employers.
> (BASW, 2018, p. 7).

The guidance above seems vague and somewhat menacing, focusing on social workers controlling their danger to others while protecting their careers and integrity.

It is helpful to look at Reamer's (2003) classification of dual relationships, which identify five themes, the latter three having particular relevance to rural social work.

1. Intimate relationships (sexual, physical contact).
2. Personal benefit (monetary gain, goods, services, information).
3. Emotional and dependency needs (promoting dependence, role reversal, confusing personal and professional lives).
4. Altruistic gestures (performing favours, giving gifts, being available out with one's professional role).
5. Unanticipated circumstances (social and community events, mutual friends, and acquaintances).
(Adapted from Reamer, 2003)

In descriptions by Pugh (2007) and Turbett (2010, 2019), dual relationships have a narrower focus with less emphasis on the risk to the client from the worker. It also confirms the inevitability of dual relationships in rural practice. Altruistic gestures in rural social work may be seen as part of the social work role or as the cultural norm. Service users, their friends, and family often approach the social worker outside of office hours or in social settings. Social workers take on tasks that would not be considered appropriate in an urban setting and will be offered small gifts, particularly food, during home visits. Emotional and dependency needs, confusing personal and professional lives are tasks all rural workers must learn to manage. When the worker is embedded in the local community, there may be regular crossovers in who is providing support and who is being supported. The 'unanticipated circumstances' in Reamer's classification are entirely anticipated in rural settings. Sharing the space where we live and work 'includes managing high-visibility, informality, self-disclosure, trust and mistrust of professionals' dual and multiple roles and blurring of professional and personal boundaries' (Green et al., 2003, p. 95).

There is little research into social workers' experience of dual relationships. With the exception of comments from notable UK-based authors, the majority of research comes from Australia, Canada, and the United States of America, where the role of a social worker varies, as does the definition of 'rural'. However, the correlation between working practices, cultures, and the rural context appears comparable.

For the majority of rural social workers, dual relationships are unavoidable (Gregory et al., 2007; Brocious et al., 2013; Brownlee et al., 2019). Social work clients *are* the community; they are teachers, chefs, hairdressers, taxi drivers, and bank workers. The nature of small communities means that people can have many intersecting roles (Turbett, 2010). For example, the school bus driver may also deliver the mail and take on odd jobs within the community. In this way, social workers' connections with their clients and their families can be multi-layered and multigenerational (Turbett, 2010). The likelihood of a social worker having no prior knowledge of their client would be slim, unless both were new to the area (Brocious et al., 2013). Working in a small community where you live; where your children attend school; where your partner works; and where you, your parents, siblings, and friends grew up makes dual relationships a part of life: 'While any social worker working in a rural community cannot manage all of the connections and relationships of their immediate family members, workers working in their community of origin would struggle significantly more' (Piché et al., 2015, p. 65).

Numerous research papers look at social workers' well-being and the impact of stress; however, there is little exploration of these issues in relation to rural social work. The limited research available indicates that dual relationships can have a significant impact on workers' well-being (Brownlee et al., 2012). A study looking at dual relationships and workers' well-being in rural Australia explored strategies social workers employed to protect their own and their family's physical and emotional safety, including withholding phone numbers and screening which clients they accepted. Several participants had 'deliberately sought to distance themselves physically from their working environment' by commuting to their workplace (Gregory et al., 2007, p. 19). Workers reported this separation of professional and personal as having a positive impact on their health and well-being. The ability to commute is not always a feasible option in rural areas. In island communities, the separation of work and home is entirely impractical, involving lengthy boat trips which may only be provided once or twice a week. The ability to screen which service users one supports is not always an option in small rural teams. There are also additional pressures faced by social workers undertaking statutory duties who are required to provide a service that is not always welcomed. Examples of harassment faced by rural social workers in Australia include, 'verbal abuse, … malicious gossip and complaints abuse, invasion of privacy at social events and in public places, … sexual references, … episodes of stalking and excessive contact…' (Green et al., 2003, p. 100).

The findings of this study concur with Canadian research completed by Halverson and Brownlee (Brownlee et al., 2012) and Piché et al. (2015). Social workers frequently employed avoidance and isolation strategies in an effort to keep themselves and their family safe and avoid conflict with clients. The concerns raised in these papers were not universal. Studies also recognised that some participants felt that rather than isolation, their well-being was supported by 'a rich social life and family involvement in the community' (Piché et al., 2015, p. 60). This sense of being accepted by the community promoted connectedness and belonging.

In rural areas, dual relationships are not limited to the social worker/ service user relationship. This crossover is interprofessional and inter-agency. The available research identifies that interprofessional dual relationships for most rural social workers are unavoidable. In the course of a working day, rural workers may come into contact with health professionals whose practice they attend, a health visitor who supported their children, police officers who are friends of their partner, and teachers who taught them when they were children. Where interagency working was discussed in the research, the consensus exhorted the benefits of trusted peers, supportive team working, and reciprocal support (Brownlee et al., 2012; Riebschleger, 2007).

One of the few papers to touch on workers who worked with a colleague or their family on a professional basis acknowledged the role conflict and ethical dilemmas involved (Brownlee et al., 2012). Workers struggled with the dichotomy between their duty to adhere to their professional codes of ethics and provide a much-needed service. The lack of specialist services in remote areas can place added pressures on social workers to support clients with whom they have a dual relationship (Humble et al., 2013; Brocious et al., 2013). With this lack of provision, there are limits to the kind of work undertaken with clients outside of the one-to-one relationship with the worker. Group work can be challenging when many participants know each other and have previous associations or preconceived ideas, both positive and negative. Limited Third Sector providers in rural areas mean that social workers have little if any choice in where to refer clients for support. Humble et al. (2013) explained that workers in rural communities are required to take on multiple roles. The lack of training opportunities available to rural workers can be seen as disadvantaging the very workers who are expected to take on diverse, generalist duties (Turbett, 2004, 2010).

In a rare study looking at dual relationships from a strength perspective, Brocious et al. (2013) maintain that there is a need for workers to be 'interwoven' with the community. The benefits of cultural sensitivity and an ability to appropriately manage prior and historical knowledge of clients were seen as essential to positive community relationships and practice. These findings were reflected in Halverson and Brownlee (2010) in Brownlee et al. (2012) and Beecher et al. (2016), where some participants felt that their close ties and prior knowledge benefited the client as they already had a trusting relationship. Gregory et al. (2007) point out that whilst workers gain information relating to their clients on many levels, this is a reciprocal process, and clients also gain the worker's information. The lack of anonymity was a feature of the reviewed literature (Riebschleger, 2007; McAuliffe et al., 2007; Green et al., 2003). The disparity between how workers are perceived in the community and how they perceive themselves can contribute negatively to workers' well-being (Shier & Graham, 2015).

How social workers managed their professional identities was the focus of research in rural Canada (Brownlee et al., 2012). This study linked how workers were viewed in the community, to their professional identity and credibility. Social Workers were aware of the need to manage their behaviour in their social and private lives to ensure they were perceived as 'professional'. The study acknowledged that this was particularly difficult for workers practising in their home community. Their past behaviour as teenagers or the behaviours of their family and friends could impact the worker's credibility and professional image. Although this experience of developing a professional identity will be similar for others in helping professions, the role of social worker seems less clear than in other professions. One only has to search for 'definition of social worker' and compare the results to a search for police officer or doctor. It can be difficult for people to know where the role of a social worker begins and ends; therefore, expectations can be unrealistic, leading to disappointment or frustration.

Never NOT the Social Worker?

In the first section of this chapter, the research base was examined, terminology defined, and factors leading to the development of dual relationships identified. This section will examine how dual relationships can impact social workers and their families. The title of this section was difficult, 'Never not the social worker?' Social work is not a 9 to 5 job: its responsibilities, duties, and values do not end with the working day. However, in remote and rural settings, the social workers are *always* the social workers. The quotations in this section have all been gathered from the author's colleagues, some informally through workplace chat, and some sought systematically through a growing interest in the subject based on reading and comparisons with workers in other settings—rural and urban. The frequency with which this subject arises in routine conversations suggests that dual relationships and their negotiation are regularly remarked upon in rural settings where workers share place with the people they serve.

One complicating aspect of dual relationships research is, ironically, dual relationships. When information is gathered, either by an inside researcher or by an external researcher, risks around confidentiality and identity are immediately faced. Although the need for confidentiality is understood and expected in research, it is not straightforward. In an environment where workers are interconnected personally and professionally, where their families and friends are equally interwoven, redacting names and ages from research is not sufficient. In a rural setting, an individual seeking care and support for their elderly parent may have required children and family's social work input as a child and mental health or justice support in later years. The knowledge held by workers in these environments can span generations. By knowledge, I refer not only to computerised data storage but to the personal, social, and anecdotal knowledge that is carried as members of a community. The most veiled reference or obscure throwaway comment can identify individuals. There are many workers new to rural areas who, in passing, have complained about the service in a restaurant or shop, only to discover they have been discussing their new colleague's family or friend. Although embarrassing, this is relatively harmless; however, when people are identified in a professional context, the breach of trust can be irreparable. Due to this, the experiences I share have been changed in all identifiable ways; however, the core and the emotional resonance remain the same. Rural social workers reading these stories may identify immediately with the experiences, like putting on an old coat. For others, these experiences will feel quite alien to their practice.

So how does it *feel* when your professional and social lives converge? How does it feel when your professional role impacts your family? Moreover, how does it feel when you need support in your private life from your colleagues and interagency professionals? *Agreement was secured to use the quotations below.*

A social worker related the story of taking their young child to a local leisure centre on a Saturday afternoon:

On arrival, they were told the activity they wished to attend was closed for a private function. The child was understandably disappointed. When consoling the child, the worker was interrupted by a service user they had supported two years previously. The service user advised that the activity was closed because they were having a party for their child. The service user asked the worker's child if they would like to come and join in with the party. After excited pleading from their child, and the recognition that their working relationship had been positive and enjoyable, the social worker felt it would be churlish to refuse. Upon entering the venue, the worker immediately realised that several current and past service users were present with their children. Delighted, the worker's child ran off to play with the other children. The social worker soon became aware that they had become the topic of conversation by the looks and less than discreet comments. Although the worker felt confident in their relationship with the party organiser, this was not the case with others present.

The worker explained their thought process and the dilemma they found themself in.

> I thought, 'Should I just leave? But if I left, it would be obvious that I was leaving because of some of the people present.' I was aware I needed to preserve working relationships, and my behaviour and reactions were being judged. Would they believe I was leaving because I did not want my child playing with theirs? Should I walk over and chat away as if I belonged? But I was aware of the hostile looks and felt vulnerable and exposed. I knew if I took my child away, they would be disappointed and vocal about leaving a party they were enjoying. I would then get comments about how badly the social worker's child behaved and my shortcomings as a parent. I felt foolish for putting myself and my child in this position.

For this worker, what was meant to be a lovely day out with their child became a source of upset and guilt. In these fleeting moments, the worker had tried to manage the positive relationship with an ex-service user, current service users where the relationship was new and tenuous, and one service user who viewed them with overt hostility. Alongside these professional thoughts, they also had their responsibilities to their child.

This situation, in one guise or another, is not uncommon in rural settings. The factors involved are so varied and complex that no written guidance or policy could possibly fit the minutiae of the situation. However, the worker involved required support to process these complex events. They needed to reflect in a safe space and to develop coping strategies transferable to the next unforeseen merger of personal and professional. This worker's child was at an age where they were oblivious to the unfolding dilemma faced by their parent. Tensions can also develop when a worker's child is aware of their parent's social work role. Social workers can be the allocated worker for children in their own child's class or social circle.

One social worker recalled returning home to find a young person who was on the Child Protection register sitting in their home, having befriended their teenager:

> I walked in and stopped dead. My child said, 'I've asked xx for dinner, is that okay?' The young person knew who I was and my job, as I had worked with them. However, my own child did not know of the connection.

Again, the thought process was explained.

> I could not disclose that I knew this young person as I would be breaching their confidentiality. However, my knowledge of the young person and their family made me uneasy. This was a complicated situation as I was concerned that the young person was looking for a relationship which I could not provide. I was worried about how the young person's family would view this situation. I also wondered if there was an agenda behind the young person befriending my child.

This was a challenging situation for the social worker who had to share the events with their supervisor. The supervisor believed they had encouraged the young person and had fostered an inappropriate dependency. There was little support offered in managing the situation going forward.

Workers hold considerable knowledge in a rural setting; this is true of all professions in health, police, and social services. This knowledge can inform decision-making in social situations such as workers' teenagers going out with a friend or being asked for sleepovers. It can also build levels of ethical stress in social situations. Workers will know that rumours and malicious gossip are wholly incorrect but be unable to intervene to correct the misinformation or defend their service users. Although upholding privacy and confidentiality is understood on a professional level, in reality, this can feel like condoning or, at worst, being complicit in misinformation. Gossip can be corrected, but only after discussion and the consent of the victim—a long-held tenet for rural social workers (Pugh, 2007).

Social workers report being approached by service users when out with their friends and family. This happens in shops, cafes, or public parks. Service users can breach their own confidentiality and privacy by discussing issues in public. This leaves the social worker to manage the disclosures when others are in hearing. Social workers talked about their family members walking away when the worker is approached by people they do not know or may know when the conversion appears work-related. One worker said,

> My family know not to ask whom I was speaking with as they know I may have difficulty responding sometimes, the best response is 'it's someone from work'.

but in this situation, not answering is, unfortunately, answer enough. Not all such meetings are confrontational or distressing; many meetings are pleasurable and friendly, a natural consequence of small community life. However, they are an additional layer that will need consideration, both through a professional and personal lens. I have spoken with many social workers who report meeting service users in the local supermarket, with the contents of the worker's trolley being brought up at the next meeting. One worker reported a service user saying, 'Well, you can't tell me I shouldn't be drinking; I saw you buying three bottles of wine last week'.

Social workers and their families can be held to high standards, and the congruence of their professional and personal identities judged. One worker reported being out with their children in a café when a service user approached them. The service user was unhappy that the worker had been unable to secure funds from their ex-partner. The service user had loudly complained that their children were going hungry when the social worker was out 'living it up'. When the worker had quietly advised that they would discuss the issue on Monday when they were at work, the service user shouted, 'You don't have time for me'. The worker had to reassure and explain to their children that they were not letting other children starve.

On other occasions, information is shared with the social worker's family when the worker is not present. A worker explained that their husband had been approached by an acquaintance at work, saying how much they appreciated the support their mother had been given when she required a care service. Saying, 'Your wife was excellent and sorted everything quickly', they added, 'we were really struggling with doing all the housework and personal care'. This was gratitude for a job well done where the person was very pleased with social work involvement. However, bits of this conversation were overheard and passed on in gossip as the worker's husband was discussing his wife's cases.

High levels of scrutiny are expected in rural settings; workers are more visible and therefore accessible to service users and professionals. We are all aware of our neighbours and have an understanding of their lives to a greater or lesser degree. The levels of scrutiny experienced by rural workers can be dismissed by some or seen as irksome by others. How scrutiny is viewed depends on the social workers' personality, role, and experiences they and their families have. A statutory role in children's services and involvement in child protection and neglect situations are not always welcomed by the families whom workers are required to support. Social workers involved with Adult Support and Protection processes can be met with distrust and hostility. Mental Health Social Workers support people who, due to their illness, can become a risk to themselves and, on rare occasions, others. The combination of feeling at risk and being scrutinised can be oppressive. When the worker's family gets drawn into their professional role, these feelings can extend to their private lives.

Social workers whose children, partners, or parents require justice services, mental health, or care services can be in the position of working side by side with the professionals providing these services. The more remote and rural the setting, the smaller the teams and the closer that working relationship will be. The worker's chances of interacting socially are also increased, either by choice or through the normal closeness of rural life.

One worker whose family member required a service reported overhearing the case being discussed in the office. They also saw references to their family in Out Of Hours information which was shared with the team. Supporting colleagues' families can be incredibly difficult for the workers involved and the team.

There is a misconception that rural social workers do not hold high numbers or complex cases. This is akin to the fallacy that the countryside is crime, drugs, and poverty-free. All issues faced in urban areas are reflected in rural settings; they may just be better concealed (Schmidt, 2020). Social workers in rural areas rarely have specialist teams, meaning workers will hold cases from initial assessment to complex protection work. Rural working at its best provides a broad range of duties and experiences, which feeds professional growth, expands skills, and provides job satisfaction. However, this lack of specialisms can leave workers feeling unprepared and insecure in their knowledge.

When the worker themselves is the person requiring a social work or health service, the stigma and lack of anonymity can compound the 'normal' levels of stress experienced by social workers. Workers experiencing stress, burnout, or other mental health concerns will be aware that their issues are unlikely to remain private at work and in the community, not necessarily by what is said, but by what is left unsaid. If no physical health reason for a long-term absence is forthcoming, the silence can speak volumes, and rumours may fill the gap. Unfortunately, for many, it still remains more acceptable to have a broken body than a damaged mind.

The typical advice for managing depression, anxiety, or stress may also be more complicated in rural settings. In seeking professional support, workers will be required to disclose their mental health concerns to managers and interagency partners whom they likely work with professionally. The worker may work on a protection case alongside a doctor or nurse who knows they are struggling with their own mental health. The advice of 'take up an activity, join a group or get outside for walks' can be difficult when, as discussed earlier, the worker comes into contact with service users as part of their day. Should they be signed off work, the issues are compounded as the worker will be seen out and about, but people will know they are off work. Social workers fight to uphold social justice, social work values, and service users' rights. Article 8 of the Human Rights Act protects the right to a private and family life. The profession must not forget that these rights also extend to workers and their families.

The events described above are not unusual. The stories that make up a rural social worker's rich mine of experiences can be upsetting, life-affirming, and downright hilarious. Sometimes, the term 'six degrees of separation' feels like a massive overestimate. So, if there is an awareness of the complexities and impact of dual relationships in rural practice, where and how does the worker seek guidance and support? Pugh answers that social workers learn the 'dynamics of rural life and practice almost entirely from their personal experiences, with little or no research support or theoretical analysis of the setting within which they operate' (2003, p. 68).

Essentially, practitioners learn 'on the go' from their personal, colleagues', and service users' experiences. The lack of support and guidance is filled with practice wisdom, an unrecognised and undervalued resource; however, social workers are registered professionals and should have access to professional, relevant, and accurate guidance. Firstly, there needs to be an acceptance that rural social work is not the same as urban social work. The way work is undertaken is diverse, as are the challenges.

Rural social workers are connected to their community in a way that is not possible or understood in urban settings. Lord Clyde showed the dichotomy rural social workers face in his 1992 report.

> The trust and confidence which each should have in the other cannot be effectively secured if the Social Worker appears as a remote occasional visitor who does not in any sense belong to the area. However, there must be

limits to this approach. The Social Worker cannot be expected always to reside in a particular area. Indeed, too constant a presence might well be counter-productive.
(Clyde, 1992, p. 340)

Social workers should be readily accessible and available to the particular community which they serve and know and be known by it.
(Clyde, 1992, p. 363)

These two statements clearly identify the balance expected from workers, to be both *readily accessible and available* and *not too constant a presence.*

Recommendations and Insights from Practice

The data gap evident in the research, which leads to policy development and practice guidance, needs to be recognised. As discussed earlier, research into dual relationships is not a simple matter, but I would argue that it is necessary, particularly in relation to the recruitment and retention of workers. The difficulties around staffing rural areas, for several reasons, are well known, but dual relationships are rarely considered a contributory factor: another data gap? This being the case, what can social workers and their managers do to support this undeniably complex issue?

- *Setting the scene, not the barrier!*
- When service users first seek support, it will be helpful to find their connections to workers as an aid to worker allocation. Social workers may be unconcerned about working with friends or distant relatives, but the service user may feel differently and vice versa. Where these situations are unavoidable, which they often are in remote areas, even where there are no apparent connections, there will likely be at some point, so it can be helpful to set the scene. Discussion around what happens when they meet in social settings, functions, or just passing on the street are better explored before they occur 'are you happy for me to say hello when we meet, or would you rather I didn't?' This can

reduce misunderstandings and uncomfortable silences when both are trying to figure out what is wanted. Someone you have said hello to for years in passing may view you differently as their social worker, so there is worth in exploring greetings. The social worker and the service user may have very different interpretations of what confidently means to them; therefore, upfront conversations are often beneficial, 'I don't speak about the work we do together as I'm aware people talk and pick up bits of information'. 'I know you are friends with my cousin, but I don't discuss our work with anyone'. A worker who is seen as indiscreet will quickly face obstacles. Nevertheless, as discussed earlier, information in a small community can be like holding water in your hands; some will always get out.

- *Sharing is caring, and it's expected.*
- Rural workers will be asked about themselves and their family in an attempt to 'place' them and establish their connection to the person they support and their community (Pugh, 2003). This is particularly evident when working with older adults. Who are your parents? Where did they come from? Or, as said in Orkney, where do you belong? An urban social worker may feel uncomfortable sharing themselves in this way, but to refuse to answer or, worse, present as officious with, 'we are here to talk about you, not me', will be met with closed looks and the likely end of a positive working relationship. If workers are going to be allowed into service users' lives, be told their troubles, and accept their help, it is seen as common decency to know a bit about them. Once the worker is satisfactorily placed, the work can commence. The modern and common equivalent is exploring social media accounts. This form of sharing is not to be confused with unethical emotional or private disclosures, which compromise the social worker's professionalism and cause damage. Feminists have long challenged the masculinist idea of the objective observer (or practitioner) and have carried ideas of sharing and reciprocity into social work practice, notably in the area of support to the victims of domestic abuse (Hardy, 1991; Wendt & Moulding, 2016).
- *Find support and hold on.*
- For some of the reasons outlined earlier, finding support can be challenging in a rural area. Where confidentiality is vital, workers must

have confidence in formal and informal support. Social workers aspire to work safely, with professional supervision that guides practice, explores decision-making, and develops confidence and skills. Open discussions may prove difficult where a supervisor is connected to clients professionally or personally. A supervisor who has been or is currently a front-line social worker may have experience with the people discussed in supervision. Here an understanding of confirmation bias needs to go hand in hand with practice wisdom. The relationship they once held will not be the same as that held by their supervisee; situations and people will have changed. Peer supervision and support can be invaluable for workers as there is likely to be a shared understanding of situations without the power differential or hierarchy that may exist in the manager/worker role. It can also be problematic to challenge budget or practice decisions in rural settings. Workers will often know the people in their line management structure well and will be interviewed by them when seeking advancement. These difficulties can be more pronounced for island workers where commuting is not practicable, and there is likely to be one employer. Making ripples in a small pond means you see the effects and feel the wake. What it takes to be a social worker in a rural community is, in the words of Hunter (2020, p. 98), 'messier than what our textbook frameworks or research protocols demand'.

- _The worker is not alone._
- If there is little research on dual relationships through the worker's lens, then research from the service users' view is an unexplored area. Personal experience can be extrapolated from service users' feelings about the contact they have with workers in their social lives. How does it feel for service users when the social worker arrives at a parents' evening? When their social worker attends weddings and social functions? When you see your social worker on a night out, or they arrive at your workplace? Where there is a positive relationship, these meetings may not feel intrusive, but if people feel judged, frightened, or powerless, unexpected contact will be viewed very differently.

And Finally ....

Rural social work can be immensely rewarding; you can actually see the difference your work makes to your community and the people you know. It can also be personally and professionally challenging for workers and their families. An understanding of rural social work's uniqueness, *not just a smaller version of urban social work*, may inform the development of national and local policy and guidance that meets workers' needs. A greater understanding of dual relationships may equip workers and their employers to make supportive decisions that aid workers' practice and their well-being. Training and induction information on rural working would give students and new starts a better idea of the work *and* the way of life they will be embracing. The Covid-19 pandemic has pushed forward remote working and training to the point where location is no longer a barrier. Independent supervision and mental health support could be arranged outside the worker's geographical area, providing safe support pathways. Workers and their family members who require services could equally be supported remotely if this was their choice. The positive aspects of working in a rural or remote community should not be understated; there is real joy and job satisfaction to be had, but by failing to recognise the strengths *and* pressures of dual relationships, we do a disservice to social workers and services users.

References

Banks, S. (2020). *Ethics and Values in Social Work* (5th ed.). Red Globe.

Beecher, B., Reedy, A. R., Loke, V., Walker, J., & Raske, M. (2016). An Exploration of Social Work Needs of Select Rural Behavioral Health Agencies in Washington State. *Social Work in Mental Health, 14*(6), 714–732.

Biestik, F. (1961). *The Casework Relationship*. George Allen & Unwin.

British Association of Social Workers. (2018). *Social Media Policy*. BASW.

British Association of Social Workers. (2021). *Code of Ethics for Social Worker*. BASW.

Brocious, H., Eisenberg, J., York, J., Shepard, H., Clayton, S., & Van Sickle, B. (2013). The Strengths of Rural Social Workers: Perspectives on Managing

Dual Relationships in Small Alaskan Communities. *Journal of Family Social Work, 16*(1), 4–19.

Brownlee, K., Halverson, G., & Chassie, A. (2012). Multiple Relationships: Maintaining Professional Identity in Rural Social Work Practice. *Journal of Comparative Social Work, 7*(1), 81–91.

Brownlee, K., Leblanc, H., Halverson, G., Piché, T., & Brazeau, J. (2019). Exploring Self-Reflection in Dual Relationship Decision-Making. *Journal of Social Work, 19*(5), 629–641.

Clyde, L. J. (1992). *Report of the Inquiry into the Removal of Children from Orkney in February 1991.* HM Stationery Office.

Galambos, C., Watt, W., Anderson, K., & Danis, F. (2005). Forum – Rural Social Work Practice. *Journal of Social Work Ethics and Practice, 2*(2), 84–93.

Green, R., Gregory, R., & Mason, R. (2003). It's No Picnic: Personal and Family Safety for Rural Social Workers. *Australian Social Work, 56*(2), 94–106.

Gregory, R., Green, R., & McLaren, S. (2007). The Development of "Expertness": Rural Practitioners and Role Boundaries. *Rural Social Work & Community Practice, 12*(2), 16–21.

Halverson, G., & Brownlee, K. (2010). Managing Ethical Considerations Around Dual Relationships in Small Rural and Remote Canadian Communities. *International Social Work, 53*(2), 247–260.

Hardy, S. (1991). *Whose Science, Whose Knowledge? Thinking From Womens' Lives.* Cornell University Press.

Humble, M. N., Lewis, M. L., Scott, D. L., & Herzog, J. R. (2013). Challenges in Rural Social Work Practice: When Support Groups Contain Your Neighbours, Church Members, and the PTA. *Social Work with Groups, 36*(2–3), 249–258.

Hunter, C. (2020). I Am with You in Your Pain: Privilege, Humanity, and Cultural Humility in Social Work. *Reflections: Narratives of Professional Helping, 26*(2), 89–100.

McAuliffe, D., Chenoweth, L., & Stehlik, D. (2007). Rural Practitioners of the Future: Views of Graduating Students About Rural Child and Family Practice. *Rural Social Work & Community Practice, 12*(1), 6–14.

Piché, T., Brownlee, K., & Halverson, G. (2015). The Development of Dual Relationships for Social Workers in Rural Communities. *Contemporary Rural Social Work, 7*(2), 57–70.

Pugh, R. (2003). Considering the Countryside: Is There a Case for Rural Social Work? *British Journal of Social Work, 33*(1), 67–85.

Pugh, R. (2007). Dual Relationships: Personal and Professional Boundaries in Rural Social Work. *British Journal of Social Work, 37*(8), 1405–1423.

Reamer, F. G. (2003). Boundary Issues in Social Work: Managing Dual Relationships. *Social Work, 48*(1), 121–133.

Riebschleger, J. (2007). Social Workers' Suggestions for Effective Rural Practice. *Families in Society: The Journal of Contemporary Social Services, 88*(2), 203–213.

Schmidt, G. G. (2020). *Social Work Practice in Remote Communities.* Ronkonkoma.

Scottish Social Services Council. (2016). *Codes of Practice for Social Services Workers and Employers* (Revised ed.). Scottish Social Services Council.

Shier, M. L., & Graham, J. R. (2015). Subjective Well-Being, Social Work, and the Environment: The Impact of the Socio-Political Context of Practice on Social Worker Happiness. *Journal of Social Work, 15*(1), 3–23.

Turbett, C. (2004). A Decade After Orkney: Towards a Practice Model for Social Work in the Remoter Areas of Scotland. *British Journal of Social Work, 34*(7), 981–995.

Turbett, C. (2010). *Rural Social Work Practice in Scotland.* Venture Press.

Turbett, C. (2019). Rural Social Work in Scotland. *Contemporary Rural Social Work Journal, 11*(1), 10.

Wendt, S., & Moulding, N. (Eds.). (2016). *Contemporary Feminisms in Social Work Practice.* Routledge.

3

Alcohol and Other Drug Harm in Rural Scotland: Addiction Looks Different Here

Heather Still

Introduction

Rural Scotland has a great image. There are plenty of areas of outstanding natural beauty, as well as consistently high levels of happiness and a strong community spirit. The Scottish overall tend to trust their neighbours, and that level of trust is even higher in rural areas (Scottish Government, 2020a).

But what happens when you or someone in your family has an addiction? Does that same level of happiness and camaraderie ring true if you are trying to recover?

Dependency and its recovery journey are hard. The shame associated is profound; often individuals and their families have to manage the addiction, the recovery and the stigma, all at the same time with huge varieties in informal and formal support. If a person dies as a result of alcohol and other drugs (AOD), then the individual's family endures a difficult and

H. Still (✉)
Greenock, Scotland, UK
e-mail: heather.still@ggc.scot.nhs.uk

confusing loss. Deaths from alcohol and drugs are the highest they have ever been in Scotland (National Records of Scotland, 2021a, 2021b). The scale of suffering this is causing the population is immeasurable and there is a real urgency for people with lived experience to get the correct support.

The focus on addiction and help for addiction is primarily on urban areas, specifically areas of severe deprivation. This makes sense as deaths and harms from AOD tend to hit the most deprived the hardest in terms of a higher mortality rate and physically poorer health (Scottish Government, 2022). But addiction is universal, it touches every area, class, sex, ethnicity and geography. Addiction can and does occur in rural Scotland and the impact can be as acutely felt by those who experience it, whether directly or through their family. By side-lining addiction in rural areas, suffering resulting from overdoses and deaths caused by AOD in these areas continue under the radar. Side-lining AOD harm is occurring throughout the policy landscape, health and social care and within our culture: complacency is as endemic as the harm AOD are causing in Scotland.

This is of major relevance to social workers as addiction issues feature in all areas of work, from safeguarding of children and vulnerable adults to preventative support duties and functions. Indeed, it is these latter tasks, so often neglected in favour of reactive and downstream statutory duties, that are emphasised throughout the chapters of this book. This factor takes the focus on addiction beyond the treatment and support of those in life-endangering situations, to those whose social circumstances place themselves at risk of harm through alcohol and drug use. These are crucial tasks that fall within the premise of community social work.

As with other areas of statutory social work intervention, there are also class issues in relation to how drug and alcohol problematic behaviours are viewed by agencies (Turbett, 2014). Those in affluent families who have children or parents with drink and other drug problems are much more likely to be missed in needing support as they are not monitored by social or health services in the same way as those with less financial means (Bernard, 2017). Adverse Childhood Experiences—particularly neglect—are presented differently in children who come from higher socioeconomic backgrounds, making neglect that stems from parental addiction harder to pick up on (Bellis et al., 2014). The usual definition of child neglect in social work does mention emotional neglect but it generally focuses on the physical effects of neglect: the absence of food, shelter, water and hygiene, of which affluence can cover these physical symptoms to a certain extent (Bellis et al., 2014; Bernard, 2017). There are also power imbalances when working with families with money or influence, leading to more reluctance by social workers to work with these families, who can use their education and social connections to intimidate staff or even to demand more time and attention than social workers can give (Bernard, 2017).

There will be two ongoing themes in this chapter: The first being that the evidence of AOD prevalence and harm in rural communities is scarce. The 'gold standard' of data science, resources and staff is in the cities, and there is also minimal investment in good quality qualitative data that can thoroughly explore the experiences of addiction in rural UK (Fecht et al., 2017). This makes it hard to analyse and recommend improvements for people living with alcohol and other drug use dependencies within rural social work, despite being a prevalent concern and an evidenced harm in our country.

The second ongoing theme is that addiction looks different depending on where you live. There are fundamental differences in how addiction manifests through individuals in urban and rural communities, as well as differences as to how the community and support services interact with people who are unwell. The same goes for how poverty looks (SHAAP, 2020; Fecht et al., 2017; Roderick et al., 2018) and how crime is committed, further impacting on how health and social care issues around addiction are presented in general.

This chapter will start to look at the general prevalence and harm in Scotland as a whole, before exploring the impact of alcohol and other drugs in rural Scotland. To help with this, I will draw relevant points from the study of alcohol and other drug harm on the Isle of Arran I conducted on a full-time basis in 2019–2020. The research was funded by the Corra Foundation upon the initiative of a local steering group composed of health and social care professionals and Third Sector organisations. They had shared concerns about the absence of data and concrete knowledge about drug and alcohol issues on the island—a discreet locality with a population of just over 4500 people. This chapter is written on the hypothesis that many of the findings and the literature review that accompanied the research have applicability across Scotland's remote communities, and quite probably in similar ones throughout the UK. The research was written up in the paper cited (Still, 2020) and made recommendations for further action on the part of agencies and funders, which are also generalised here.

Alcohol and Other Drug Use and Harm in Scotland

Alcohol Use and Associated Physical Harm in Scotland

It is important to note that 'harm' expands outside of illness and mortality paradigms: alcohol and other drugs can cause substantial harm to a person, their family, the community and society. It is however more difficult to establish AOD harm in more subjective ways.

The first consideration in this section concerns alcohol consumption and consequential alcohol harm. In 2019 the equivalent of 9.9 litres of alcohol were sold per person in Scotland, which corresponds to 19.1 units being drunk by adults every week (Public Health Scotland, 2020). To put that in perspective, harmful alcohol consumption is defined as drinking more than 14 units of alcohol a week and 24% of the Scottish population drink over these levels on a weekly basis, with men (32%) predominantly drinking above recommended safe limits (Scottish Government, 2019a).

Just over half of 13-year-olds and 70% of 15-year-olds have had alcohol at least once. Young people aged between 13 and 15 are most likely to acquire alcohol from family members or the family home than from friends or attempting to purchase from shops (Scottish Government, 2019b).

Precisely 96% of people believe that alcohol is a problem in Scotland, with 74% considering it a big problem (Scottish Government, 2020b). Scotland is aware of the harm alcohol is causing on society.

Deaths where alcohol was an underlying cause totalled 1190 people in 2019, an increase of 17% since the previous year. Men accounted for 826 of the total number of deaths (National Records of Scotland, 2021a), and a total of 35,124 alcohol-related hospitalisations were accounted for.

The most direct innocent victims of harmful alcohol consumption are unborn babies. Drinking alcohol during pregnancy, irrespective of stage, is linked to foetal alcohol spectrum disorder (FASD). FASD is a lifelong neurodevelopmental disorder that takes place 'when an unborn baby is exposed to alcohol' (Healthcare Improvement Scotland, 2019, p. 5). FASD can affect memory, cognition, language, emotional regulation, overall brain structure and development. There are a large proportion of children and young people with FASD who are under the care of social services either in care or fostering, with many foster or adoptive parents being unaware that the child or young person may have FASD (Gralton, 2014), and it is estimated that up to 80% of children who are care-experienced will not have access to their developmental history, making a diagnosis of FASD difficult (Streissguth et al., 2004). Parents or guardians who have children with FASD may also need social work support due to the additional needs these children may have (Gralton, 2014). At the time of writing, there is only one specialist healthcare service in Scotland concerned with FASD community care—NHS Ayrshire.

Evidence on needs of adults with FASD in Scotland is slim but healthcare professionals suggest that they have a higher rate of mental ill health and suicide attempts (Dirks et al., 2019), unemployment, incarceration and substance dependency (NHS Ayrshire & Arran Foetal Alcohol Advisory and Support Team, n.d.). It is likely that social workers will have contact with adults who have diagnosed or undiagnosed FASD throughout their career.

It is thought that drinking during pregnancy in the UK is the highest of the World Health Organisation European Region (WHO, 2018). In Scotland, about 54% of women have had alcohol leading up to or in the early stages of pregnancy. Eleven per cent of women will continue to drink alcohol when they find out they are pregnant (Scottish Government, 2017). One study in Glasgow suggested around 40% of babies have been exposed to alcohol in utero, with 15% at significant levels. There were no differences in consumption in relation to deprivation, postcode or ethnicity (Abernethy et al., 2018). Midwives have expressed difficulty in starting honest conversations with pregnant women and note that self-reporting methods alone are insufficient in determining alcohol drunk during pregnancy (Schölin & Fitzgerald, 2019).

Despite this, FASD is being called a 'governmental blind spot' (Sher et al., 2019) with policies being built around 'lessons learned' and crisis management (Sher, 2017), missing preventative measures to limit FASD occurring as well as underinvestment in interventions to limit harm caused by FASD within individuals and the family.

There is also little research globally on how alcohol may contribute towards sperm damage resulting in neurodevelopmental or physical health disorders. Since males in Scotland are some of the heaviest drinkers globally, this is an urgent research issue due to the impact FASD has on family and on social services.

Other Drug Use and Associated Physical Harm in Scotland

Consumption of other drugs is harder to recognise because there is no legalised market. The Scottish Crime and Justice Survey (2020b) says the highest amount of seized illicit drugs were cannabis, benzodiazepines and heroin. Self-reported measures indicate that 9.7% of respondents used illicit drugs within the last reporting year. The top three most commonly reported illicit drugs were cannabis, followed by cocaine and ecstasy (Scottish Crime and Justice Survey, 2020b). Prevalence of dependence on illicit drugs in Scotland is estimated to be around 1.62% of the Scottish population, 71% of whom are male (NHS National Services Scotland, 2019).

There were 1339 drug deaths in Scotland in 2020, the highest ever recorded (National Records of Scotland, 2021b). There were 14,310 drug-related hospital stays in 2020/21, lower than in previous years, but this is thought to be due to the COVID-19 pandemics (NHS National Services Scotland, 2019). Approximately 3.8% of people who inject drugs are thought to have HIV in Scotland (UK Health Security Agency, 2021), and 1423 new cases of Hepatitis C were reported in people who inject drugs (MacLeod et al., 2019).

As with FASD, unborn babies also suffer the consequences of illicit (unprescribed) parental drug use. Between 2019 and 2020 drug use was recorded in 1.6% of 47,676 pregnancies (Public Health Scotland, 2021). Cannabis, cocaine and opiates (including prescription opiates) were the most common drugs used during pregnancy. Neonatal Abstinence Syndrome (NAS) takes place when a newborn is in withdrawal from drugs absorbed during pregnancy. A newborn with NAS can be premature and have a low birth weight, difficulty with latching, mottled skin, high-pitched excessive crying, vomiting and tremors. It is thought that 0.2% of births in Scotland have NAS (Public Health Scotland, 2021). Due to the physicality and almost instant symptoms of NAS, there are guidelines for referral to social services (Ellis & Grant, 2019).

Harm Caused to Families

There are significant amounts of people in Scotland who have lived or are living with parents/guardians with an AOD dependency. Precisely 21% of adults reported living with a parent/guardian who has AOD dependency, whilst 17% of children are thought to be currently living with a parent(s)/ guardian displaying harmful alcohol behaviour or dependence (Scottish Government, 2019a).

The consequences of this are deep and complex. Most of the literature around family members is based on the needs of children (Holleran, 2020). Growing up with a loved one who has AOD dependency features in the literature and official reports as Adverse Childhood Experience (ACE) and can impact on a person's behaviour, mood and physical health throughout their lives (Marryat & Frank, 2019). Children of family members with AOD dependency often become carers for their loved ones, something they carry through to adulthood (Church et al., 2018). Orford et al. (2010) analysed two decades of research into family experiences and noted that family members have significant amount of stress and worry on a daily basis about whether their loved one will die or is dead, about money, and fear of safety if their loved one becomes aggressive whilst intoxicated. Caring responsibility seemed to overwhelmingly affect women and girls.

Family members will often take on the role of support services for their loved ones: advocating on their behalf, meeting basic needs such as food and shelter, encouraging attendance to recovery services and providing a source of empathy and care, but this can go unnoticed or unappreciated by recovery services (Scottish Families Affected by Alcohol and Drugs, 2019). Some families feel that support for people with AOD dependency and their families was lacking because dealing with these cases was deemed too difficult or too risky. Families have also described feeling blamed, judged or ignored by statutory services, as often they are sharing the same stigma as those personally experiencing AOD dependency and have historically been blamed societally as causing or contributing to a person's dependency (Holleran, 2020; Church et al., 2018; Orford, 2017). I have heard of cases where family members are kept out of meetings by social services or hospital staff for reasons of confidentiality, despite being the main carer or living with their loved one. Consequently they are left to deal with the caring aspects of their loved one without any understanding as to why they were in hospital or being visited by social services (Fig. 3.1).

Prevalence of Alcohol and Other Drug Use in Rural Scotland

Alcohol is the most normalised drug and can be seen more openly in rural areas than other drugs, especially in winter where most other activities are closed (SHAAP, 2020). It seems that alcohol is the drug of choice in rural Scotland, as it is nationally, primarily due to the accessibility, normalisation and affordability in comparison to other drugs. Alcohol is woven into rural culture, particularly with whisky in the highlands where the whisky distillery industry took off in the 1800s (MacDonald, 2020) and it is commonplace to offer whisky as a drink instead of or alongside tea (SHAAP, 2020). Due to whisky being a historic part of the rural economy, it has become an integral part of the romanticised versions of Scottish identity, minimising the harm chronic drinking or dependence can cause (MacDonald, 2020).

The prevalence of drinking manifests itself in how boredom, a lack of non-drinking social opportunities and low mood interact in rural settings. There have been examples of people acknowledging that they would drink less if there were more non-drinking social facilities available

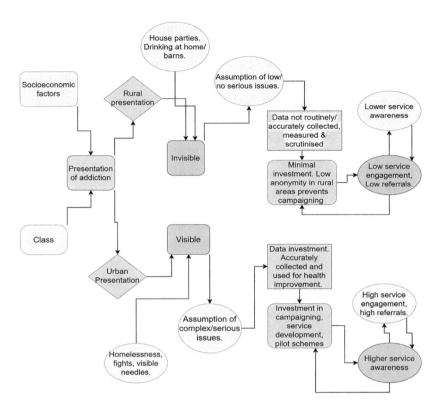

Fig. 3.1 Presentation for Dependency on Urban Versus Rural Settings

to them (Galloway et al., 2007). Adolescents are also more likely to drink for negative reasons in remote areas in comparison to urban centres, suggesting that adequate mental health support is less available to certain areas of Scotland (Martin et al., 2019) or that the stigma of mental health prevents people from accessing support (Daly, 2014).

Whilst these insights offer an understanding as to how alcohol harm might form in rural Scotland, they have not developed into a national evidence base. Harm from alcohol and other drugs on a national scale is separated through deprivation levels, rather than urban/rural demographics (SHAAP, 2020), as exemplified by the Rights, Respect and Recovery action plan (Scottish Government, 2018) which measures differences in alcohol and other drugs through deprivation, missing the different context of rural poverty (SHAAP, 2020). There is no distinction or understanding for urban/rural differences in governmental alcohol and other drug policy.

Illicit drug use is not thought to be as common in rural areas compared to urban areas (Scottish Crime and Justice Survey, 2020b), although with better Wi-Fi connectivity more drug dealing to larger rural areas has been noted (Matthews et al., 2021). Older studies however suggested that illicit drug use in rural Scotland (Forsyth & Barnard, 1999) and UK (Vivancos et al., 2006) is either as prevalent or more prevalent than originally thought. One study of illicit drug use in Norfolk even suggested that some illicit drug use is higher in rural areas (Roderick et al., 2018).

Hidden in Plain Sight

It is important to note that whilst mental health in rural areas is starting to be discussed in the policy landscape, the same is not true for alcohol and other drugs. An example of this is the Scottish Government's National Islands Plan (Scottish Government, 2019c) where they mention that mental health 'was frequently mentioned during consultation as being an area of crucial importance that can be overlooked and under resourced in relation to health and wellbeing on the islands' (p. 47). Arguably, alcohol and other drugs are also of crucial importance and can be overlooked and under resourced in island location; however, they were not mentioned in the plan at all, effectively helping the narrative that alcohol and other drug harms do not materialise in island communities. This is partially because poverty, crime and addiction look different in remote areas, and this is down to our own biases of the 'type' of person that develops an addiction. The stereotyped links between addiction, criminality, poverty and unemployment are entrenched in how we approach dependence.

Crime

Crime in general is lower in rural areas, although it is noted that theft of money or possessions is likely to occur within the family (Stallwitz & Shewan, 2004). Theft from within the family was also something mentioned on Arran by police and health services.

As a way for rural communities to distance themselves from the issue of illicit drugs being within their vicinity, crime associated with illicit drugs as well as the illicit drugs themselves are generally seen as being 'brought in' from urban areas and is portrayed this way in the media. Examples of this include *'Orkney drugs dog helps police in Glasgow sniff out £10,000 substances'* (Munro, 2020); *'Heroin had taken hold, couriered in by drugs gangs from Liverpool and Glasgow'* (Carrell, 2008). This tactic reinforces the belief that certain illicit drug use is an urban problem. Some rural areas have also been known to associate illicit drug use in general as something that afflicts 'incomers' rather than locals (Scottish Executive Interventions Unit, 2004).

Illicit drug use that is more accepted tends to be seen as recreational, lifestyle or counterculture, such as cannabis and cocaine (Duffy & Smith, 2016). These illicit drugs are not associated with poverty or significantly play a part in the *official* drug deaths, therefore are more tolerated. Drugs such as cannabis and cocaine however are not immune from causing harm: they contribute towards poor mental health and suicidal ideation. Furthermore the Scottish Families Affected by Alcohol and Drugs report (2020) mentions cocaine as the most reported drug (after alcohol) to their helpline, suggesting that cocaine is having a significant burden on the family dynamic.

Poverty and Employment

Considering urban manifestations of poverty and crime do not exist in rural locations, the association society has got from what addiction looks like is difficult to compute with a different geographical community. On Arran, there were informal foodbanks that were connected to church rather than the formal charity or social sector and there were no referrals needed to access food. There were also food swap initiatives brought on by environmental concerns, that meant people were able to access free food without it being associated with poverty. These initiatives certainly helped with removing stigma and should be encouraged; however, they kept the extent of poverty on the island hidden.

A qualitative study on heroin use in the Shetlands noted that the presentation of heroin addiction looked different in island and rural communities compared to urban Scotland, with people using heroin often in employment (Stallwitz & Shewan, 2004). The association between addiction and long-term unemployment plays out in our statutory services. People with alcohol use disorder who are in employment and attempt to get help from recovery support are at risk of being rejected as they are not seen as 'severe' enough for support (SHAAP, 2018). Rural Scotland tends to have higher employment rates, and it can mean people from these locations could be getting missed as they do not fit the traditional urban criteria of addiction. Additionally the moralistic notion that in order for someone to be truly dependent means that an individual has to have lost everything, to have hurt others around them, to suffer immeasurably and to hit a rock bottom is still prevalent in our culture. It contradicts the concept of preventative community-based social work (Turbett, 2020) as well as harm reduction guidelines in healthcare that were intended to prevent a person from reaching the point of crisis and to limit our over-reliance on crisis management in the public sector.

There are barely any visible markers of addiction in a traditional sense, although rural communities are aware of individuals who struggle with AOD dependencies and people do talk about this with their friends and neighbours (Krentzman & Glass, 2021). The low anonymity and the high social capital of gossip in these places makes it hard for someone to struggle in private. This is why it is 'hiding in plain sight'. There's an acknowledgement that suffering is happening, but a low level of responsibility—collectively or nationally—is in place that minimises supporting those who are suffering.

Affluence

Whilst health inequalities demonstrate those in most acute poverty are more likely to suffer the worst health outcomes from alcohol (Institute of Alcohol Studies, 2020), socioeconomic levels are not a strong indicator for alcohol consumption (Pape et al., 2018; Schölin & Fitzgerald, 2019). Alcohol given by parents to adolescents is higher in rural populations (Chan et al., 2016). Teenagers with the most money to spend (£30 + per week) were three times more likely to drink alcohol than those with no money to spend (National Statistics Scotland, 2018).

There is an element of community denial when it comes to the extent of AOD harm in rural society (SEIU, 2004; Cragg, 2003). The level of affluence can coincide with the level of deniability on whether alcohol and other drugs are a prevalent issue where they live (SEIU, 2004). Nevertheless the rural communities are not the only ones in denial over the extent of the hold addiction has over the countryside. A peer mentor in rural England recalled local officials saying: 'we haven't got a drug problem in this part of the country… They are there, but they don't want them there' (Whiteford et al., 2016, p. 79). Local officials and commissioners in rural areas have also been known to deny the extent of AOD dependency in rural areas mirroring the popular view (SEIU, 2004).

The traditional markers of addiction—poverty, criminality, poor health—are not only stigmatising; they are unrepresentative of a sizeable proportion of the population. When addiction is seen as not prevalent, therefore not relevant, communities find it easier to deny that addiction is a problem in their area even if they know of or admit to knowing others in their community with a dependence on alcohol and other drugs. This lack of visibility leads to less investment in recovery services and a lack of clarity for people to know where to get help (SEIU, 2004). It keeps the addiction hidden.

Barriers to Recovery Services and Seeking Support

Access to Services

Access begins with knowing where to go. Without this, your chances of starting a recovery journey are slim. SHAAP (2020) undertook qualitative research and asked service users/patients and professionals in rural communities throughout Scotland what they would like to know most about alcohol support and their top concern was to know what support was available, who to talk to and how to access help.

When there is a lack of access to services or awareness of where to get support, family members are often the first port of call to absorb the crisis (Holleran, 2020). Living in rural areas will likely exacerbate the pressure on family members to support their loved ones.

A lack of access to health and social care services in remote areas is something well established in Scotland. Alcohol and other drugs can be more accessible than the recovery services themselves, a fact which is not lost on rural communities. Those enduring mental health problems find alcohol is more accessible as a method of self-medication, effectively masking the underlying mental health problem (Chandler & Nugent, 2016). Both alcohol and illicit drugs can be delivered to the house, making them more accessible than ever regardless of income.

Accessing support however is often a lot harder. Recovery services tend to be centralised to more urban centres and can house medical support such as medication, harm reduction and help from withdrawing from substances safely as well as social, psychological and peer support. Dependence is multifaceted, and often there is close working with housing, employment, welfare, criminal justice and mental health services. Charities tend to work with more assertive outreach, peer support groups and family support.

Centralised services were originally conceived to improve the quality of care, as they pooled expertise into one building and it was hoped to increase communication. Having these resources available during a period of acute vulnerability is really important for a person's recovery journey. But a centralised service is not always easy to access, particularly for more rural communities (Skerratt, 2018). Communities who have had their services centralised have reported feeling 'disabled' and find it harder to live with a physical or mental health condition (Skerratt, 2018).

Some services can be delivered over the phone or online, something that has been promoted more since COVID. These types of services, known as telehealth, can be beneficial to people who are time-poor or have difficulty in accessing support, but there are inequalities in this telehealth for people in remote areas. Offering a tele service instead of a face-to-face to people in remote areas, whilst offering face-to-face support in urban centres is a disparity of care and results in a differing quality of relationship-based support, an important factor in recovery (Radley et al., 2020).

Transportation

Public transport in rural communities is notoriously poor (SHAAP, 2020; Skerratt et al., 2017; Skerratt, 2018; Whiteford et al., 2016; SEIU, 2004). It is important to understand that often people who are dependent on alcohol or other drugs are unlikely to be able to drive a car due to their condition, or perhaps their licence has been revoked temporarily or permanently (Whiteford et al., 2016). The dedication it takes for a person who is seeking recovery in rural Scotland is to be commended: to travel in multiple forms of transportation, waiting for long periods of time or rushing quickly in-between connections, with questionable weather and temperature for a good portion of the year whilst feeling unwell and vulnerable is tough.

For island communities, particularly those who live within mainland-based Councils, it is likely you will need to rely on a ferry to access some recovery services. The unreliability of ferries is only one factor to contend with when attempting to access recovery services. Not all ferries have private rooms, and where they exist they are usually designated for people who are requiring an ambulance or receiving health treatments such as chemotherapy.

Relying on public transport connections from the ferry to centralised recovery service puts an additional accessibility barrier in place; however placing a specialist outreach worker from mainland services onto an island is time-consuming for the worker, who will spend most of their time travelling (SEIU, 2004). The focus on commissioning recovery services is based on the number of people within an area (SEIU, 2004), which means that island communities often featuring low population density, are less likely to receive investment for services if they are part of Local Authorities that are primarily based on the mainland. It is more likely that island-based Local Authorities have an island recovery worker, whereas islands within mainland-based council areas tend to have outreach recovery workers dependent on an unreliable ferry service.

Urban Bias in Co-producing Recovery Services

Co-creating or co-producing comprises getting the community involved in the creation of services (Filipe et al., 2017). There are some good examples of community-based co-production research on urban populations (Brown & Head, 2019; Greer et al., 2019; Damon et al., 2017); however issues such as anonymity and privacy are not held in the same regard in rural populations (Turbett, 2019; Skerratt et al., 2017), making recruitment, training and facilitating of people with lived experience exceptionally difficult. This means services are shaped with an urban population in mind as this has the highest empirical evidence base, often supported by city universities who fund the research and theory. Rural issues are not seen with the same academic interest as urban issues (Turbett, 2019; Skerratt et al., 2017). Whilst this has resulted in a reliance on anecdotal evidence as a substitute for normal research methods, carrying a danger of not being taken seriously (NICE, 2016), perhaps these stories contain a depth and richness for social work scholarship that deserves better recognition—an argument made in the concluding chapter of this book.

Poor Communication and Dilution of Expertise

Rural social and health care staff tend to be generalists. Whilst this can be the most effective way of working with small populations, the lack of AOD expertise again means a disparity of care for people who need specialist recovery support, particularly in medical knowledge. This dilution is worsened through cutting community social and health care to invest in centralised services, although there are still underinvestment and lack of expertise in urban areas, suggesting overall cuts to services and a difficulty in retaining staff are national issues.

On Arran there was no known alcohol or other drug support worker on the island, although there was sporadic support from mainland services dependent on the ferry. This lack of visible presence contributed to low referral numbers to recovery services. For example, there was a noticeable rise in cocaine dependency but GPs admitted to not referring to recovery services as they were unsure about what recovery services did. This left a lot of work to the community psychiatric nurse, whose caseload included both mental health and recovery patients.

Poor communication from both centralised services and the rural community-based services results in people not getting referred despite coming forward and asking for support. From a recovery services point of view if a remote area has low referral numbers, little communication from their local GPs, little to no data on any issues surrounding AOD and statistically has a high quality of life, there will not be a desire to extend already stretched resources to these locations (SEIU, 2004). Likewise when centralised services focus on urban types of addiction, the emphasis on naloxone and opiate replacement therapy can alienate rural practitioners and make them reluctant to openly discuss rural AOD dependency.

Stigma

It is difficult to talk about alcohol and other drug dependencies without looking at stigma (a matter considered in the opening chapter of this book). The definition of stigma is that a person is 'marked' or 'stained' by something that is socially frowned upon. The use of shame and stigma as a coercive population tool in the UK has been in place for centuries. Stigma is a form of social control; it uses shaming to coerce people into hiding, repressing or denying their behaviour. Within AOD dependencies there is a hierarchy of stigma: factors such as type of drug, route of administration, class, gender, race, violence, and committal of crime will dictate where you fit into that hierarchy (Scottish Drugs Death Taskforce, 2020). Due to the nature of AOD dependency when a person is no longer able to hide, repress or deny the extent of their problems, the shaming increases to keep that person away from society and prevents them and their family from seeking support (Scottish Drugs Death Taskforce, 2020). Stigmatising issues such as AOD dependency allows a society to lessen its responsibility towards helping those it stigmatises, keeping addiction a very personal and individual issue. This happens throughout Scotland regardless of geography.

There are some differences however in how stigma manifests in remote areas. The preconceived notions of a community's geographical location affect the expectations we have of individuals in those communities. The binary of cities being dirty and countryside being clean go back to the 1800s, when wealthy people would flee to the countryside to avoid overcrowding and contagious disease within the city (MacDonald, 2020). The Scottish poet Walter Scott often romanticised the sparse landscape and began to pave the way for richer citizens to spend their leisure time in 'untouched' lands.

This narrative continues to this day for people who live with AOD dependencies. There is an expectation that addiction is prevalent in urban communities; therefore we see this as a social issue that we try to resolve. Whilst in rural communities there is an idealised way of life, focusing around the link between nature, health and wholesomeness (SHAAP, 2020; Skerratt, 2018) against which the individual with AOD dependencies (and their families) are seen to be a threat to this ideal.

Stigma in urban areas can be 'placed-based'. For example, saying a certain area is a 'shithole' means an area has negative connotations due to the association of poverty, homelessness, degeneration, crime or illicit drug use (Butler et al., 2018). Living in a place that is stigmatised alienates entire communities. Whilst this place-based stigma is fundamentally harmful to the community it tarnishes, from a social care perspective it makes pinpointing and targeting resources easier, resulting in fewer barriers to commissioning services in these locations.

This is unlikely to happen outside of cities and towns and perhaps some accessible rural areas. The no-go areas of remote rural places are minimal and this place-based stigma does not play out as openly. This means communities are not likely to be tarnished with placed-based stigma, leaving individuals in rural areas who are AOD dependent more open to individual and familial stigma, as they would be seen to be putting the rural idyll at risk.

Stigma is also fuelled by gossip. As discussed briefly in Chap. 2, gossip is a prevalent aspect of life but holds a higher social capital in remote areas. In rural Scotland, gossip leads to community exclusion and bullying for people with mental health problems (Parr et al., 2004). Krentzman and Glass (2021) noted that gossip for those in recovery in rural America actively prevented individuals from seeking help and made recovery harder. Social workers were known within the community; therefore if any individual was 'seen' with a social worker gossip about them would manifest, whether it was accurate or not. Gossip-based stigma has prevented people and their families from accessing housing, employment (Bailey et al., 2004) and basic medical care (Krentzman & Glass, 2021).

Is It All Bad?

The good image typically portrayed of rural Scotland needs to be remedied with some realism. There is a serious underinvestment in rural services, from housing, diverse employment, transportation to health and social care. This underinvestment leads to very well-hidden poverty, isolation, and unattended mental, physical and addiction-based conditions. All of this will impact how a person can feel confident and safe enough to get help, and for that help to be sustained throughout their recovery journey.

That being said, there are benefits to living in rural locations when it comes to AOD dependency. Living in a place where there is little anonymity allows for greater social cohesion. Whilst gossip was noted earlier as disruptive for some people with AOD dependency in their recovery, gossip can also be positive. Whilst in recovery, gossip about how healthier and happier an individual looks can bolster a person's self-esteem. As one participant mentioned in Krentzman and Glass's study (2021), 'I would rather you talk about me going to recovery meetings than you talk about me going to the bar and peeing my pants' (p. 2578). The difficulty in hiding a dependency can work in a person's benefit when they are in recovery because a person in recovery is trying to get better and that can be reinforced positively by the community. This positive reinforcement has also been noted in mental health (Parr et al., 2004). Rural social workers are also better placed (after appropriate discussion and with consent) to correct misinformation caused by local gossip and have a stronger role of advocating for their service users (Pugh, 2007).

There is a Scottish government policy shift towards empowering rural communities to be more independent, such as the Community Empowerment Scotland Act (Scottish Government, 2015). Whilst one can look at this sceptically as a way of not investing further in rural services, there are some advantages to community empowerment particularly when it comes to rural social work. Social workers are seen as positive agents for people in recovery, they are able to be a 'critical friend'—a voice that offers honest feedback and sometimes uncomfortable but necessary truths. They can also help deal with the socioeconomic issues around AOD dependency such as housing and benefit entitlement (Cree et al., 2016). Rural social workers will also have a better understanding of transportation issues and can use this to mitigate punitive measures of missing appointments in some health services.

Community-based services can build higher quality relationships with their clients. In recovery, being cared for and shown respect is seen as the most crucial element of their support and people would rather wait longer to be seen if they knew they were going to be treated with respect than for a more 'efficient' yet uncaring service (Radley et al., 2020). Social workers have a vital role to play in community-based AOD recovery as there are embedded socioeconomic or complicated familial issues surrounding AOD dependency that are difficult to unpick in healthcare settings.

Since rural localities do not produce the same numbers of alarming health harms and inequalities, the scrutiny is not as severe as it is in cities and towns. This leaves room for creativity and flexibility as to how communities respond to AOD. For example, both Shetland and Orkney have their own trained drug dogs to sniff out postal drugs. From this they have been able to understand what drugs are coming to the island, information that would have been more difficult to access beforehand. Within rural social work there is capacity to accommodate the needs of people outside of the individual, such as the whole family approach towards AOD. On Arran staff performed welfare checks, whereas people on the mainland did not have this service unless their needs were very high. They were able to do this on Arran because they knew the person and this minimised risk and safety concerns for the worker. These checks made people feel safe and cared for. Having local, in-depth knowledge of a community allows quicker decision making. There is capacity for rural social work to perform higher quality care, but the issue remains as to whether a person gets referred to a service to begin with.

Conclusion

> People value landscapes and places, not communities and their skills; … remote rural living is seen as a choice, so rural people feel 'blamed' for any difficulties they experience; and … the majority of real rural issues are hidden from view, because 'green space' equates to peace, holidays and relaxation, not poverty, deprivation and service centralisation.
> Skerratt (2018, p. 9)

Although not specifically mentioning alcohol and other drugs, this quote from Skerratt sums up the issues people who live with AOD dependency face living in the countryside quite accurately. The thing that struck me about my time on Arran was how often people who worked in mainland services would holiday to the island. Wanting to separate yourself from work is natural, and to minimise the suffering you see in your holiday destination allows you to enjoy your destination more. That is how rural locations get romanticised.

The main issue for people living with AOD addiction in rural Scotland is that addiction looks different. Addiction is harder to locate, there are few areas of visible and obvious deprivation, so poverty and stigma are experienced differently. Affluence can mask a lot of addiction harm to an individual and their family, particularly where children are involved. Additional issues facing people with AOD addiction are lack of service availability, accessibility and a confusion of what rural and urban services do. Mention has also been made about the possibility of differing services emerging that deal with remoteness and distance by offering a virtual service rather than a face to face one. This might be beneficial to some but also disadvantage others: the substitution of cheap convenience for quality might well be challenged by those who live and work in remote areas.

However, on the positive side, rural locations can reinforce a sense of camaraderie—when people are in recovery usually (there will always be exceptions) the community are very encouraging. Rural social workers are some of the best placed individuals to work with people with AOD. If adopting the type of Community Social Work model suggested elsewhere in this book, they may not have the same pressure of target culture and red tape, allowing more flexibility for an illness that naturally lends itself to chaos. There is often time and space to allow relationship building, allowing people with AOD addiction and their families to feel the safety and worthiness they deserve. Being aware how rural AOD addiction looks and works can help us tailor our care and empathy. Social work are good advocates for their service users, and they can be good advocates to promote the regional and national change desperately needed in rural care. Being aware of the issues equips social workers and their health and social care colleagues for a proactive approach to change the status quo.

It seems cliché to say this, but more research needs to be done. There should not be one or two papers coming out every 10 years saying the same thing, as this demonstrates a severe lack of progress. In order for services and the government to take rural addiction seriously, there needs to be more high quality research. Without an evidence base denial can continue, as can the lack of imperative to change. It is suggested earlier, and in the concluding chapter of this book, that the stories of rural social workers and the people they serve can form a rich basis for future qualitative research.

Most importantly, we are all responsible in how we treat those suffering with AOD and their families, and we are all responsible for being vocal about changing current practice to best accommodate those living in rural areas.

It may be your drink. It may be your drugs. But it is *Our Problem*.

References

Abernethy, C., McCall, K. E., Cooper, G., Favretto, D., Vaiano, F., Bertol, E., & Mactier, H. (2018). Determining the Pattern and Prevalence of Alcohol Consumption in Pregnancy by Measuring Biomarkers in Meconium. *Archives of Disease in Childhood. Fetal and Neonatal Edition, 103*(3), 216–220.

Bailey, N., Spratt, J., Pickering, J., Goodlad, R., & Shucksmith, M. (2004). *Deprivation and Social Exclusion in Argyll and Bute - Report to the Community Planning Partnership*. Accessed April 2022, from https://www.researchgate.net/publication/237760118_Deprivation_and_social_exclusion_in_Argyll_and_Bute_Report_to_the_Community_Planning_Partnership

Bellis, M. A., Hughes, K., Leckenby, N., Perkins, C., & Lowey, H. (2014). National Household Survey of Adverse Childhood Experiences and Their Relationship with Resilience to Health-Harming Behaviours in England. *BMC Medicine, 12*, 72.

Bernard, C. (2017). An Exploration of How Social Workers Engage Neglectful Parents from Affluent Backgrounds in the Child Protection System. *Child Family & Social Work, 24*(2), 340–347.

Brown, P., & Head, B. (2019). Navigating Tensions in Co-production: A Missing Link in Leadership for Public Value. *Public Administration, 97*(2), 250–263.

Butler, A., Schafran, A., & Carpenter, G. (2018). What Does It Mean When People Call a Place a Shithole? Understanding a Discourse of Denigration in the United Kingdom and the Republic of Ireland. *Transactions of the Institute of British Geographers, 43*(3), 496–510.

Carrell, S. (2008). Heroin Death Exposes Shetland Drugs Blight. *The Guardian Online*. Accessed April 2022, from https://www.theguardian.com/uk/2008/apr/23/scotland.drugstrade

Chan, G. C. K., Leung, J., Quinn, C., Kelly, A. B., Connor, J. P., Weier, M., & Hall, W. D. (2016). Rural and Urban Differences in Adolescent Alcohol Use,

Alcohol Supply, and Parental Drinking. *The Journal of Rural Health, 32*, 280–286.

Chandler, A. & Nugent, B. (2016). *Alcohol Stories: A Lifecourse Perspective on Self-Harm, Suicide and Alcohol Use Among Men.* Accessed December 2022, from http://www.meldap.co.uk/data/uploads/finalreport-alcohol-stories.pdf

Church, S., Bhatia, U., Velleman, R., Velleman, G., Orford, J., Rane, A., & Nadkarni, A. (2018). Coping Strategies and Support Structures of Addiction Affected Families: A Qualitative Study from Goa, India. *Families, Systems & Health, 36*(2), 216–224.

Cragg, A. (2003). *Drugs in Rural Areas: Qualitative Research to Assess the Adequacy of Communications and Services.* Home Office.

Cree, V., Jain, S., & Hillen, P. (2016). The Challenge of Measuring Effectiveness in Social Work: A Case Study of an Evaluation of a Drug and Alcohol Referral Service in Scotland. *The British Journal of Social Work, 46*(1), 277–293.

Daly, C. (2014). *Mental Health Services and Social Inclusion in Remote and Rural Areas of Scotland and Canada: A Qualitative Comparison.* [Dissertation]. Accessed March 28, 2022, from https://pure.uhi.ac.uk/portal/files/3084034/Clare_Daly_thesis.pdf

Damon, W., Callon, C., Wiebe, L., Small, W., Kerr, T., & McNeil, R. (2017). Community-Based Participatory Research in a Heavily Researched Inner City Neighbourhood: Perspectives of People Who Use Drugs on Their Experiences as Peer Researchers. *Social Science & Medicine, 176*, 85–92.

Dirks, H., Francke, L., Würz, V., Kretschmann, C., Dehghan-Sanij, S., & Scherbaum, N. (2019). Substance Use, Comorbid Psychiatric Disorders and Suicide Attempts in Adult FASD Patients. *Advances in Dual Diagnosis, 12*(1/2), 6–13.

Duffy, C., & Smith, C. (2016). *Community Attitude Research on Alcohol and Other Drugs, Qualitative Research Report.* Australian Government Department of Health. Accessed March 25, 2022, from https://www.health.gov.au/resources/publications/community-attitude-research-on-alcohol-and-other-drugs-qualitative-report

Ellis, L. & Grant, J. (2019) *NHS GGC Guidelines on Neonatal Abstinence Syndrome.* Accessed December 18, 2021, from https://www.clinicalguidelines.scot.nhs.uk/nhsggc-guidelines/nhsggc-guidelines/neonatology/neonatal-abstinence-syndrome-nas/

Fecht, D., Jones, A., Hill, T., Lindfield, T., Thomson, R., Hansell, A. L., & Shukla, R. (2017). Inequalities in Rural Communities: Adapting National Deprivation Indices for Rural Settings. *Journal of Public Health, 2*, 1–425.

Filipe, A., Renedo, A., & Marston, C. (2017). The Co-production of What? Knowledge, Values, and Social Relations in Health Care. *PLoS Biology, 15*(5), e2001403.

Forsyth, A., & Barnard, M. (1999). Contrasting Levels of Adolescent Drug Use Between Adjacent Urban and Rural Communities in Scotland. *Addiction, 94*(11), 1707–1718.

Galloway, J., Forsyth, A. & Shewan, D. (2007) *Young People's Street Drinking Behaviour: Investigating the Influence of Marketing & Subculture.* Glasgow Centre for the Study of Violence. Accessed March 2022, from https://alcoholchange.org.uk/publication/young-peoples-streetdrinking-behaviour-investigating-the-influence-of-marketing-subculture

Gralton, E. (2014). Foetal Alcohol Spectrum Disorder (FASD) – Its Relevance to Forensic Adolescent Services. *Journal of Intellectual Disabilities and Offending Behaviour, 5*(3), 124–137.

Greer, A. M., Pauly, B., Scott, A., Martin, R., Burmeister, C., & Buxton, J. (2019). Paying People Who Use Illicit Substances or 'Peers' Participating in Community-Based Work: A Narrative Review of the Literature. *Drugs: Education, Prevention and Policy, 26*(6), 447–459.

Healthcare Improvement Scotland. (2019). *Foetal Alcohol Spectrum Disorder: A Booklet for Parents, Carers and Families of Children and Young People Exposed to Alcohol During Pregnancy.* ISBN 978-1-909103-72-6. Accessed December 2021, from https://www.sign.ac.uk/assets/pat156_fasd.pdf?msclkid=aa90bf16a2fd11ec8a1aafdebe41fa98

Holleran, J (2020) *Constantly Just Holding It Up and Together. Exploring Family Support in Relation to Problem Substance Use in Scotland.* Scottish Families Affected by Alcohol and Drugs. Accessed January 20, 2022, from rhttps://www.sfad.org.uk/content/uploads/2020/12/Constantly-Just-Holding-It-Up-and-Together-Report.pdf

Institute of Alcohol Studies. (2020). *Alcohol and Health Inequalities.* Accessed January 2022, from https://www.ias.org.uk/wp-content/uploads/2020/12/Alcohol-and-health-inequalities.pdf

Krentzman, A., & Glass, L. (2021). Gossip and Addiction Recovery in Rural Communities. *Qualitative Health Research, 31*(14), 2571–2584.

MacDonald, S. (2020). Whisky, Women and the Scottish Drink Problem. A View from the Highlands. In M. McDonald (Ed.), *Gender, Drink and Drugs.* Routledge.

MacLeod, A., Glancy, M., Went, A., Smith, S., Weir, A., McAuley, A., Hutchinson, S., & Goldberg, D. (2019). *Surveillance Report: Surveillance of*

Hepatitis C Testing, Diagnosis and Treatment in Scotland, 2019 Update. Accessed April 2022, from https://hpspubsrepo.blob.core.windows.net/hps-website/nss/2834/documents/1_hcv-testing-diagnosis-treatment-scotland-2018.pdf

Marryat, L., & Frank, J. (2019). Factors Associated with Adverse Childhood Experiences in Scottish Children: A Prospective Cohort Study. *BMJ Paediatrics Open, 3,* e000340.

Martin, G., Inchley, J., Marshall, A., Shortt, N., & Currie, C. (2019). The Neighbourhood Social Environment and Alcohol Use Among Urban and Rural Scottish Adolescents. *International Journal of Public Health, 64*(1), 95–105.

Matthews, B., Collier, B., McVie, S., & Dibben, C. (2021). Understanding Digital Drug Markets Through the Geography of Postal Drug Deliveries in Scotland. *European Journal of Criminology.* https://doi.org/10.1177/1477370821997323

Munro, C. (2020). Orkney Drugs Dog Helps Police in Glasgow Sniff Out. £10,000 Substances. *The Press and Journal.* Accessed April 2022, from https://www.pressandjournal.co.uk/fp/news/highlands-islands/2590348/orkney-drug-dog-efforts-lead-to-woman-charged-in-glasgow/

National Records of Scotland. (2021a). *Alcohol Specific Deaths in Scotland Increase.* Accessed April 2022, from https://www.nrscotland.gov.uk/news/2021/alcohol-specific-deaths-in-scotland-increase

National Records of Scotland. (2021b). *Drug-Related Deaths Rise.* Accessed April 2022, from https://www.nrscotland.gov.uk/news/2021/drug-related-deaths-rise

National Statistics Scotland. (2018). *Scottish Schools Adolescent Lifestyle and Substance Use Survey (SALUS).* Scottish Government. Accessed October 2021, from https://www.gov.scot/publications/scottish-schools-adolescent-lifestylesubstance-use-survey-salsus-alcohol-report-2018/

NHS Ayrshire & Arran Specialist FASD Centre. (n.d.). Accessed April 2022, from https://www.nhsaaa.net/media/7953/fasd-a-lifelong-condition-blog.pdf

NHS National Services Scotland. (2019). *Prevalence of Problem Drug Use in Scotland.* Accessed April 2022, from https://www.isdscotland.org/Health-Topics/Drugs-and-Alcohol-Misuse/Publications/2019-03-05/2019-03-05-Drug-Prevalence-2015-16-Report.pdf

NICE. (2016). Chapter 6 Reviewing the Evidence. In *Social Care Guidance Manual*. Accessed March 2022, from https://www.nice.org.uk/process/pmg10/chapter/reviewing-the-evidence

Orford, J. (2017). How does the common core to the harm experienced by affected family members vary by relationship, social and cultural factors? *Drugs: Education, Prevention and Policy, 24*(1), 9–16. https://doi.org/10.1080/09687637.2016.1189876

Orford, J., Velleman, R., Copello, A., Templeton, L., & Ibanga, A. (2010). The Experiences of Affected Family Members: A Summary of Two Decades of Qualitative Research. *Drugs: Education, Prevention and Policy, 17*(s1), 44–62.

Pape, H., Rossow, I., Andreas, J. B., & Norström, T. (2018). Social Class and Alcohol Use by Youth: Different Drinking Behaviors, Different Associations? *Journal of Studies on Alcohol and Drugs, 79*, 132–136.

Parr, H., Philo, C., & Burns, N. (2004). Social Geographies of Rural Mental Health: Experiencing Inclusions and Exclusions. *Transactions of the Institute of British Geographers, 29*, 401–419.

Public Health Scotland. (2020). *Monitoring and Evaluating Scotland's Alcohol Strategy (MESAS)*. Accessed November 2021, from https://publichealthscotland.scot/media/3089/mesas-monitoring-report-2020-english-updated-march-2021.pdf

Public Health Scotland. (2021). *Births in Scottish Hospitals*. Accessed March 2022, from https://publichealthscotland.scot/publications/births-in-scottish-hospitals/births-in-scottish-hospitals-year-ending-31-march-2021/

Pugh, R. (2007). Dual Relationships: Personal and Professional Boundaries in Rural Social Work. *The British Journal of Social Work, 37*(8), 1405–1423.

Radley, A., de Bruin, M., Inglis, S. K., Donnan, P. T., Hapca, A., Barclay, S. T., Fraser, A., & Dillon, J. F. (2020). Clinical Effectiveness of Pharmacist-Led Versus Conventionally Delivered Antiviral Treatment for Hepatitis C virus in Patients Receiving Opioid Substitution Therapy: A Pragmatic, Cluster-Randomised Trial. *The Lancet Gastroenterology & Hepatology, 5*(9), 809–818.

Roderick, E., Penney, J., Murrells, T., Darganl, I., & Norman, J. (2018). Epidemiology of Adolescent Substance Use in Norfolk Schools. *QJM: An International Journal of Medicine, 111*(10), 699.

Schölin, L., & Fitzgerald, N. (2019). The Conversation Matters: A Qualitative Study Exploring the Implementation of Alcohol Screening and Brief Interventions in Antenatal Care in Scotland. *BMC Pregnancy and Childbirth, 19316*, 1–11.

Scottish Drugs Death Taskforce. (2020). *A Strategy to Address the Stigmatisation of People and Communities Affected by Drug Use - We All Have a Part to Play.* Accessed January 2022, from https://drugdeathstaskforce.scot/media/1111/stigma-strategy-for-ddtf-final-290720.pdf

Scottish Executive Interventions Unit. (2004). *Rural and Remote Areas: Effective Approaches to Delivering Integrated Care for Drug Users.* ISBN-10:0755925912. Accessed March 2022, from https://core.ac.uk/download/34711094.pdf

Scottish Families Affected by Alcohol & Drugs. (2020). *Helpline Report 18th March to 30th July 2020.* Report Available upon request from https://www.sfad.org.uk/

Scottish Families Affected by Alcohol and Drugs. (2019). *Behind the Numbers Findings Report.* Accessed January 2022, from https://www.sfad.org.uk/content/uploads/2020/05/Behind-the-Numbers-Findings-Report.pdf

Scottish Government. (2015). *Community Empowerment (Scotland) Act.* Accessed November 2021, from https://www.legislation.gov.uk/asp/2015/6

Scottish Government. (2017). *Scottish Maternal and Infant Nutrition Survey.* Accessed April 2021, from https://www.gov.scot/binaries/content/documents/govscot/publications/statistics/2018/02/scottish-maternal-infant-nutrition-survey-2017/documents/00531610-pdf/00531610-pdf/govscot%3Adocument/00531610.pdf

Scottish Government. (2018). *Rights, Respect and Recovery: Scotland's Strategy to Improve Health by Preventing and Reducing Alcohol and Drug Use, Harm and Related Deaths.* Accessed December 2021, from https://www.gov.scot/binaries/content/documents/govscot/publications/strategy-plan/2018/11/rights-respect-recovery/documents/00543437-pdf/00543437-pdf/govscot%3Adocument/00543437.pdf?forceDownload=true

Scottish Government. (2019a). *Scottish Health Survey.* Accessed January 2022, from https://www.gov.scot/publications/scottish-health-survey-2019-volume-1-main-report/

Scottish Government. (2019b). *Scottish Schools Adolescent Lifestyle and Substance Use Survey (SALSUS): national overview 2018.* Accessed November 2021, from https://www.gov.scot/publications/scottish-schools-adolescent-lifestyle-substance-use-survey-salsus-national-overview-2018/documents/

Scottish Government. (2019c). *National Islands Plan.* Accessed March 2022, from https://www.gov.scot/publications/national-plan-scotlands-islands/documents/

Scottish Government. (2020a). *How Is Social Capital Distributed in Scotland? – Social Capital in Scotland Report.* Accessed October 2021, from https://www. gov.scot/publications/social-capital-scotland-measuring-understanding-scotlands-social-connections/pages/6/

Scottish Government. (2020b). *The Scottish Crime and Justice Survey 2019/2020.* Accessed March 2022, from https://www.gov.scot/publications/scottish-crime-justice-survey-2019-20-main-findings/pages/2/#:~:text=The%20 2019%2F20%20Scottish%20Crime%20and%20Justice%20Survey%20% 28SCJS%29,of%20being%20a%20victim%20of%20crime%20since%20 2008%2F09

Scottish Government. (2022). *Long-Term Monitoring of Health Inequalities.* Accessed April 2022, from https://www.gov.scot/publications/long-term-monitoring-health-inequalities-march-2022-report/

SHAAP (Scottish Health Action on Alcohol Problems). (2020). *Rural Matters: Understanding Alcohol Use in Rural Scotland. A Qualitative Study.* Accessed November 2021, from https://shaap.org.uk/our-work/alcohol-rural-communities.html

SHAAP (Scottish Health Actions on Alcohol Problems). (2018). *Dying for a Drink: SHAAP Report on Alcohol Related Mortality in Scotland.* Royal College of Physicians. Accessed November 2021, from https://www.shaap.org.uk/ images/dying-for-a-drink-text_for_web.pdf

Sher, J. (2017). Accessed March 2022, from https://www.holyrood.com/comment/view,prevention-means-never-having-to-say-youre-sorry_7227.htm

Sher, J., Frank, J. W., Doi, L., & Caestecker, L. (2019). Failures in Reproductive Health Policy: Overcoming the Consequences and Causes of Inaction. *Journal of Public Health, 41*(2), 209–215.

Skerratt, S., Meader, E., & Sprencer, M. (2017) *National Rural Mental Health Survey Scotland: Report of Key Findings.* Scottish Rural University College. Accessed April 2022, from https://www.sruc.ac.uk/downloads/download/1239/national_rural_mental_health_survey_scotland_report_of_key_ findings

Skerratt, S. (2018). *Recharging Rural. Creating Sustainable Communities to 2030 and Beyond.* The Prince's Trust Countryside Fund. Accessed April 2022, from https://www.princescountrysidefund.org.uk/our-impact/our-research/ recharging-rural/

Stallwitz, A., & Shewan, D. (2004). A Qualitative Exploration of the Impact of Cultural and Social Factors on Heroin Use in Shetland (Scotland). *Journal of Psychoactive Drugs, 36*(3), 367–378.

Still, H. (2020). *Paradise Explored – Investigating the Experiences of Alcohol and Drugs on Arran – Health and Social Communication and Barriers to Care.* Arran Council of Voluntary Service.

Streissguth, A. P., Bookstein, F. L., Barr, H. M., Sampson, P. D., O'Malley, K., & Young, J. K. (2004). Risk Factors for Adverse Life Outcomes in Fetal Alcohol Syndrome and Fetal Alcohol Effects. *Journal of Developmental Behaviour in Pediatrics, 25*(4), 228–238.

Turbett, C. (2014). *Doing Radical Social Work.* Palgrave.

Turbett, C., (2019). *Rural Social Work in Scotland.* Iriss. Accessed April 2022, from https://www.iriss.org.uk/resources/insights/rural-social-work-scotland

Turbett, C. (2020). *Rediscovering and Mainstreaming Community Social Work.* Iriss. Accessed April 2022, from https://www.iriss.org.uk/resources/insights/rediscovering-and-mainstreaming-community-social-work-scotland

UK Health and Security Agency. (2021). *Shooting Up: Infections and Other Injection Related Harms Among People Who Inject Drugs in the UK 2020.* Accessed March 2022, from https://assets.publishing.service.gov.uk/government/uploads/system/uploads/attachment_data/file/1053202/Shooting_Up_2021_report_final.pdf

Vivancos, R., Maskrey, V., Rumball, D., Harvey, I., & Holland, R. (2006). Crack/Cocaine Use in a Rural County of England. *Journal of Public Health, 28*(2), 96–103.

Whiteford, M., Haydock, W., & Cleave, N. (2016). Two Buses and a Short Walk: The Place of Geography in Recovery. *Drugs and Alcohol Today, 16*(1), 72–83.

World Health Organisation. (2018). *Global Status on Alcohol and Health.* Accessed November 2021, from https://www.who.int/publications/i/item/9789241565639

4

Rural Social Work with Romani and Travellers

Allison Hulmes and Peter Unwin

Introduction

<u>Par O Mulotan Ki Abram Wood</u>

*Puro Romani baro noiyelus keldos o gillia ta akai ando konya tan maskal
O playna
Ando jota ki O baval man Shenesa O Gillia ta puri parramisha
Arch ando mi Sherro sar perdoben katar patriana
Old Romani Harp plays the tune and here in the quiet valley
between mountains
I hear a song in the sound of the breeze and memories are dripping from
the leaves.*

A. Hulmes (✉)
Swansea University, Swansea, Wales, UK
e-mail: a.e.hulmes@swansea.ac.uk

P. Unwin
University of Worcester, Worcester, UK
e-mail: p.unwin@worc.ac.uk

© The Author(s), under exclusive license to Springer Nature Switzerland AG 2024
C. Turbett, J. Pye (eds.), *Rural Social Work in the UK*, Rethinking Rural,
https://doi.org/10.1007/978-3-031-52440-0_4

91

(Frances Roberts-Reilly, Welsh Kale Gypsy - Translated into Welsh Romanus by Bob Lovell, Kumalo, Welsh Kale Gypsy)

In common with the majority of the population, most social workers will hold traditional images of rural Romani and Traveller life, which might typically include a brightly painted bow-topped wagon, cooking on an open fire, women making pegs or weaving baskets and children playing happily in a meadow. This romanticised idyll, however, is a far cry from the reality of coping with harsh weather, subsistence living and continual persecution and discrimination, the latter of which continues to the present day. This chapter will contrast romantic notions of rurality with the realities of everyday living for Romani and Travellers and will challenge social work to play its part in addressing the racism that still affects this ethnic minority, who have been an intrinsic part of our countryside for centuries. The particular forms of racism discussed below are not exclusive to rural settings and many of the concerns discussed below pertain equally to urbanised environments. However, the changing socio-economic make-up of the countryside, greater isolation and traditional rural stoicism perhaps add particular complexities to lived experiences of racism. One of the authors' lived and living experience is as a Welsh Kale Gypsy, and many of the references in the chapter will be from the Welsh context, alongside other examples from across the UK. Contemporary images held across the UK regarding Romani and Traveller life are likely to have been shaped by representations such as those in '*My Big Fat Gypsy Wedding*' (Channel 4, 2010) or '*60 Days with the Gypsies*' (Channel 4, 2022), with their flamboyant and dysfunctional presentations of Romani and Traveller culture, which are just not recognised by most Romani and Travellers.

Gypsy, Roma and Travellers as Distinct Ethnic Groups

Before discussing issues of rurality, it is important for readers to have a basic understanding of the different Gypsy, Roma and Traveller cultures, often referred to under the umbrella term 'GRT.' The term 'GRT' is an administrative convenience which homogenises very different cultures, hence the preference is to always use the full term 'Gypsy, Roma and Travellers'. In regard to the communities living in rural UK, it is primarily Gypsy and Traveller communities who are present, with Roma tending to be more recently arrived into the UK, often finding work and housing in urban areas. Where Roma are present in the UK countryside, for example as seasonal labourers, they are more likely to self-identify by country of origin rather than ethnicity, mainly for fear of discrimination. Statistics are very difficult to ascertain across Gypsy, Roma and Traveller communities for two main reasons, data on ethnicity has not always included Gypsy, Traveller and Roma people and a reluctance to not self-declare ethnicity, for fear of discrimination, a fear that is often justified (The Traveller Movement, 2017). Estimates of the number of Gypsies and Travellers in the UK range widely, but 300,000 is a figure often cited (The Traveller Movement, 2023). Gypsies and Travellers could only self-identify in the census, for the first time in 2011 and Roma in 2021. There is only one category for Gypsy/Traveller in the census and this, in itself, reinforces a lack of understanding, as Gypsies and Travellers are distinct and separate ethnicities, with wholly different origins. Without disaggregated census data, a more accurate estimate of population sizes is not available and service provision, which flows from the data, is not properly designed or targeted to meet the distinct and separate needs of Gypsies and Travellers.

Accommodation

Contrary to popular belief, it is now only a small minority of Gypsies and Travellers who lead a nomadic lifestyle. The 2011 Census found that the majority (76%) of Gypsies and Irish Travellers in England and Wales lived in conventional bricks-and-mortar accommodation (e.g., house, bungalow, flat). This compared to 99% of the population as a whole. 24% of Gypsies and Travellers in England and Wales lived in a caravan or other mobile or temporary structure (Cromarty, 2019). The Ministry of Housing, Communities and Local Government (2020, p. 4) estimated that England contained some 23,000 Traveller caravans, of which 6506 (29%) were on socially rented sites; 13,461 (59%) were on privately funded sites; 2049 (9%) were unauthorised developments on land owned by travellers; and 694 (3%) were unauthorised encampments on land not owned by travellers. In Wales, the July 2021 count revealed the total number of Gypsy and Traveller caravans was 1095. There were 928 caravans on authorised sites with planning permission, accounting for 85% of all caravans. Of these, 618 (67%) were on socially rented sites and 310 (33%) were on privately funded sites. It is important to understand that Gypsies and Travellers do not cease being ethnic Gypsies and Travellers once they move (in many cases because of forced assimilation) into bricks and mortar. They take their culture, practices, social mores, values and history with them.

Many settled families still adopt traditional summer visiting of friends and relatives and are nomadic in this sense during the summer months, but the vast majority of Gypsies and Travellers in the UK now live in houses or are settled on sites. The passing of the Police, Crime, Sentencing and Courts Act 2022, which now criminalises 'intentional trespass' will serve to further curtail the nomadic lifestyles practised for centuries by Gypsies, Travellers, showmen and circus people who are nomadic in the course of their employment. This Act is also likely to initiate increased social work intervention in private and family life, especially if caravans (i.e., family homes) are confiscated and homelessness ensues. The social work profession's response to the passing of this racist Act was muted, and although the British Association of Social Workers (BASW, 2021a) was vocal in opposing the legislation on human rights grounds, it was a minority voice in a society where discrimination against Gypsies, Roma and Travellers has been termed 'the last acceptable form of racism' (The Traveller Movement, 2017).

The Gypsies and Travellers who inhabit the UK countryside are variously Welsh (Kale) Gypsies, English Gypsies (Romanichal), Scottish Gypsy Travellers (Nawkin) and Irish Travellers (Minceir). All of these groupings have protected ethnic status unlike other travelling populations such as showmen, boaters and new travellers, who are also sometimes rural dwellers. Ethnicity is not a fixed characteristic, and it is possible that at some point in the future any of the other non-ethnic travellers could make out a legal case for establishing themselves as an ethnic minority, according to the Mandla case which established a set of criteria for determining ethnicity (Equal Rights Trust, 1983).

Origins

The origins of all Romani Gypsies are firmly established as the Indian subcontinent; this fact is based on academic study of the various Romani dialects and points to a separation from India some 1000 years ago. As the populations migrated further West, borrowed words added to the vocabulary, and this has provided scholars with a linguistic map of the migration roots followed by Romani people. Travellers of Irish decent and Scottish Travellers are indigenous to Ireland and Scotland and have suffered a similar history of discrimination and 'othering' by the state. Romani Gypsies along with Irish and Scottish Travellers have travelled throughout the UK in harmony, although their ethnicities are distinct and separate. *Travellers Times* is a magazine for all Gypsy, Roma and Traveller communities, and their short video *'Roads from the Past'* (Travellers' Times, 2019), which gives an excellent introduction to community origins, should be shown to all social workers in education and practice.

Along with a dispersal across Eastern Europe and onwards (Hancock, 2017), came discrimination and, in some cases (e.g., Romania), slavery. This discrimination continues to the present day in the UK, through government, the media and popular culture. The Channel 4 programmes noted above and examples such as the comedian, Jimmy Carr, whose 2021 Netflix show 'joked' that the only good thing to come of the Holocaust was the genocide of thousands of Gypsies (BASW, 2022). It is not only popular culture that promotes discrimination but the UK government's Police, Crime, Sentencing and Courts Act (2022) will have the additional effect of outlawing a nomadic lifestyle by criminalising trespass, which was previously a civil offence. If the conditions for initiating this draconian new offence are met, sanctions include being arrested, having a vehicle removed (which in many cases is a home), being fined up to £2500, and/or being imprisoned up to 3 months and being prevented from returning to the land within 12 months of a notice being given.

This is a law that not even the police establishment supports (Friends, Families and Travellers, 2020) but it is viewed by many as a vote winner for those in conservative constituencies who object to Travellers parking on their land. Nomadic lifestyles involve stopping on land that has been used for centuries by Travellers and can be seen as part of a social policy that seeks to eliminate nomadism, rather than actively promoting and supporting nomadic ways of life.

Activism and the Gypsy, Roma and Traveller Social Work Association

For decades, councils have not provided or invested in stopping sites, even where a statutory duty exists to assess and meet the culturally appropriate needs of nomadic Gypsies and Travellers. In Wales, for example, local councils have consistently failed to meet their statutory duties under Part 3 of the Housing Act (2014). Where stopping sites do exist, they are often in very poor condition with few amenities regarded as essential for safe and dignified living (Quarmby, 2022). When Travellers stop on unauthorised land, the local authorities regularly refuse to provide water and toilet facilities and recycling centres refuse to accept waste from their vans without local permits. Such attitudes and behaviours might be construed as 'Anti-Gypsyism' (Walach, 2020), a construct which parallels discriminations such as racism and disablism, being stereotypically negative in the characteristics and behaviours ascribed to a specific group or culture. Allen and Riding (2019) wrote about the 'aversive racism' they saw in child protection services, noting that social workers might publicly ascribe to being non-discriminatory and committed to equality of opportunity, but they actually harboured prejudices. The numbers of Gypsy, Roma and Traveller children in state care, from both rural and urban backgrounds is a serious concern, with Allen and Hamnett (2022) drawing attention to the lack of reliable and authoritative statistics about the actual numbers of children from Gypsy Roma and Traveller backgrounds who are in state care. It was partly due to issues such as this, that the Gypsy, Roma, Traveller Social Work Association (GRTSWA) formed in

2019 to combat Anti-Gypsyism and aversive racism, which they considered endemic in both social work and wider society. The GRTSWA is primarily made up of community members who have been at times, reluctant to share their ethnicities because of lived and living experiences of discrimination and racism. This group has noted the almost complete absence of training and practice guides for work with adults and children from Gypsy, Roma, Traveller, Showmen and Boater backgrounds and is determined to develop training, guidance and models of practice, co-productively with community members.

The lack of knowledge about Gypsy, Roma and Traveller lifestyles, norms and mores leads to prejudice. How many social workers might relate to the colleague cited by Allen and Hulmes (2021, p. 9) below:

> …. if I am asked to work with a Gypsy family. I will be afraid and have low confidence in my ability to dig deep and to carry out a detailed assessment. I would be so fearful of getting through the front door and if I thought that the parents will become more aggressive my ambition will be to get the kids out.

The challenge for social workers in rural settings is to find ways of ensuring they have sufficient knowledge and understanding about the Gypsy, Roma or Traveller families in their locality, their origins, beliefs, cultural practices and lifestyles.

The journalist, Katharine Quarmby, has recently researched authorised and unauthorised Gypsy and Traveller sites across the UK, and she regards their locations and state of repair as a form of environmental racism which should be regarded as a national scandal. One particular site in Cardiff was condemned by the council decades ago due to contamination, a public inquiry in 1973 having reached the conclusion that even though the site was not acceptable for ordinary citizens, it could be suitable for Gypsies (Quarmby, 2022). Note the language and the placing of Gypsies and Travellers outside of the framing of 'ordinary' residents in this text-book example of 'othering.' The Cardiff site still exists in the same place in 2022, next to a steel works which produces red dust that coats the trailers and washing and is breathed in by the residents. The red dust alone would be enough to contend with, but sites are often plagued by rats and flies because of their proximity to refuse sites. Gypsies and Travellers have strict rules around cleanliness, these form part of the culture and social mores by which the communities abide. The rules are known as 'marime' or 'mochadi' and being forced to live in environmental conditions, which infringe upon these strict hygiene rules, is a daily grind, reinforces feelings of being second class citizens and is no doubt a factor which adds to the health inequalities experienced by Gypsies and Travellers on these sites.

Impact of Changing Rural Economy

One of the many problems facing Gypsy and Traveller communities in the countryside is the lack of available employment opportunities as agricultural work has radically changed with mechanised and computerised farming methods leading to less demand for casual and seasonal workers. Additionally, Eastern European workers have become dominant in the agricultural sector over recent decades, often at the expense of Gypsy and Traveller labour. Health and Safety regulations have also become increasingly prescriptive for traditional manual jobs such as tree surgery and landscaping while trades such as tinsmithing and sharpening of tools have also become redundant, and the once symbiotic relationship between farmers and itinerant seasonal Gypsy and Traveller labour has changed. The cash economy is also in serious decline and many current working-age Gypsies and Travellers have not been educated in the skills needed in a computerised era. These socio-economic challenges also bring with them a worsening mental health crisis across Gypsy, Roma and Traveller communities; research by Greenfields and Rogers (2020) established an evidence base that highlighted the 'ripple effect' of hate crime experiences on mental health. Participants in this latter study repeatedly stressed the persistent grinding and demoralising effect of hate crime/hate speech and discriminatory representations of their communities on their lives. The data from Greenfields and Rogers (2020) further reinforces previous evidence for other populations, that being a victim of hate crime has a greater impact on the emotional wellbeing of victims than non-hate crimes, with potentially devastating effects which may be linked to, and exacerbate, the risk of suicide. This same study found that 100% of Welsh Gypsies; 82% of Irish Travellers, 80% of Scottish Travellers and 32% of Romani Gypsies respondents reported having relatives who had attempted suicide in the previous five years. These figures are very significantly higher than for all other ethnic minorities in the UK.

So how, then, might a social worker (who represents the same 'authority' which discriminates) begin to work with Gypsy and Traveller communities in the countryside, especially when the likelihood is that they will not have received any training or orientation toward Gypsy and Traveller communities, despite the profession's expressed commitment to diversity and equality of opportunity. A first port of call might be to contact the nearest Gypsy, Roma and Traveller voluntary organisation, who do exist around the UK. Some may be grassroots led like GATE Herts (https://gateherts.org.uk/) or Moving for Change (https://www.moving-forchange.org.uk/). Other organisations such as Friends, Families and Travellers (https://www.gypsy-traveller.org/) or The Traveller Movement (https://travellermovement.org.uk/) will give advice regardless of the geographical location of the enquiry, although their local knowledge outside of their geographical headquarters can be limited. The 'aware' social worker may be able to find a local 'community connector' (Unwin et al., 2020, p. 2) who can introduce the social worker to the community, and advise on mores and norms that are real, rather than based on myth and prejudice. It would be important to ask how the family wish to be identified—as Irish Travellers/English Gypsies/Scottish Gypsy Travellers/Welsh Gypsies- and to show cultural respect by asking about the mores and norms around the issue initiating the social work involvement—how much supervision might young children expect?/what might be acceptable relationships among teenagers?/how might a disabled person be cared for?/how are mental health concerns viewed and articulated in that community?

As readers of this book will have noted, social work does not have a high profile within rural areas, the majority of social work being associated with urban settings. There is comparatively little written about social work and rurality, authors such as Pugh (2000), Pugh et al. (2007), Pugh and Cheers (2010) and Turbett (2010, 2019) being among the exceptions. This present chapter is believed to be one of the very few to address the particular issues of Gypsies, Roma and Travellers in rural settings, apart from the co-produced work '*Gypsy Travellers: Human rights and social work's role*' by MacLennan et al. (2017) and Turbett (2010) both of which specifically addressed issues within the Scottish context. Social work services, which have little contact, limited knowledge and poor understanding of Gypsy and Traveller communities, will tend to have apprehensive and negative views towards this population, as will health professionals (Heaslip et al., 2019). The reluctance to approach social work services can be partially attributed to the preference of Gypsies and Travellers to take care of themselves and their family, but also because of real fears that children will be removed (Allen & Hamnett, 2022), as has happened throughout time and across nations in respect of Gypsies, Roma and Travellers. Van Cleemput (2018, p. 205) interviewed 27 Gypsies and Travellers and found that their

> …own poor health and of extended family members was normalised and accepted. Four main themes emerged relating to health beliefs and the effect of lifestyle on health for these respondents: the travelling way; low expectations of health; self-reliance and staying in control; fatalism and fear of death. Among Gypsies and Travellers, clear cultural beliefs and attitudes underpin health-related behaviour, and health experiences must be understood in this context. In this group, ill health is seen as normal, an inevitable consequence of adverse social experiences, and is stoically and fatalistically accepted.

These above phenomena regarding health interactions could be equally applicable to social work—mutual contact and respect being one way forward to help change this antipathy. There is some literature about the particular nature of domestic violence in rural areas which gives pointers to the ways in which rural contexts can bring dynamics not associated with urban contexts (Stalford et al., 2003; Eastman et al., 2007). Issues here that social workers should heed include physical isolation, the lack of specialised organisations, the difficulties of keeping confidentialities in close-knit settings and the culture of not seeking outside help, but of sorting out your own problems. Gypsy and Traveller communities are known to express feelings of shame and stigma about mental illness; men in particular are loath to acknowledge any weaknesses in a tradition where men are perceived as being strong and the breadwinners. Unwin et al. (2020 p. 17) reported the following views from rural Gypsies and Travellers:

> Nobody talks about their disabilities. It's shameful; we don't do that sort of thing because your business is your business isn't it? (Welsh Gypsy)

> I think it's fear, because of being discriminated against in the past. I mean Gypsy Travellers have moved on a lot from years ago from the way they used to be, but the older generation are still there, and I think it's fear because of being discriminated against so much in the past. (Scottish Gypsy Traveller).

In respect of men's issues the following quote from a Welsh Gypsy sums up the problems health and social workers are likely to encounter with male Gypsies and Travellers:

> Too many of them kill themselves … they are taking their lives, they really are. Men in particular … Men don't talk, they're too macho, well maybe they're macho. (Unwin et al., 2020, p. 19).

A distrust of mainstream services has often built up over decades, even centuries, and some communities find their own solutions—for example, some rural Gypsies and Travellers will travel many miles to see an empathic doctor- the logistics in such realities meaning that health problems often are not addressed until they are acute (Unwin et al., 2020). This distrust is likely to similarly mean that 'early help' type social work services are unlikely to be taken up, the challenge to social work being how, then, to effectively reach out to Gypsy and Traveller rural communities and build up this much-needed trust. Rural communities in general are short of community resources and are all the harder to access if you are 'othered' by mainstream communities and professional staff. Feelings run deep in Gypsy and Traveller communities about historical discrimination and there is sometimes a reluctance to even believe that services not run by Gypsies and Travellers would ever do anything but discriminate (Unwin et al., 2020). Hence, the challenges, say, of a social worker encouraging a disabled person to try attending day services or care at home are all the greater.

Little (1999) brought academic attention to the complexity and fluidity of rural 'otherness', through which lens the nature of identities in rural settings are seen and debated. A contemporary example of this would be the phenomenon of many well off second-home owners buying up rural property which once would have been sold to local people, and post-Covid-19 working from home patterns meaning that many people can now work outside of urban setting and enjoy a different quality of life. Greenfields (2014) notes that the continuing romantic notions of the countryside do not include visualisations of living alongside Gypsy and Traveller communities, whose ancestors dwelt there centuries before the urban elite. Holloway (2003) sets this rural othering in exploring the positioning of Gypsies and Travellers in the English rural context across the late nineteenth and early twentieth centuries, drawing on public attitudes expressed about the traditional annual Gypsy fair held in Appleby, Cumbria. Her methodology, which involved analysing the ways in which the Appleby Fair was written about in the local paper, the '*Cumberland and Westmoreland Herald*' is interesting as it provides a local, albeit journalistic, representation of how the fair was viewed. Holloway posits that this local approach brought forward less romanticised characterisations of Gypsy and Traveller culture than did traditional academic views of the countryside. These latter views, which heralded Gypsies and Travellers as 'noble savages,' living a natural way of life devoid of the trapping of materialism, often came from urban scholars such as those within the Gypsy Lore Society and have since been widely critiqued as inaccurate (Sibley, 1995; Mayall, 1988). Such idealised images of the countryside have been criticised for privileging particular white rural identities at the expense of ethnic minorities such as Gypsies and Travellers. (e.g., Cloke et al., 2000; Philips, 1998).

Sibley (1995) unpicked the romanticised rural idyll model in which Gypsies and Travellers were seen to lead idealised, largely harmonious, if rather hidden, lives alongside other agricultural workers, moving as harvests and seasons dictated. This work goes on to contrast the 'idyll' model with views around Gypsies and Travellers being idle, wanton and criminal, views which had become dominant by the late nineteenth century and early twentieth century when mechanisation and other changes in agriculture, meant the need for their labour greatly lessened. These negative stereotypes of Gypsies and Travellers are still prevalent today, modern media showcasing programmes such as '*My Big Fat Gypsy Wedding*' (Channel 4, 2010) which grossly distort Gypsy and Traveller cultures and emphasise criminality, violence and excess. UK government-level oppression of Gypsies and Travellers has a long history and is still apparent even after the passing of the Equality Act (2010) and the granting of ethnic minority status to English Gypsies, Welsh Gypsies, Irish Travellers and Scottish Gypsy Travellers. As far back as the sixteenth-century, laws were passed to expel Gypsies and Travellers from the country (Mayall, 1995), and later came the Vagrancy Act (1824) and the Highways Act (1835), which criminalised nomadic lifestyles. Scholars such as Elder et al. (1998) discuss the racialisation of many colonial peoples, a discourse which placed Gypsies, Roma and Travellers on the less-valued side of the nature, often being perceived as lacking a higher moral code.

Returning to Holloway's (2003) historical study of representations of the Appleby Fair, she notes that local newspaper reporting of the Appleby Fair developed a racialised tone over the years. Pre-World War One, reports on crimes such as camping on the highway, furious driving, allowing horses to stray on the highway and being drunk and disorderly were sometimes included in articles about the fair itself, but these articles were not racialised and included non-Gypsy offenders. After World War One, comments began to appear in the *Cumberland and Westmoreland Herald* about the wealth of some of the Gypsies and the presence of motorised rather than horse-drawn vehicles, which were seen to dilute notions of 'authentic' Gypsies based on romanticism and a bucolic harmonious countryside. During the interwar years, the *Cumberland and Westmoreland Herald* started to report the Appleby Fair along racial lines, seeing the 'authentic' Gypsies as superior to other Gypsies and Travellers. This type of rural prejudice is also noted later by Halfacree (1996) who observed that New Age Travellers were not welcome in the countryside because they were not seen as 'real' Gypsies, rather they were seen as social deviants.

'The Last Acceptable Form of Racism'

A Traveller Movement (2017) report into racism against Gypsies, Roma and Travellers was entitled *'The last acceptable form of racism'* and found that most Gypsy, Roma and Traveller communities experienced pervasive and constant racism from all sides of life. Greenfields and Rogers (2020) called their report into hate crime against the same communities *'Hate as Regular as Rain'*, finding that Gypsies, Roma, and Travellers suffered intense and insidious forms of discrimination, both from bottom up and top down. Prejudice at an everyday level can still be heard in all kinds of settings, both rural and urban. The same comments can be heard in everyday talk today—*"where do they get their money from?;" "Do you know how much those vans cost?;" "They don't pay any tax?;" "They'll rip you off"* As regards 'top-down' prejudice, the current Police, Crime, Courts, and Sentencing Act (2020) has been brought in largely to satisfy the prejudices of well-off communities, often rural in nature, who object to a nomadic lifestyle which means that groups of Gypsies or Travellers will pitch up on local, traditional sites and sometimes leave a mess behind. Sanitary or waste disposal facilities are rarely provided in such cases and the (deliberate) failure of many councils to provide transit or permanent sites over the past 50 years mean that the small minority still wishing to pursue their nomadic lifestyles have no alternatives open to them other than to set up camp in ways that will now involve their criminalisation, seizure of their homes and possible removal of their children into state care. This racist Act serves to further endorse Anti-Gypsyism as acceptable and reveals a racist underbelly in the countryside. The Countryside Alliance is the lead UK campaigning organisation that promotes the rural way of life in Parliament and in the media, yet its website (https://www.countryside-alliance.org/), which claims to stand shoulder to shoulder with other country people, makes not one mention of ethnic minorities such as Gypsies or Travellers. This exclusion suggests that Gypsies and Travellers do not qualify as 'other country people' but are 'othered' people with no legitimacy as rural dwellers. Such approaches encourage the perpetuation of a white monocultural construct of the countryside, whose values do not embrace Gypsies and Travellers as 'insiders', especially now that much of their synergy as essential parts of the agricultural economy has faded.

Perhaps the most shocking example of racism in the 'idyllic' country-side took place in the Sussex village of Firle in 2003 when residents 'symbolically purged their village of Gypsy-Travellers by burning a mock caravan complete with effigies at their annual Bonfire Night celebrations' (Holloway, 2007, p. 7). Burning in the caravan were effigies of young children and scantily dressed women, while the caravan's number plate read 'P1 KEY' ('pikey' is an offensive term for Gypsies and Travellers). Subsequent arrests were made for inciting racial hatred, but no prosecutions followed. The clear message from this 'respectable' country town was that not only do Gypsies and Travellers not fit with the mainstream view of rural dwellers, but that violence and murder would befall those who transgressed their 'rural idyll.' Holloway (2007, pp. 11–13) cites the following examples of mixed public reaction to the effigy burning, taken from letters' sections in national newspapers:

Well done on your choice of effigy. To all the bleeding-heart do-gooders out there crying racism, try living next door to pikeys and see whether you still feel the same way (Payne (2003) in *The Daily Telegraph*)

I would just like to thank everyone involved for an excellent show on Saturday. Keep up the good work! Don't let the PC *[Politically Correct]* mob get you down (McGreevy (2003) in *The Sunday Times*)

The last people to burn Gypsies that I heard of were the Nazis in their concentration camps. We all like to think things are so different now, but are they? Will it be effigies of Jews we burn at Firle bonfire next year? (Shaikh (2003) in *The Times*)

Imagine an English village building an effigy of a car, with caricatures of black people in the windows and the number plate "N1 GGER" and burning it in a public ceremony ... It is, or so we should hope, unimaginable. But something very much like it happened last week (Monbiot (2003) in *The Guardian*).

There is little written about discrimination in the countryside, and racial hatred is generally associated with urban towns and cities. Garland and Chakraborti (2006) have written about the need to recognise ethic minorities' experiences of discrimination in rural settings, while Neal

(2002, p. 445) notes that: 'English pastoralism represents a place of security away from the commonly perceived urban malaise of English cities which have, in the post-war period, become increasingly diverse ('unEnglish') and synonymous with an undesirable black/Other presence'. So, social workers in rural areas have a different challenge in upholding the codes of ethics that underpin their profession (e.g., BASW, 2021b) and may find that racism is more covert than overt.

Gypsies and Travellers sit at the uncomfortable crossroads between having been given rights as ethnic minorities, but it is perhaps unlikely many country dwellers know about this status, indeed many Gypsies and Travellers do not know of these rights, nor of the Equality Act, 2010 (Unwin et al., 2020). Gypsies and Travellers are not seen as black people in the UK (although they are in parts of Europe) but perhaps they are seen more as part of a white underclass who do not 'fit in,' especially since changes in the nature of agricultural employment have led to less close working relationships between communities.

The tensions which exist between Gypsies and Travellers and rural councils are reflected in the recent decision of Powys County Council not to support the achin tan (stopping place) at the 2022 Royal Welsh Show. The temporary stopping site at the 'Ysgiog' was granted planning permission in 2013 and was jointly funded by Powys Council and the Royal Welsh Show. Families would pay a fee which covered all the necessary amenities. This stopping place has a long history of use by Gypsies and Travellers who travelled from across the UK to stay at the annual Royal Welsh Show. The 'Ysgiog' was unique in Wales and held up as an exemplar of not only supporting but also enabling the legally protected nomadic traditions of Gypsies and Travellers in Wales and the UK. There is even a FaceBook page especially for the stopping site. This decision to not fund the 'Ysgiog' may be viewed as symptomatic of an erosion in the of the role the Royal Welsh Show plays in the cultural life of Gypsy and Traveller communities, a place where old traditions are maintained and where families and friends meet to share news and to trade with one another. This is especially insensitive as the decision not to support the stopping site, was announced on the day that the Police, Crime, Courts, and Sentencing Act (2022) came into force. The following notice appeared on the Facebook page 'Any unauthorised encampments will be assessed by Powys County Council and Dyfed-Powys Police, in line with the Welsh Government guidance.' This notice can be construed as a threat, and not as the supportive and enabling approach that is enshrined in the Welsh Government's diversity legislation and policies. The decision not to support the stopping site was apparently made approximately two years ago with no consultation and no impact assessment on how this decision would affect the communities.

In Wales there is a legal duty on councils to assess and meet the need for permanent and temporary accommodation and councils have a legal duty to provide these kinds of sites so that Gypsies and Travellers can travel to, and stay on, suitable land with necessary facilities. Given that the Police, Crime, Courts, and Sentencing Act (2020) is now in force in Wales, it is even more important that local authorities provide transit or temporary sites, otherwise families have no legal place to site their trailers while visiting shows or other cultural events, which will make them vulnerable to criminal sanction and potential removal of their homes.

The police, local authorities and other public bodies should undertake welfare considerations before evicting an encampment, because existing government guidance in England and Wales regarding this practice is still in force. The GRTSWA in collaboration with BASW, has recognised that social workers and others, who may be involved in undertaking welfare checks, do not have access to guidance which is human rights gold-plated, strengths-based, and family-focused. Therefore, good practice guidance with associated welfare enquiry forms has been developed. This Good Practice Guidance (Allen & GRTSWA, 2022) and associated welfare enquiry protocols are aimed at professionals, including social workers, in local authorities and any other organisations tasked with undertaking welfare assessments on unauthorised encampments.

The above Good Practice Guidance provides a brief introduction to the types of conversations that can lead to a reliable and verifiable understanding of welfare considerations that result from police action. This information may then be used to support a legal challenge or appeal against the Police, Crime, Courts, and Sentencing Act (2022), on the grounds that the act of eviction is incompatible with the Human Rights Act in England and Wales. It is critical that social workers and others undertaking these assessments, are absolutely clear that it is the application of the Police, Crime, Courts, and Sentencing Act (2022)—the eviction—which creates the inherent vulnerability, and not perceptions of family dysfunction or judgements about parenting or lifestyle.

Conclusion

In conclusion, this chapter has given a historical and contextual view of Gypsies and Travellers in the UK countryside and, to date, social work as establishment, has been part of the problem, rather than part of the solution. Much lost ground has been made up since the formation of the GRTSWA, however, and all social workers should make it their business to gain knowledge and competencies in working with Gypsies, Roma and Travellers, just as with all other ethnic minorities. The chapter has illuminated how lifestyles and the nomadic traditions of Gypsies and Travellers have been under threat since they first came into the UK in the sixteenth Century and were greeted with the Egyptian Acts (1530 & 1554) which were designed to either force Gypsies out of the UK, or to enforce their assimilation into the mainstream. If neither of these outcomes occurred, the penalty for being a Gypsy or associating with a Gypsy, was death. It could be argued that the state has almost come full circle with the passing of the Police, Crime, Courts, and Sentencing Act (2020) and the outlawing of nomadism, so central to ethnic identity. It is also chilling to be reminded that the Porrajmos (Roma and Sinti Holocaust) started with the removal of trailers.

One of the authors of this chapter, a Welsh Gypsy, asked her mother who was forcibly removed into state care in the 1940s, and then moved into bricks and mortar accommodation, away from the achin tans/stopping places and nomadism which represented her family life—what a home means to her, she replied "No walls … open countryside … moving with family … the open sky. I only ever wanted to live in a caravan, and I want to die in one."

Is that so very much to ask?

References

Allen, D., & Hamnett, V. (2022). Gypsy, Roma and Traveller Children in Child Welfare Services in England. *The British Journal of Social Work, 52*(7), 3904–3922. https://doi.org/10.1093/bjsw/bcab265

Allen, D., & Hulmes, A. (2021). Aversive Racism and Child Protection Practice with Gypsy, Roma and Traveller Children and Families. *Seen and Heard, 31*(2), 40–55. Accessed September 01, 2022, from https://www.nagalro.com/_userfiles/pages/files/allen_hulmes_aversive_racismjs.pdf

Allen, D., & Riding, S. (2019). *The Fragility of Professional Competence: A Preliminary Account of Child Protection Practice with Romani and Traveller Children.* Project Report, European Roma Rights Centre. Accessed March 21, 2022, from https://e-space.mmu.ac.uk/623526/1/the-fragility-of-professional-competence-january-2018.pdf

Allen, D., & The Gypsy Roma Traveller Social Work Association (GRTSWA). (2022). *Good Practice Guidance: Understanding the Welfare Impact of the Police, Crime, Sentencing & Courts Act.* Accessed July 19, 2022, from https://www.basw.co.uk/what-we-do/equality-diversity-and-inclusion-edi-social-work/supporting-grt-communities

British Association of Social Workers (BASW). (2021a). *BASW and SWU Oppose Part 4 of the Police, Crime, Sentencing and Courts Bill.* Accessed July 21, 2022, from https://www.basw.co.uk/media/news/2021/jun/basw-and-swu-oppose-part-4-police-crime-sentencing-and-courts-bill

British Association of Social Workers (BASW). (2021b). *The BASW Code of Ethics for Social Work.* BASW. Accessed December 15, 2022, from https://www.basw.co.uk/system/files/resources/basw_code_of_ethics_-_2021.pdf

BASW. (2022). *Social Workers Tell Comic Jimmy Carr to Stand Down from Welsh Show.* Accessed September 06, 2023, from Social Workers Tell Comic Jimmy Carr to Stand Down from Welsh Show | www.basw.co.uk

Channel 4. (2010). *My Big Fat Gypsy Wedding.* Accessed April 11, 2022, from https://www.channel4.com/press/news/big-fat-gypsy-weddings

Channel 4. (2022) *60 Days with the Gypsies.* Accessed July 22, 2022, from https://www.channel4.com/programmes/60-days-with-the-gypsies

Cloke, P., Milbourne, P., & Widdowfield, R. (2000). Homelessness and Rurality: 'Out-of-Place' in Purified Space. *Environment and Planning D: Society and Space, 18,* 715–735.

Countryside Alliance. (2022). *Still Standing Your Ground.* Accessed March 21, 2022, from https://www.countryside-alliance.org/about-us

Cromarty, H. (2019, May 9). *Gypsies and Travellers*. House of Commons Briefing Paper, 08083. Accessed December 15, 2022, from https://research-briefings.files.parliament.uk/documents/CBP-8083/CBP-8083.pdf

Eastman, B., Bunch, S., Hamilton, G., Williams, A., & Caravan, L. (2007). Exploring the Perceptions of Domestic Violence of Service Providers in Rural Localities. *Violence Against Women, 13*(7), 700–716.

Elder, G., Wolch, J., & Emel, J. (1998). La Pratique Sauvage: Race, Place and the Human Animal Divide. In J. Wolch & J. Emel (Eds.), *Animal Geographies* (pp. 72–90). Verso.

Equal Rights Trust. (1983). *Mandla (Sewa Singh) and Another v Dowell Lee and Others [1983] 2 AC 548*. Accessed June 21, 2022, from https://www.equal-rightstrust.org/ertdocumentbank/Microsoft%20Word%20-%20Mandla.pdf

Friends, Families and Travellers. (2020). *Police Repeat Calls for More Sites Rejecting Home Office Proposals to Criminalise Trespass*. Accessed April 4, 2022, from https://www.gypsy-traveller.org/news/police-repeat-calls-for-more-sites-rejecting-home-office-proposals-to-criminalise-trespass/

Garland, J., & Chakraborti, N. (2006). 'Race', Space and Place: Examining Identity and Cultures of Exclusion in Rural England. *Ethnicities, 6*(2), 159–177.

Greenfields, M. (2014). Gypsies and Travellers in Modern Rural England. In G. Bosworth & P. Somerville (Eds.), *Interpreting Rurality, Multidisciplinary Approaches* (pp. 219–234). Routledge.

Greenfields, M., & Rogers, C. (2020). *Hate: "As Regular as Rain" – A Pilot Research Project into the Psychological Effects of Hate Crime on Gypsy, Traveller and Roma (GTR) Communities*. Accessed August 2023, from https://gate-herts.org.uk/wp-content/uploads/2020/12/Rain-Report-201211.pdf

Halfacree, K. (1996). Out of Place in the Country: Travellers and the 'Rural Idyll'. *Antipode, 28*(1), 42–47.

Hancock, I. (2017). *We Are the Romani People, Ames am e Rromane dzene*. University of Hertfordshire Press.

Heaslip, V., Vanceulebroeck, V., Kalkan, I., Kömürcü, N., & Solanas, I. (2019). Student Nurse Perceptions of Gypsy Roma Travellers. A European Qualitative Study. *Nurse Education Today, 829*, 1–7.

Holloway, S. (2003). Outsiders in Rural Society? Constructions of Rurality and Nature—Society Relations in the Racialisation of English Gypsy-Travellers, 1869–1934. *Environment and Planning D: Society and Space, 21*(6), 695–715.

Holloway, S. (2007). Burning Issues: Whiteness, Rurality and the Politics of Difference. *Geoforum, 38*, 7–20. Accessed July 19, 2022, from https://www.academia.edu/6623626/Burning_issues_Whiteness_rurality_and_the_politics_of_difference

Little, J. (1999). Otherness, Representation and the Cultural Construction of Rurality. *Progress in Human Geography, 23*, 437–442.

MacLennan, K., McPhee, R., McPhee, S., & Turbett, C. (2017). Gypsy Travellers: Human Rights and Social Work's Role. *Insight, 35*. Accessed January 20, 2022, from https://www.iriss.org.uk/resources/insights/gypsy-travellers-human-rights-and-social-works-role

Mayall, D. (1988). *Gypsy-Travellers in Nineteenth-Century Society*. Cambridge University Press.

Mayall, D. (1995). *English Gypsies and State Policies*. University of Hertfordshire Press.

McGreevy, R. (2003, November 2). Traveller Bonfire in Sussex Village 'Incited Racial Hatred.' *Sunday Times*, p. 8. in Holloway S. (2003). Outsiders in Rural Society? Constructions of Rurality and Nature—Society Relations in the Racialisation of English Gypsy-Travellers, 1869 – 1934. *Environment and Planning D: Society and Space, 21*(6), 695–715.

Ministry of Housing, Communities and Local Government. (2020). *Count of Traveller Caravans, January 2020, England*. Accessed March 21, 2022, from https://assets.publishing.service.gov.uk/government/uploads/system/uploads/attachment_data/file/891229/Traveller_caravan_count_2020_stats_release.pdf

Monbiot, G. (2003, November 4). Acceptable Hatred: Beneath the Enduring Hostility to Gypsies Lies an Ancient Envy of the Nomadic Life. *The Guardian*. Accessed September 01, 2022, from http://www.coldtype.net/Assets/pdfs/GM.36.pdf

Neal, S. (2002). Rural Landscape, Representations and Racism: Examining Multicultural Citizenship and Policy-Making in the English Countryside. *Ethnic and Racial Studies, 25*(3), 442–461.

Payne, S. (2003, October 30). Effigies of Gipsies Are Set Alight at Village Party. *The Daily Telegraph*, p. 15. Accessed September 01, 2022, from https://www.cpfc.org/forums/archive/index.php/t-43148.html

Philips, M. (1998). The Restructuring of Social Imaginations in Rural Geography. *Journal of Rural Studies, 14*, 121–153.

Pugh, R. (2000). *Rural Social Work*. Russell House Publishing.

Pugh, R., & Cheers, B. (2010). *Rural Social Work: International Perspectives*. Policy Press.

Pugh, R., Scharf, T., Williams C., & Roberts, D. (2007). *Obstacles to Using and Providing Rural Social Care*. Research Brief 22, Social Care Institute for Excellence. Accessed March 22, 2022, from https://www.research.manchester.ac.uk/portal/en/publications/obstacles-to-using-and-providing-rural-social-care(1ed99526-da32-44aa-9418-22a377c7506e).html

Quarmby, K. (2022, July 3). The Scandal of Authorised Gypsy, Roma and Traveller Sites in Wales. *The National*. Accessed June 22, 2022, from https://www.thenational.wales/news/20249600.scandal-authorised-gypsy-roma-traveller-sites-wales/

Shaikh, T. (2003, October 30). Villagers Burn an Effigy of Gypsies. *The Times*, p. 16. in Holloway S. (2003) Outsiders in Rural Society? Constructions of Rurality and Nature—Society Relations in the Racialisation of English Gypsy-Travellers, 1869 – 1934. *Environment and Planning D: Society and Space, 21*(6), 695–715.

Sibley, D. (1995). *Geographies of Exclusion*. Routledge.

Stalford, L., Barker, H., & Beveridge, F. (2003). *Children and Domestic Violence in Rural Areas. A Child-Focused Assessment of Service Provision*. Save the Children. Accessed March 22, 2022, from https://resourcecentre.savethechildren.net/pdf/children_and_domestic_violence_in_rural_areas.pdf/

The Traveller Movement. (2017). *The Last Acceptable Form of Racism? The Pervasive Discrimination and Prejudice Experienced by Gypsy, Roma and Traveller Communities*. Accessed January 18, 2022, from https://travellermovement.org.uk/policy-and-publications/the-last-acceptable-form-of-racism

The Traveller Movement. (2023). *Gypsy, Roma and Traveller Culture*. Gypsy Roma and Traveller History and Culture | The Traveller Movement. Accessed September 06, 2023.

Travellers Times. (2019). *Roads from the Past*. Accessed April 11, 2022, from https://www.youtube.com/watch?v=1bhBbMrF8Z0

Turbett, C. (2010). *Rural Social Work Practice in Scotland*. Venture Press.

Turbett, C. (2019). Rural Social Work in Scotland. *Contemporary Rural Social Work Journal, 11*(1), 1–14.

Unwin, P., Meakin, B., & Jones, A. (2020). *The Missing Voices of Disabled People in Gypsy, Roma and Traveller Communities*. Report to Disabled Research into Independent Living and Learning (DRILL). Accessed January 18, 2022, from http://www.drilluk.org.uk/wp-content/uploads/2020/12/Missing-Voices-FINAL-report.pdf

Van Cleemput, P. (2018). Health Needs of Gypsy Travellers. *InnovAiT, 11*(12), 681–688.

Walach, V. (2020). Envy, Corruption and 'Hard Racism': Studying Antigypsyism as an Ideological Fantasy. *Slovenský národopis, 68*(4), 324–339.

Part II

Environment

5

Re-Imagining Rural Social Work During the Time of Covid-19 and a Climate Crisis

Lena Dominelli

Introduction

The UK is a highly industrialised society. However, most of its land is rural, and half of it is devoted to agriculture. Only 6% is built upon, but 83% of the population lives on that (Rae, 2017). In 2020, the urban population of the UK had reached 56.4 million, and the rural population about 10.8 million. Since 1960, the rural population has decreased by 480,000 while the urban population grew by 15.3 million (Statista, 2022). The rural economy is more reliant on individuals providing their own job opportunities as self-employed entrepreneurs. Additionally, in 2019, home working was proportionately greater in rural areas—around 1.1 million or 22% of the rural workforce, compared to 3 million or 13% of the urban one. The depopulation of rural areas can be ascribed to the lack of affordable housing, well-paid jobs, and good transportation and

L. Dominelli (✉)
Programme Director of Disaster Interventions and Humanitarian Aid,
University of Stirling, Stirling, Scotland, UK
e-mail: lena.dominelli@stir.ac.uk

© The Author(s), under exclusive license to Springer Nature Switzerland AG 2024   **115**
C. Turbett, J. Pye (eds.), *Rural Social Work in the UK*, Rethinking Rural,
https://doi.org/10.1007/978-3-031-52440-0_5

communication infrastructures (DEFRA, 2021). This can challenge the Tory government's 'Levelling Up' agenda, as a 'one-size fits all' approach will not meet the multiple complexities that must be addressed in rural areas.

The countryside, or rural areas that provide the lungs for the cities dotted throughout the British Isles, are formed by fragments of human imagination as places of leisure and harmony. While this presupposes a commitment to care for the resources harboured in the countryside to meet human needs, these areas are often exploited for commercial gain. This has resulted in environmental degradation and a climate crisis of extreme weather events including cold-snaps, heat waves, droughts, floods, storm surges, and wildfires as demonstrated by recent statistics highlighting the changing climate (ONS, 2023).

How humans have extracted the bounty of nature in rural areas has been historically conditioned by humanity's approach to creating the goods and services that supply food, clothing, shelter, medicines, and the built infrastructures that ensure the necessities of life. Since industrialisation and agribusiness replaced small-scale farming following the Enclosure Acts in the seventeenth century, nature's bounty –the countryside's rivers, soils and other resources have been harnessed to meet human need and make money. These resources provided water to power mills and steam-engines; land for railways and cars to transport people from one end of the country to the other; and air for airplanes to carry people across continents cheaply, conveniently and rapidly. Systems of agriculture predicated on the rhythms of and harmony with nature gave way to agribusiness embedded in a green revolution that increased productivity through mechanisation, the use of chemical herbicides, pesticides, and fertilisers, and genetically modified (GM) crops. Following a strong campaign by environmental activists, GM crops were rejected for use in the European Union (EU) which then included the UK. The rejection of GM foods remains fragile because large corporations stand to make substantial profits if allowed to grow these. Permitting their growth would initiate a step-change in controlling farming equivalent to the time when agribusiness swallowed up small-holding farmers.

The processes of industrialisation have eroded the balance and harmony between human activity and nature, and its spread throughout the countryside has been called *rurbanisation* (Dominelli, 2012). Thus, urban patterns of housing, street lighting and commuting lifestyles erode rural spaces and their close links with the physical environment and starlit skies. Another threat to traditional forms of farming is the lack of interest in agricultural jobs by young people, due to low pay, job insecurity, lack of housing, and poverty which is persistent, though often invisible. These changes have made defining rural social work and rurality contentious (Francis & Henderson, 1992; Richardson, 2019; Pugh & Cheers, 2010; Daley, 2010; Lohman & Lohman, 2005; Richardson, 2019). As these are elaborated at great length in other chapters, I define rural social work as practice occurring among populations sparsely distributed in the countryside, living in geographic locations with limited public services including health facilities, educational services, and good communication and transportation systems.

This chapter is innovative in that it considers rural social work from a green social work perspective that focuses on how social workers can play roles in retaining the countryside as a place of leisure and employment activities that include caring for the environment as its resources are used to produce the necessities of life, especially food, clothing, water, medicines, and shelter. I begin by defining green social work (GSW) including its rural variant (RGSW) by drawing on Dominelli (2012) as the inspiration behind this emerging paradigm for practice. I then link RGSW to practice that widens the profession's portfolio to discuss social workers' roles in climate change; disaster interventions to address environmental degradation caused by industrial and farming processes; create renewable, sustainable energy to reduce and eventually eliminate fossil fuel consumption; engage in valuing local or indigenous knowledges alongside scientific expertise; and incorporate RGSW in life's daily routines among rural inhabitants. I conclude that RGSW has a critical role to play in developing resilient, sustainable, and inclusive communities.

Defining Rural Green Social Work

Rural social work from a green perspective or rural green social work (RGSW) has emerged from green social work (GSW). GSW is defined as a form of social work practice that:

> focuses on how the social organisation of relationships between peoples and their interaction with the flora and fauna in their physical habitats create [today's] socio-economic and physical environmental crises that undermine the well-being of human beings and planet earth (Dominelli, 2012:25).

Green social work is global in scope. It is, therefore, a holistic transdisciplinary theory and practice that acknowledges global interdependencies; links between people, their activities and the physical environment or ecosystem; values local, indigenous, and scientific expertise; and engages people in coproducing solutions to their problems. GSW critiques the social organisation of production and consumption of goods and services based on the exploitation of fossil fuels and nature in rural areas, green field sites, including pristine tropical and temperate forests, as sources of cheap materials. Under neoliberalism, the current form of capitalist modernity, this approach promotes low pay for those employed by the 'entrepreneurs', and environmental degradation to maximise profits for the few. Meanwhile, poverty, structural inequalities, and climate crises proceed apace for the majority being buffeted by economic crises and cost-of-living (CLC) increases.

As the economy catered for the accumulation of wealth among the few (Oxfam, 2016), the number of billionaires rose from 946 holding $6.3 billion in 2007 when the economic financial crisis initiated by unsustainable modes of making money erupted, to 2755 holding $13.6 trillion in 2021 by which time Covid-19 lockdowns had further decimated the economy globally (Peterson-Withorn, 2021). This astonishing achievement remains primarily a privilege of men. Gender inequality continues in their midst despite the growth in the number of women billionaires which reached 328 women holding $1.53 trillion in 2021. Meanwhile, more than 700 million people live in absolute poverty, or less than $1.90 per day (Peterson-Withorn, 2021).

Most of these poor people live in rural areas in the global South. In the UK, there are 8.1 million working-age adults, 4.3 million children and 2.1 million pensioners, or 14.5 million people, living in poverty (JRF, 2022). Poverty tends to be higher in urban and suburban areas, with Scotland having lower rates of poverty than Wales and England. This is largely due to lower housing costs in Scotland (JRF, 2022). However, such statistics hide other aspects of poverty that are significant in the countryside. These include poor infrastructures including in power, communications and other utilities, high costs of transportation, fewer recreational amenities, limited services including of health, education, and employment opportunities. Rural poverty is often hidden (Chandini et al., 2019; Bloomer, 2022) and requires community development initiatives to overcome it (Dominelli, 2012).

Ironically, despite having been developed in the UK, GSW has taken off in countries across the world more than here (Dominelli, 2018). Consequently, explaining what constitutes GSW and rural green social work draws on some global developments. The definition of rural social work remains contested, despite various attempts to define it (Force-Emery Mackie et al., 2015). In this chapter, I focus on two key contemporary disasters—climate change and the COVID-19 pandemic. Both are global challenges with local repercussions due to interdependencies between the macro- and micro-levels. I define rural social work as practice occurring in a geographically based small community located within the rural hinterland or countryside and containing limited amenities for any age group living there. The literature on rural social work remains sparse compared to the vast range referring to urban landscapes. This is unsurprising given that human development has been one of migration from rural areas to urban ones, often in search of work. A recent form of this movement is exemplified by the migration of rural dwellers in China to its megacities regardless of whether they hold permits under the *houkou* (rehousing) system promulgated by the Communist Party to control people's access to jobs, housing, health, and educational opportunities to restrict individual, ad hoc population movements. This system has had limited success because rural dwellers have left the countryside for the cities in huge numbers to earn incomes that could support both them and family members left in the countryside. Those left behind were older people who cared for their grandchildren and agricultural plots. Those entering the cities disregarded the privations they endured through unauthorised entry into the cities (Xue, 2018). Despite this population shift, rural social work in China has been innovative and promoted traditional forms of crop production, especially in places where agribusiness had failed (Ku & Dominelli, 2018; Ku et al., 2019). These developments encouraged the growth of rural green social work, innovation, and sustainable development in that country (Ku, 2011; Dominelli, 2018; Dominelli & Ku, 2017; Ku & Dominelli, 2018; Ku et al., 2019). The Chart below captures the RGSW Model visually (Fig. 5.1).

Rural green social workers (RGSWRs) have engaged residents in re-imagining their communities in transformative directions by resisting commercial disregard of the environment as an entity in its own right, supported mutual self-help among residents and referred people to necessary services at all points of the disaster cycle—immediate relief, recovery and reconstruction. During these activities, RGSWRs have performed the following roles:

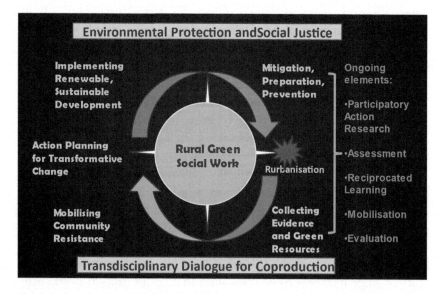

Fig. 5.1   Rural green social work model

- Facilitators
- Coordinators
- Community mobilisers
- Lobbyists
- Resource mobilisers
- Coordinators
- Negotiators
- Mediators
- Consultants
- Advocates
- Educators
- Trainers
- Cultural interpreters
- Representatives at decision-making tables
- Psychosocial therapists and counsellors
- Scientific translators conveying scientific knowledge to communities and local expertise to scientists (Dominelli, 2011).

Rural areas, like urban ones, must reduce fossil fuel consumption to achieve 'Net Zero'. Green social workers can mobilise communities to focus the West's attention on addressing its historical legacy of damaging the environment identified in the Rio Summit of 1992 as the basis for the Kyoto Protocol of 1997. Doing nothing exacerbates the current climate crisis. Under the Kyoto Protocol, each Annex 1 country (all those in the West) was given targets in reducing greenhouse gas emissions by cutting their use of fossil fuels. At that time, the USA was the largest emitter of such gases. However, this picture has changed as the emerging economies and their substantial populations seek rapid industrialisation. China overtook the USA as the largest emitter in 2005. By 2022, the largest emitters of GHG emissions were China, the USA, India, Russia, Japan, Germany, Korea, and Iran, in that order. Both historical and current GHG emissions must be contained to eliminate the climate crisis that is destroying life as we know it (Friedrich et al., 2023). RGSWRs can also engage in consciousness-raising and educational activities to provide residents with the information they need to change their behaviours.

Other emerging economies, for example, Brazil, Mexico, Indonesia, and South Africa will soon be adding to this list of polluters. All these countries justify such growth as essential in reducing poverty by industrialising. The right to development is a human right and needs to be disentangled from using fossil fuels. Hence, RGSWRs can raise consciousness and demonstrate that fossil fuel-based development is not the only option available for human and social development. There are renewable energies available, although these technologies have to be shared equitably to make it possible for sustainable development to occur throughout the world, regardless of population size and level of industrialisation in any country (Dominelli, 2012). However, this requires a sharing of such technologies by large multinational firms which are reluctant to do so. Green, renewable energies (e.g., solar panels, wind turbines, heat pumps) should be accessible to all at low cost to show solidarity and improve life for people, the flora, fauna, and physical world. Additionally, rising levels of GHG emissions impact primarily on countries with largely rural populations who contribute little to GHG emissions (WWF, 2020). Nonetheless, they are most likely to experience the highest levels of air pollution, sea level rises, and ocean acidification. Countries with large rural populations experiencing the most deleterious effects of climate change are Bangladesh, Pakistan, Mongolia, Afghanistan, India, Indonesia, Bahrain, and Nepal in that order (Kharas et al., 2022).

Social work in the UK has discounted the relevance of environmental disasters in its theory and practice. However, Covid-19, as a zoonotic disease based on the SARS-CoV-2 coronavirus raised the significance of the ecosystem in allowing the transmission of a virus harboured in the animal kingdom into the human one. Human beings lacked immunity to this unknown coronavirus, and by bringing it into social settings, it became a health pandemic, leaving numerous casualties in its wake, and highlighting the destructive impact of existing inequalities along many social attributes and physical environments. Climate change played a role in this scenario because the destruction of pristine ecosystem to grow crops like palm oil and soya beans in tropical forests promoted the transmission of this disease between animals and humans (WWF, 2020).

Now, social workers across the globe are examining the impact of Covid-19 on their practice and are becoming aware of the impact of climate change on both their environment and working lives. Practitioners have also had to engage with the controversies around the role of climate change in precipitating the pandemic and have highlighted various environmental concerns ranging from air pollution which adversely impacts health especially that of children to degraded ocean waters which place people's lives and livelihoods at risk. Green social workers have been working on these issues for several years (Dominelli, 2012, 2021), and activities that seemed remote five years ago, are becoming commonplace in both urban and rural settings today.

Consequently, the urbanisation of the countryside or rurbanisation (Dominelli, 2012) calls on rural green social workers to resist the further encroachment of agribusiness and industrial production methods relying on fossil fuels in rural areas. This strategy has to be enacted without ignoring the traps that ensure the continuation of livelihoods under the industrial production models favoured by neoliberalism, industrialists and agribusinesses as these contribute to climate change. Rural social workers working from a RGSW seek to replace fossil fuel-based development by using coproduction with local communities to innovate and find alternative ways of addressing the degradation that burning fossil fuels imposes upon their environment. This has occurred in the Isle of Eigg in Scotland where renewable energies provide a model of a self-sufficient rural community development and growth that has eschewed the use of fossil fuels favoured by our societies generally. Thus, the inhabitants of Eigg exemplify how the destruction and degradation of wildlife habitats can be avoided by becoming a renewable energy sufficient community (Gardiner, 2017). RGSW argues that people have a duty to care for and protect planet earth so that it can provide for living things to exist into the long-term future as a healthy, sustainable place for living beings to thrive (Dominelli, 2012). RGSWRs living in rural and remote areas can assist in protecting the physical environment, its flora, its fauna, and its unique cultural life.

RGSWRs have important roles in enabling people to maintain mental health and well-being. This includes promoting initiatives that secure sustainable jobs in the countryside and protecting its rural nature. The lost links between people and nature, especially those living in highly urbanised or hyper-urbanised areas within megacities was acknowledged during the lockdowns of the Covid-19 pandemic that restricted people indoors. In the UK, some of those living in high-rise apartment blocks began a minor exodus from the cities to the countryside in search of closer links to the natural environment (*The Telegraph*, 2020) by buying houses with gardens. This demand for rural housing throughout the UK heightened demands for houses with land in rural areas (Currie et al., 2021). This placed pressure on housing prices that had already escalated beyond local people's purchasing power as city dwellers bought second homes as havens from highly pressured city life. Such tendencies exacerbated tensions between local residents and the 'outsiders' because children born in rural areas were priced out of houses in their birth villages. Nor could they find well-paid jobs in such locales which tend to have limited employment opportunities based around tourism and hospitality (Glass et al., 2021).

Self-Care

Climate change, disaster interventions including during Covid-19 have emphasised the importance of peer support and self-care. Having each person assess the risks they faced and define what self-care means personally is part of this concern. Details for accessing support and supervision informally among peers and formally with managers, and debriefing regularly are other elements to include in a self-care plan. Forming and using peer-support groups to consider different scenarios and ethical dilemmas encountered during home visits, agency visits, or delivering services is an important function of these groups. If you become traumatised by your experiences, speak to your line manager, and obtain appropriate psychosocial support. This may be needed for some time and should be delivered in a non-stigmatising manner. Peer support provides invaluable help in talking through issues, especially if peer group members have had similar experiences and have understood your situation.

Learning from other people's experiences (professional and personal), whether local or from overseas can enhance professional competence, assist in improvising solutions, and seeking further information when safe to do so. Trust, reflective, critical, and innovative capacities can be utilised to check out ideas.

Be prepared when going into the field, whether it is to deliver humanitarian aid or do home visits during a pandemic. This may include taking a thermos flask of tea/coffee; wearing disposable gloves; disinfecting surfaces at home, in the office or car and disposing of personal protective equipment (PPE) carefully to protect the environment. Think about sustainability and the environment in everything, including when disposing of PPE. Wash hands with soap and water often.

If feeling ill, stay home. If this happens during a COVID-19 pandemic, self-isolate to avoid spreading the coronavirus. Discuss your situation with your line manager. Obtain the best possible online medical advice and support initially and seek face-to-face health care if needed. Keep yourself informed in a constantly changing COVID-19 environment. Keep and make available records of your visits to enable test and tracing to occur easily.

Finally, stay calm, stay safe, and stay connected while keeping your social and physical distance (2 metres—WHO guidelines during the COVID-19 pandemic) and get vaccinated (including boosters unless you are exempt). Vaccines are also useful to avoid catching various diseases including hepatitis during a flood (Dominelli, 2021).

Rurbanisation: The Demise of Rural Living

Building affordable housing is often seen as an economic driver, and rural areas have been allocated a disproportionate number of new-build developments, with few units of affordable housing. This is undesirable, as often these highly priced houses are out of the reach of the pocketbook of rural residents, especially young people (Gallent et al., 2019). Moreover, these housing developments are built without due provision of highly paid jobs that would enable rural residents to earn enough to apply for mortgages to remain living in these areas. Also, the attractions of urban life—leisure facilities, schools, cultural amenities, and basic infrastructures including roads, high quality broadband, and cheap energy supplies are usually not made available in rural areas. Government policies to reduce GHG emissions will mean that the burden of climate change will be higher in rural areas, for example, eliminating burning wood, relying on electricity or oil for heating due to the lack of natural gas supplies, all mean higher costs for poor people living in rural areas. Heat pumps (air or ground) and solar panels are expensive for individuals to purchase. The Green Deal that subsidised some energy improvement measures which began in 2013 was terminated in 2015. It resumed in 2017, but with private providers subsidising the switch, not the UK government. Consequently, take up remains low including in rural areas, and it does not help low users of energy because their energy bill savings would be insufficient to make the necessary changes (Green Deal Guide, 2021). Understanding these complexities of rural life is critical for rural green social workers who want to support residents in rural areas take effective measures to reduce their carbon footprint. RGSWRs joining community-based alliances could help achieve such aims. Rural green social work is community-based and often draws upon collective action. However, there are no guarantees that the protection of rural areas will be successful, because the opponents who want to develop its resources, especially those wishing to build housing on green field sites have more influence, money, and lawyers at their disposal. Thus, they can shape discussions in ways that prioritise their interests and get approval for the planning permissions they seek, even if the battles over these are protracted ones (Vincent, 2021), as is exemplified in the case study below.

Rurbanisation in Rural Warwickshire

In 2014, a developer applied to build 4000 houses on a plot of former farmland in rural Warwickshire. It was strongly opposed by residents from all surrounding villages. The local residents argued long and hard within the planning process over a lengthy period and had a minor victory of sorts. The developer reduced the number of houses to be built to 3000 and succeeded in gaining approval for building this many on part of the overall plot. None of the residents' concerns about increased traffic on rural roads not originally built for the potential increase in population of around 12,000–16,000 people, the lack of built infrastructures, the absence of leisure amenities on the estate, and the loss of agricultural land were addressed. Meanwhile, increased street lighting around the houses and on the streets of the estate brought light pollution to an area that did not have any before. The struggle continued over the other parcel of land which had an original plan submitted for a further 2000 dwellings. This was reduced to 1000 houses as a result of the protracted resistance to any houses being built on both parcels of land. By 2021, construction began on these disputed developments, and from the prices of the houses that have been completed already, most are unlikely to be purchased by local people. Consequently, this large population—the size of a new town of around 16,000 people when completed, will become a dormitory town, as people (Vincent, 2021), unless they work from home will have to commute to jobs outside the area. Home working favours middle class people coming into such locations, where few job opportunities will exist once the house construction period ends. As the newcomers will have to drive to a nearby town to catch a train or drive elsewhere for jobs and shopping, the carbon footprint in the area will rise appreciably when reduction in all GHG emissions is required to meet 'net zero'. Additionally, teenage boredom will become an issue as they will have to get lifts into town for cultural and recreational reasons as well as schooling. This reality will add more to the GHG emissions as the young people will have to be driven there. Bus services in the area are limited, and not a viable alternative to driving or being driven. Moreover, relying on parents to engage in external activities will increase young people's dependence on them, and lead to their greater isolation from peers if parental acquiescence to their needs is not forthcoming. These difficulties could increase mental ill health among such populations. Moreover, while demand for mental health support is likely to rise, treatment facilities in rural areas are scarce and unlikely to increase (Hodges et al., 2007).

The community group that was created to oppose this development drew on a range of stakeholders that included elected representatives who were on their side. A couple of strong women leaders organised and coordinated much of the resistance. They and the other stakeholders were local residents, and pooled their skills and expertise. Those who had professional skills that could be used to collect data and create the arguments that had to be put formally offered their skills. Funds had to be raised to pay for lawyers at different points in the proceedings. Individual residents, whether members of the community group or not, were encouraged to voice their opposition to the scheme. Individuals were also supplied templates of the arguments to put forward. The community group leaders knew who many of these people were, and often emailed them reports of progress or lack of it. They also shared information with them so that their objections were grounded in strong evidence. One green social worker was incorporated into these endeavours as an articulate resident that helped pull arguments together. The analysis of need and impact submitted by the developer was flawed, but although these errors were pointed out, the planners accepted the developer's evidence above that provided by the residents. This response highlighted the power disparities between the developer and the community. The outcome was a sad result for local democracy, and the local people will be living with its consequences forever. More tensions are likely to arise in future as the results of inadequate planning regarding amenities become evident. Social isolation will begin to seep in, transportation problems will become more obvious and start creating traffic chaos on limited country roads. Also, the solidarity that held the community together around a single-issue campaign has ended, and the local group has been disbanded, as is often the case. Thus, skills and experiences in rural mobilisation and resistance become fragmented or lost and have to be reconstituted when a further occasion arises. RGSWRs could maintain continuity of knowledge of such events so that others could learn from their experiences.

Climate Change: A Rural Issue

Climate refers to long-term weather patterns and not the variations in precipitation and temperatures that are experienced day-to-day. The United Nations defines climate change as a change in climate patterns during the last 100 years that can be attributed largely to the increased carbon dioxide emissions produced by using fossil fuels to sustain modernity as currently practiced. Climate change as a phenomenon has been greeted with scepticism in many quarters. Giddens (2009) divided the British population into the sceptics who denied the existence of (hu) man-induced climate change and the greens who went out of their way to reduce their carbon footprint on the environment and urge others to do likewise.

Climate change is likely to increase the frequency and intensity of extreme weather events (Oven et al., 2012), especially droughts and flooding. These disasters are likely to impact a wide range of human activities essential to maintaining everyday life—economic production, health, food security, water security, and risks associated with heat, especially for susceptible groups such as children, adolescents, young people, and older people. Furthermore, such events are likely to have tipping points and cascading risks associated with them, for example, flooding can lead to landslides and diseases in the aftermath of the flood, especially if contaminated water gets into cuts and grazes or is imbibed.

Fossil fuels are used directly in rural areas for heating, lighting, cooking, transportation and other purposes where industrial firms and warehouses are sited in rural landscapes. Additionally, there is the substantial contribution to environmental degradation arising from agricultural production, especially that using chemical herbicides, pesticides, and inorganic fertilisers. Thus, environmental degradation is evident in rural soils, waters, and air, regardless of distances from large urban populations and urban cityscapes (WWF, 2020).

Rural green social workers have been involved in rewilding schemes, promoting organic food production, the growth of legumes to replenish nitrogen in the soil, and the use of traditional animals, especially cattle and sheep to rebuild soils without the use of inorganic chemical fertilisers (Dominelli, 2012). All plants need appropriate combinations of nitrogen, phosphorus, and potassium to grow. Inorganic compounds are used to create fertilisers, for example, ammonium nitrate. These find their way into ground water and increase water pollution. Limiting the amounts of nitrates, phosphates, and potassium used in agriculture is important in cleaning up the rivers that are polluted with these chemicals through runoff water, and get into the water-table (Carson, 1964; Buckler, 2017). Similar problems can arise through agribusinesses such as megafarms used to raise pigs or turkeys and factories raising battery hens where faecal discharges can seriously pollute the soil and groundwater (Fridrich et al., 2014).

Green social workers haves been prime advocates of changing the social relationship between the industrialised Global North and the industrialising Global South through solidarity and the sharing of green technologies for some time. Rural green social workers can work alongside climate activists to insist that this sharing takes place. Additionally, they can help local communities mobilise and organise to enhance wellbeing and caring for people, the environment and planet. In this capacity, they can oppose deforestation which can increase heat waves and the severity of storms (Dominelli, 2012). RGSWRs' espousal of the duty to care for the earth has been used by Maori people in New Zealand/ Aotearoa in their long-standing struggle to demand that their sacred river, the Whanganui, was cleaned of its pollution in a landmark case that has inspired others (Lurgio, 2019). The Whanganui was granted personhood through an Act of Parliament in 2017, and then acquired the right to be cleaned up and kept free of pollution. Implementing this is a challenge, especially given the presence of a hydroelectric plant upstream which discharges water that has caused turbidity in the water downstream. RGSWRs have a role to play in assisting local people (Pakeha (Europeans) and Maori) to insist that the river that is home to specific cultures, people, fish, birds, algae and other living beings retains its pristine waters for everyone.

Climate Migrants

Another area of concern to green social workers is the rise in climate refugees. Climate refugees will reach significant numbers—up to one billion, according to estimates from the United Nations. Yet, there is no requirement on any country to accept these refugees as they are not covered by international law, including the provisions of the 1951 Geneva Convention. Failures in implementing policy regarding the reduction of GHGs and lack of provision for the people who will experience the most severe aspects of climate degradation despite having contributed least, will lead to both decreased hope and increased anger among those affected, whether they are seeking asylum or receiving those that do. Currently, most asylum seekers prefer to go to places where there are communities that share their nationality, ethnicity, languages, and cultures (Vince, 2022). Most of these migrants are located in rural areas. However, as climate change is likely to push people Northwards, and into rural areas where the impact of climate change is likely to be less, then rural areas will need to prepare to receive these refugees. This will require additional resources, infrastructures including housing, clinics, and schools. RGSWRs can lobby for such provisions before the newcomers arrive, and also assist local residents in welcoming them and helping them to settle and contribute to the locality.

The United Nations Framework Convention on Climate Change, Conference of the Parties (UNFCCC COP)

The UNFCCC COP26 meeting in Glasgow, Scotland, from 31 October to 13 November 2021, was the 26th yearly meeting (the one for 2020 was postponed due to Covid-19). People were full of hope and ambition before it began. Most participants anticipated the overcoming of many of the barriers that had held progress back for years as countries elevated national self-interest before the imperative of reducing GHG emissions to mitigate the damage that was already visible in many locations, especially the Small Island Developing States (SIDS) that are sinking under the sea (Dominelli, 2012, 2023). This situation was especially poignant for those like Kiribati which were already preparing to leave their island, much of which had already sunk, if they could be given an island by one of the many island-owning nations in the southeast Pacific Ocean. This has proved elusive thus far. Moreover, promises to provide funds for adaptation measures including $1 billion yearly, the Green Fund, actions to reduce GHG emissions had been made many times before without being fulfilled. This had led to huge disappointment among participants, including young people who have demonstrated against the lack of action, especially through the Fridays for Futures young climate activists' movement started by Greta Thunberg (2022).

Within Scotland's Glasgow, the city hosting COP26, people hoped to use COP26 to transform systematically the Region's economy, society, and natural environment and enable it to flourish within a decade. The city's rulers realised that this would mean 'hard choices' now, but possibly less harsh ones in future. Moreover, they were committed to strengths-based approaches to enhance social justice and resilience so as not to increase vulnerability or exacerbate existing inequalities through any of the adaptive measures that they enacted. Although Glasgow is Scotland's largest urban centre, economic prosperity was intended to apply to its rural areas to 'leave no one behind' (Robinson, 2019).

Recognising that transformative change required a step change and a new approach, Glasgow City Council outlined a strategy that sought to be:

- *Systems focused* so that it could initiate the required structural changes.
- *Inclusive* to enable local communities to lead their development, while allowing the private sector to contribute to this development.
- *Collaborative* to create dynamic partnerships and engage new actors in devising collective outcomes.
- *Innovative and transformative* by involving all stakeholders.

This strategy raised questions about what new governance structures might have to be developed to ensure that agreed plans could be subjected to oversight, ensure delivery of agreed action plans, promote community ownership, and facilitate residents' agency in decision-making. Additionally, substantial amounts of new funding would be necessary. These might be difficult to procure, but the task could be facilitated by using public funds strategically and unlocking private sector investment.

By 2025, Glasgow City Council was anticipating the following outcomes from their endeavours:

- Increasing resilience among 140,000 of the people most liable to feel the impact of climate change. Achieving this goal is linked to the UN's 'Race to Resilience' Campaign led by one of its members, Climate Ready Clyde. The UN's initiative aims to build resilience among 4 billion people who are most vulnerable to the impact of climate change globally.

- Becoming financially sound by closing an adaptation finance gap of £184m annually.
- Involving 125 new organisations, community groups and businesses in enabling the City Region to adapt to climate change (GCC, 2021).

Social work representation at COP26 in Glasgow was limited. The International Association of Schools of Social Work (IASSW) representative engaged in transdisciplinary activities, including participating in activities under the auspices of the COP26 Universities Network. It mounted an exhibition entitled *Making Visible the Roles of Social Workers in Climate Change*, and organised a seminar, *Living on the Edge: Young People Talk About Climate Action*, which empowered young people to speak for themselves and showcase the activities that they had undertaken to promote behaviour to mitigate climate change, especially at their school, and assisted in *Building a Terrarium* session focusing on soil improvement. IASSW also sponsored these young people on three day passes to visit the Green Zone and engage with COP26 activities and exhibitions being showcased there. However, much remains to be done to enhance the role of social workers in climate change decision-making fora, reduce fossil fuel usage and methane emissions, demand a sharing of green renewable energy technologies globally, and argue for the provision of funds for low- and middle- income countries to protect themselves from current climate destruction of their countries (Dominelli, 2012). The hosting of COP26 (Conference of the Parties or government delegates in its 26th year) for the UNFCCC (the United Nations Framework Convention on Climate Change) summit in Glasgow raised the issue of climate change as a disaster that needed to be addressed as a matter of urgency (Robinson & Bedford, 2022; Richardson, 2019). The settings for these tectonic shifts in the profession's interests are both rural and urban. IASSW continues to be involved in the COP meetings on behalf of social work.

Covid-19 Requires an End to Environmental Degradation in Rural Habitats

Covid-19 is a novel zoonotic disease caused by a coronavirus that has crossed the animal-human barrier as people destroy pristine habitats while increasingly encroaching on the lands where wild animals live. Covid-19 is linked to climate change because it depicts the transgression of human action into the wild biosphere, especially in tropical forests to plant cash crops such as soya beans and grow palm oil plantations (WWF, 2020). This wanton environmental destruction encourages animal-people contact and provides zoonotic diseases a foothold in society. This includes viruses that can adapt to survive in a human host, especially if natural immunity is absent. Covid-19 comes from a virus called SARS-CoV-2, a coronavirus like SARS and MERS, which entered human societies earlier. Covid-19 first emerged in Wuhan, China in December 2019. However, much remains unknown about Covid-19, a new respiratory disease. 'Patient Zero' and 'Ground Zero' remain elusive, but they must be found for humanity to learn how to respond to further viral incursions into the human domain. Preventing diseases and ensuring sustainability becomes a duty for every person, including rural green social workers. Treating nature as a means to the profit-making prerogative needs to be replaced with caring for the environment so that it can take care of all living things.

In comparison to Covid-19, SARS and MERS did not reach pandemic proportions of spreading globally. Instead, although all were previously unknown coronaviruses, SARS was limited to small numbers being infected in China and North America, and MERS to the Middle East. Why not? Part of the reason has to be the rapid global response initiated by Gro Brundtland, the then Head of the World Health Organisation who brought together politicians, scientific researchers, medics and other stakeholders to find out what was causing these diseases and how they could be controlled. Solidarity, quarantining people and stopping their travel to different places was an essential part of her plan. Eventually, the coronavirus was identified as causing SARS, and scientists started looking for a vaccine. This work proved invaluable later in developing a vaccine for Covid-19, and the Astra-Zeneca one drew heavily on this work. The World Health Organisation defined it as a pandemic (which is about spread and not infectiousness) on 11 March 2020. There have been many variants of Covid-19. And Omicron is a recent highly infectious one that spreads quickly and easily, especially as many infected people are asymptomatic. Moreover, older people and those with existing health conditions are more susceptible to the disease. Urban areas seem to have had higher numbers of Covid-19 cases within their populations, at least to begin with because population density; connectivity facilitated through public transport; crowded living conditions; and exposed occupations placed individuals at greater risk (WHO, 2022). This may begin to shift as greater interaction between urban and rural areas follows the removal of restrictions and leisure activities are once more permitted in national parks and small cities and hamlets. Moreover, there appears to be little difference in mortality rates between urban and rural populations, although more research needs to be undertaken to explore the reasons for this.

Covid-19, with its emphasis on working from home encouraged the use of remote technologies to conduct work activities from a rural base without a long commute. City workers who had now moved into rural areas could maintain contact with one's work colleagues, undertake home schooling, and conduct other daily activities from cooking to yoga through the internet. Other city dwellers who had relocated to their second homes also discovered that they could work from their alternative home. This meant they could forego their daily commutes and ensuing expenses, lost time and drain on the environment when consuming fossil fuels to get to and from the office. However, this luxury was not available to the bus drivers, railway workers, porters, retail clerks, and others who risked their own lives and those of others to keep critical aspects of the economy going during lockdowns. Nor was it available to those who were excluded through the digital divide. Both issues were more exclusionary of those living in rural areas due to inadequate transportation (Tracks, n.d.) and communication infrastructures.

Covid-19, an outcome of environmental degradation and the climate crisis, occurred because a virus escaped the reservoirs of countless viruses harboured in the animal kingdom and began to stalk societies where humans who lacked immunity to their attacks lived (WWF, 2020). Covid-19, is the result of an interaction between Ground Zero—the actual reservoir for the SARS-CoV-2 coronavirus that caused Covid-19, and Patient Zero, the first person who carried the virus into the human world. Neither of these are currently known, but it is crucial that they are found so that the evidence they provide can be used to contain novel viruses and/or control the further spread of this virus and its continually evolving variants. Controlling SARS-CoV-2 will involve a range of interventions through vaccinations, various types of medical regimes, and the transformation of human behaviour, to make it more respectful of the interconnectivities and interdependencies between the human, plant and animal kingdoms and the physical environment that sustains all. Rural areas as keepers of many wild species have to respect the boundaries between human beings and the animal inhabitants of diverse ecosystems (WWF, 2020).

Rural green social workers have a role to play in raising consciousness about this issue. They also have the generic skills that enable them to respond to crisis situations, using a range of theoretical perspectives and practice methods ranging from crisis interventions to counselling, following the principles of anti-oppressive practice (Dominelli, 2002). They also undertook many of their normal duties during the pandemic including safeguarding children and older people, responding to disabled people and those with mental ill health. RGSWRs performed new roles during COVID-19. These varied according to the country in which they worked (IASSW, 2020). For example, in China, they undertook many community work tasks, disinfected community buildings and streets, and tested people's temperatures in the streets. As in the West, they also supported people at a distance, online, and by coordinating resources and information to meet people's daily needs. Western social workers found that the limitations in home visiting placed them in ethical dilemmas linked to fears of missing the signs of child and elder abuse (Dominelli, 2021). Social workers working from a green perspective have lobbied against the exploitation of nature for a few shareholders to make substantial profits. For example, the Maori people in New Zealand/Aotearoa sued a company to clean-up their sacred Whanganui River (O'Donnel & Talbot-Jones, 2017). Green social workers were involved in that initiative (email communication to the author). They also protested at the low pay of the workers they employed in agribusiness and non-environmentally friendly businesses and their neglect of initiatives to prevent future pandemics from emerging. RGSWRs will also argue for the protection of indigenous cultures, tropical and temperate rainforests, assistance for climate migrants, and reduction of fossil fuel usage. They will also lobby for climate change initiatives that will maintain temperature increases to 1.5 °C as demanded by in the 2015 Paris Accord.

Conclusions

Climate change and the Covid-19 health pandemic have challenged many myths that endorse the idea of a globalised world in the thrall of neoliberalism. They also promoted calls for the envisaging of an alternative reality that respects nature, particularly that found in the rural hinterland and a weaning away of fossil fuel consumption and the misuse of the resources contained in the rural hinterlands of the world to avoid an enduring climate crisis. These insights highlight the importance of upholding:

- Sustainability—environmentally and in lifestyles.
- The public good over private greed.
- Non-consumerist lifestyles and livelihoods.
- Civic duty and neighbourliness.
- Communal support systems.
- Solidarity.
- Mutuality.
- Interdependence.
- Equality.
- Human rights and a decent quality of life for all.
- Climate change initiatives to keep greenhouse gases down to 1.5 °C.
- Concern for the physical environment.
- Increased investment in renewable energy sources.

These features are also crucial in constructing a new world after the Covid-19 pandemic that respects and celebrates the biosphere in both rural and urban areas. Covid-19 arose because humans transgressed the human-animal environmental barrier and brought viruses back into society. Green social workers can lobby for this vision, use green perspectives in daily practice, whether working in urban or rural areas. If people work together to tackle climate change, a new world order that values Planet Earth can emerge. Its rural areas can also become environmentally respected, cleaned up and their environmental leisure treasures protected.

Rural green social workers begin their interventions by assessing the risks posed by hazards that produce disasters like climate change and health pandemics. Following their analysis of a situation, these practitioners argue for:

- profound holistic conceptual and social transformations in society, especially in moving away from fossil fuel usage in production and consumption of goods and services.
- sustainable relationships among peoples, other living things, and the inanimate world and a duty to care for Planet Earth.
- transdisciplinarity to ensure that all sciences and professions engage fully with local communities/residents to coproduce solutions to contemporary social challenges such as climate change and health pandemics.
- solidarity in sharing renewable energy technologies (Dominelli, 2012; 2023).

Rural green social workers also mobilise residents by engaging with them to reimagine their communities differently—transformatively. This is in keeping with developing inclusive, resilient, and sustainable rural communities in which there is space for everyone and a dedication to protecting and caring for our beautiful planet.

References

Bloomer, N. (2022). Rural Poverty: 'People Are Struggling but It's Hidden Here'. *NN Journal,* 19 October. Accessed from https://www.nnjournal.co.uk/p/rural-poverty-people-are-struggling

Buckler, L. (2017). *The Hidden Dangers of Chemical Fertilizers.* Accessed February 1, 2022, from https://eponline.com/Articles/2017/12/07/The-Hidden-Dangers-of-Chemical-Fertilizers.aspx#:~:text=Environmental%20Issues,Nitrogen%20is%20especially%20tricky

Carson, R. (1964). *The Silent Spring.* Penguin.

Chandini, R. K., Kumar, R., & Prakash, O. (2019). The Impact of Chemical Fertilizers on Our Environment and Ecosystem. In *Research Trends in Environmental Sciences.* AkiNik Publications. Accessed February 1, 2022, from www.Chemical%20Fertilisers%20Chapter-5.pdf.

Currie, M., Wilson, R., Noble, C., & Gurd, J. (2021). *The Ongoing Impacts of Covid-19 in Scotland's Rural and Island Communities Summary Report.* Accessed October 5, 2023, from https://sefari.scot/document/the-ongoing-impacts-of-covid-19-in-scotland%E2%80%99s-rural-and-island-communities

Daley, M. (2010). A Conceptual Model for Rural Social Work. *Contemporary Rural Social Work, 2*(1), 1–8. Accessed from https://digitalcommons.murraystate.edu/cgi/viewcontent.cgi?article=1011&context=crsw

DEFRA (Department of Rural Affairs). (2021). *Statistical Digest of Rural England Population.* Accessed from https://assets.publishing.service.gov.uk/government/uploads/system/uploads/attachment_data/file/1028819/Rural_population__Oct_2021.pdf

Dominelli, L. (2002). *Anti-Oppressive Social Work Theory and Practice.* Palgrave Macmillan.

Dominelli, L. (2011). Climate Change: Social Workers' Contributions to Policy and Practice Debates. *International Journal of Social Welfare, 20*(4), 430–439. https://doi.org/10.1111/j.1468-2397.2011.00795.x

Dominelli, L. (2012). *Green Social Work: From Environmental Degradation to Environmental Justice.* Policy Press.

Dominelli, L. (Ed.). (2018). *The Routledge Handbook of Green Social Work.* Routledge.

Dominelli, L. (2021). A Green Social Work Perspective on Social Work During the Covid-19 Health Pandemic. *International Journal of Social Welfare, 30*(1), 7–16.

Dominelli, L. (2023). *Social Work During Times of Disaster: A Transformative Green Social Work Model for Theory, Education and Practice in Disaster Interventions.* Routledge.

Dominelli, L., & Ku, H. B. (2017). Green Social Work and Its Implications for Social Development in China. *China Journal of Social Work, 10*(1), 3–22.

Force-Emery Mackie, P., Zammit, K., & Alvarez, M. (2015). *Practicing Rural Social Work.* Oxford University Press.

Francis, D., & Henderson, P. (1992). *Working with Rural Communities.* BASW Macmillan.

Fridrich, B., Krčmar, D., Dalmacija, B., Molnar, J., Pešić, V., Kragulj, M., & Varga, N. (2014, March 31). Impact of Wastewater from Pig Farm Lagoons on the Quality of Local Groundwater. *Agricultural Water Management, 135,* 40–53. Accessed from https://www.sciencedirect.com/science/article/abs/pii/S0378377413003570.

Friedrich, J., Ge, M., Pickens, A., & Vigna, L. (2023, March 2) *This Interactive Chart Shows Changes in the World's Top 10 Emitters.* World Resources Institute. Accessed from https://www.wri.org/insights/interactive-chart-shows-changes-worlds-top-10-emitters

Gallent, N., Hamiduddin, I., Stirling, P., & Kelsey, J. (2019). Prioritising Local Housing Needs Through Land-Use Planning in Rural Areas: Political Theatre or Amenity Protection. *Journal of Rural Studies, 66,* 11–20.

Gardiner, K. (2017). Some 1.3 Billion People Lack Regular Access to Electricity. With Its Reliable Independent Grid Powered by Wind, Water and Solar, a Remote Scottish Island Could Hold the Key to a Solution. *BBC News,* 30 March. Accessed from https://www.bbc.com/future/article/20170329-the-extraordinary-electricity-of-the-scottish-island-of-eigg

GGC (Glasgow City Council). (2021) *Glasgow City Region Economic Strategy.* Accessed from https://glasgowcityregion.co.uk/regional-economic-strategy/

Giddens, A. (2009). *The Politics of Climate Change.* Polity Press.

Glass, J., Shucksmith, M.D., Chapman, P. & Atterton, J. (2021). *Covid-19, Lockdowns and Financial Hardship in Rural Areas: Insights from the Rural Lives Project.* Accessed October 5, 2023, from https://pure.sruc.ac.uk/en/publications/covid-19-lockdowns-and-financial-hardship-in-rural-areas-insights

Green Deal Guide. (2021). *2021 Green Deal Guide.* Accessed January 21, 2022, from https://powercompare.co.uk/green-deal/

Hodges, C., O'Brien, M., & McGorry, P. (2007). National Youth Mental Health Foundation: Making Headway with Rural Young People and Their Mental Health. *The Australian Journal of Rural Health, 15*(2), 77–80.

IASSW. (2020). Covid-19 and Social Work: A Collection of Country Reports. https://www.iasswaiets.org/2020/07/19/covid-19-and-social-work-a-collection-of-country-reports/ accessed March 2024.

JRF (Joseph Rowntree Foundation). (2022) *UK Poverty 2022: The Essential Guide to Understanding Poverty in the UK.* JRF. Accessed March 20, 2022, from https://www.jrf.org.uk/report/uk-poverty-2022.

Kharas, H., Fengler, W., Sheoraj R., Vashold, L., & Yankov, T. (2022, November 29). *Tracking Emissions by Country and Sector.* Brookings. Accessed from https://www.brookings.edu/blog/future-development/2022/11/29/tracking-emissions-by-country-and-sector/

Ku, H. B. (2011). Yingxiu Mother' as Agent of Development—A Case Study of Rural Social Work Intervention in a Sichuan Post-Disaster Community in China. *Korean Journal of Rural Welfare Studies, 7*, 33–54.

Ku, H. B., & Dominelli, L. (2018). Not Only Eating Together: Space and Green Social Work Intervention in Hazard Affected Area in Ya'an, Sichuan of China. *British Journal of Social Work., 48*(5), 1409–1431.

Ku, H. B., Qi, H., & Zhang, H. (2019). Rural Social Work in China. *Oxford Bibliographies.*

Lohman, N., & Lohman, R. (Eds.). (2005). *Rural Social Work.* Columbia University Press.

Lurgio, J. (2019). Saving the Whanganui: Can Personhood Rescue a River? *The Guardian*, 29 November. Accessed November 12, 2021, from https://www.google.com/search?q=Which+sacred+river+did+the+Maori+demand+was+cleaned+up+of+its+polluted+waters&rlz=1C1CHBF_en-GBGB860GB860&oq=Which+sacred+river+did+the+Maori+demand+was+cleaned+up+of+its+polluted+waters&aqs=chrome..69i57.30281j0j15&sourceid=chrome&ie=UTF-8

O'Donnel, E., & Talbot-Jones, J. (2017). Three Rivers Are Now Legally People – But that's Just the Start of Looking After Them. *The Conversation*, 23 March. Accessed October 5, 2023, from https://theconversation.com/three-rivers-are-now-legally-people-but-thats-just-the-start-of-looking-after-them-74983

Office For National Statistics (OFS). (2023). *Climate Change Insights, Families and Households, UK: August 2023.* Accessed October 5, 2023, from https://www.ons.gov.uk/economy/environmentalaccounts/articles/climatechangeinsightsuk/august2023#:~:text=The%20latest%20estimates%20from%20our,April%20to%201%20May%202023

Oven, K. J, Curtis, S. E., Reaney, S., Riva, M., Stewart, M. G., Ohlemuller, R. & Holden, R. (2012). Climate change and health and social care: Defining future hazard, vulnerability and risk for infrastructure systems supporting older people's health care in England. *Applied Geography*, 33, 16–24.

Oxfam. (2016). *An Economy for the 1%*. Oxfam International.

Peterson-Withorn, C. (2021) Here's How Much Richer the World's Billionaires Have Gotten in 2021. *Forbes*, 8 December. Accessed March 26, 2022, from https://www.forbes.com/sites/chasewithorn/2021/12/08/the-worlds-billionaires-have-gotten-16-trillion-richer-in-2021/

Pugh, R., & Cheers, D. (2010). *Rural Social Work: International Perspectives*. Policy Press.

Rae, S. (2017). *The Land Cover Atlas of the United Kingdom*. University of Sheffield. Accessed March 13, 2022, from https://www.sheffield.ac.uk/news/nr/land-cover-atlas-uk-1.744440

Richardson, A. (2019). *Glasgow's Climate Plan Our Response to the Climate and Ecological Emergency*. Glasgow. Accessed from https://www.glasgow.gov.uk/CHttpHandler.ashx?id=50623&p=0.

Robinson, S. (2019) *Promise of £33 Million for Rural Areas in Scotland*. Reinstated in 2022. Accessed from https://www.thescottishfarmer.co.uk/news/23604076.shona-robison-33m-funding-returned-rural-budget/

Robinson Z., & Bedford, T. (2022). *Universities and the Climate Emergency: Action Following COP26*.

Statista. (2022). *Urban and Rural Population of the United Kingdom from 1960 to 2021*. Accessed from https://www.statista.com/statistics/984702/urban-and-rural-population-of-the-uk/

The Telegraph (2020) Dreaming of a Rural Life? You're Not the Only One Wanting to Escape to the Countryside. *The Telegraph*, 29 June. Accessed March 25, 2022, from https://www.telegraph.co.uk/family/life/dreaming-rural-life-not-one-wanting-escape-countryside/

Thunberg, G. (2022). *The Climate Book*. Penguin.

Tracks. (n.d.). *The Future of Rural Bus Services in the UK*. Better Transport. Accessed March 21, 2022, from https://bettertransport.org.uk/sites/default/files/research-files/The-Future-of-Rural-Bus-Services.pdf

Vince, G. (2022). The Century of Climate Migration: Why We Need to Plan for the Great Upheaval. *The Guardian*, 18 August. Accessed from https://www.theguardian.com/news/2022/aug/18/century-climate-crisis-migration-why-we-need-plan-great-upheaval

Vincent, P (2021). *Without Affordable Housing, Rural Communities Are at Risk of Becoming Lifeless, Dormitory Settlements*. ACRE (Action with Communities in Rural England). Accessed from https://acre.org.uk/without-affordable-housing-rural-communities-are-at-risk-of-becoming-lifeless-dormitory-settlements/

WHO (World Health Organisation). (2022). *Global Research on Coronavirus Disease (COVID-19).* WHO. Accessed from https://www.who.int/emergencies/diseases/novel-coronavirus-2019/global-research-on-novel-coronavirus-2019-ncov

World Wide Fund for Nature (WWF). (2020). *Living Planet Report 2020.* Accessed October 5, 2023, from https://www.worldwildlife.org/publications/living-planet-report-2020

Xue, H. (2018). *The Happiness of Rural-to-Urban Migrant Workers in Shanghai: Comparing Migrant Workers and Shanghai's Urban Residents.* Durham University, School of Applied Social Sciences. Accessed March 20, 2022, from http://etheses.dur.ac.uk/12722/1/H_Xue_2018_thesis.pdf?DDD34

6

Food, Farming and Rural Relationships with the Land

Tina Laurie

Introduction

The British rural landscape is diverse encompassing varied landscapes, communities and activities. In places, it is made beautiful with rolling hills, lakes, rivers, trees, coastline and beaches, inhabited by all manner of interesting wild birds, insects, plants and animals. It is the home of many; inhabited by people with their distinct relationships to the land; from the white sandy beaches of the Western Isles of Scotland to the rugged coastline of north Devon. Within these varied, rural, communities people encounter the challenges of living in the twenty-first century and, consequently social workers are often in high demand. While many of the social problems faced by those dwelling in rural areas are no different from urban counterparts, the social worker living, working and being a practitioner in a rural area can have unique character and require a subtly different skills base (Turbett, 2010). In this chapter I would invite fellow

T. Laurie (✉)
University of the West of Scotland, Dumfries, UK
e-mail: Tina.Laurie@uws.ac.uk

© The Author(s), under exclusive license to Springer Nature Switzerland AG 2024
C. Turbett, J. Pye (eds.), *Rural Social Work in the UK*, Rethinking Rural,
https://doi.org/10.1007/978-3-031-52440-0_6

social workers to reflect on their own experiences of working in their communities, what rural means to them, and the impact on their practice that they may experience as a result. My own experiences, as represented here, may not be typical of all social workers in rural areas or communities but I believe that it is an important element of understanding myself as a practitioner in this space and to express that understanding. I would encourage others, in their reflections, to do the same.

Land Changes and Agriculture

When writing about climate change and food from a green social work perspective Gordon describes food needs as a "critical issue … [that] needs to be a central part of social work's engagement in the environment" (2017, p. 157). In rural communities, where food is potentially produced, this is significant and links back into theoretical social work principles, for as it is acknowledged, wellbeing is connected to the wider environment (Jones, 2010). To apply social work principles such as fairness, inclusivity, dignity and even anti-oppression to food and food distribution is challenging in Western society as this fundamental human need is influenced so strongly by the capitalist nature of our farming and food markets. Acknowledging that no two areas, rural or otherwise, are the same recognises experiences of social and ecological issues are not homogeneous. Regardless, I would invite any reader to take this as a jumping off point for their own reflections on both their practice as a social worker and their participation in the world as a global citizen.

Although not immediately obvious to the untrained eye, no matter how wild it may feel, there is an element of human management in the British countryside. Agricultural policy and economics have shaped everything from the structure of the rivers to the treeline in the distance, and the need to use land to produce food has altered the human landscape across the globe for millennia. The changes to the look of the countryside and the impact of our farming systems have had an accelerated growth, driven by policies to enhance food security and production. As a result, there have been substantial increases to the intensity of agricultural land management in the past century (Dallimer et al., 2009).

In order to be profitable, farms across the world but particularly in the UK have had to intensify and specialise. It is these things which have changed the way that our farms produce food that has subsequently had an impact on the people working and living in the communities to which they belong. In modern times there is a distinct distance between those producing our food and those consuming it, there being many layers of distribution, packaging and processing between what is grown on farms and what is ultimately purchased

> most people would never set foot in the fields that feed them – which was either liberation from a kind of endless drudgery, or a loss of contact with the vital process that sustains us, depending on your point of view (Rebanks, 2020, p. 137).

At the turn of the last century, British farms, in the most part, looked a little different than they do today. They had a wider variety of animals, wildlife and human activity going on in the landscape, and our older service users may remember small fields and small tractors (or even horses), walking cows up into the hills for summer grazing and throwing kitchen scraps to the pigs. They might remember curlews calling over-head, a brace of grey partridges on the kitchen table or growing vegetables in the garden. The farms were small and populated: at certain times of the year, many hands would gather for important jobs, harvesting, clipping, ploughing and neighbours would help neighbours. The land connected working people, and the reminisces from our elders are one of commu-nity, and co-operation. The natural environment had to be respected, nourished and understood if it was to continue to yield for the future. These basic principles echo in what we now call eco-social work (Boetto, 2017), community or green social work (Dominelli, 2012). This respect for the natural environment, working in partnership with one another and the land is recognisable in these perspectives and would imply that aside from the barriers we face more generally in our profession we already have some of the foundations to advocate in an impactful way to future policy. That is not to say that the notion of community should be regarded as unproblematic and homogenous. There are long standing issues of

discrimination and exclusion in all communities as explored in the introduction to this book.

Alongside discrimination and exclusion there was (and is) poverty, and
in the past when crops failed due to droughts, floods, blights or pests
there was little support for communities to fall back onto. There were
difficulties to be overcome and over the past hundred years farming and
agriculture has been transformed by technologies to solve these problems
and to further the use of land to produce food for a growing population
(Dallimer et al., 2009). Mechanical advances, tractors and machinery
now take the place of horses, and crops are enhanced by artificial fertilisers, herbicides, pesticides. Animals can be kept in smaller more intensive
conditions because farmers have access to the antibiotics, medicines and
disinfectants needed to keep them healthy in these environments. For
instance, between ten and fifteen square kilometres is needed to produce
food to support one hunter gatherer living in the simplest environment
whereas modern farming can feed four thousand people in a ten-kilometre
area (Malhi, 2014). These advancements have transformed the physical
landscape and altered the way that people in rural areas live, and they
have not come without a cost.

Not only have these things happened exceptionally quickly but they
continue to advance. Dairy production for instance advances at an alarming rate. As the price of milk is kept so low by competing supermarkets
dairy farmers have had to adapt their business models or give up entirely,
farms have increased in size and cows have been selectively bred to maximise efficiency. It used to take a person one hour to milk six cows by hand
whereas now one hundred cows can be milked in an hour with the use of
robotic milking. The animals themselves have also changed dramatically;
traditionally cows would have been "dual purpose" they would have produced ample milk and also grown well for beef, but as things have inten-
sified dairy farms have prioritised breeds with high milk production and
selectively bred from the most proficient animals within a herd.

The changes in farming and food logistics have consequently had a
significant impact on the food itself. The beef that was traditionally part
of the "dual purpose" herd, providing small scale farmers with a bit of
everything, tended to be reared on pasture. Cows put out onto hill ground
would eat fauna which is indigestible to our human stomachs converting

it into the beef superfood packed with vitamins, minerals and complex omega-3 fatty acids. In the modern system, this way of farming is not efficient enough. It does not make the best use of the land and traditional breeds which are suited to this style of grazing are hardy but slow growing, meaning profit margins are squeezed and farms are less able to compete with a global market. Instead, cows are no longer put out onto hill ground to graze and instead kept in sheds and fed on grains. Cows are not as well suited to eating these grains, and although it helps them to gain weight quickly, the resulting beef is loaded not with omega-3 rich muscle but with omega-6 fats (Harvey, 2016). The detailed science of this is beyond the remit of this chapter but is it notable as it is demonstrative of a significant change to our diet which has happened within a generation. Omega-3 is an essential component to a good diet which is increasingly absent and according to Oxford University Professor of Physiology John Stein, "The lack of omega-3 in our diet is going to change the human brain in ways that are as serious as climate change" (Stein, 2015, cited in Steel, 2020, p. 56).

Carrots have undergone a similar transformation. As farmers have turned to artificial fertilisers and pesticides, they have depleted the fertility of the soil (Steel, 2020).

> New farming has taken two mutually beneficial things – grazing animals and fertilising fields – and separated them to create massive industrial-scale problems in separate spaces. The farms with thousands of animals have more muck than their land can possibly accommodate, while the crop farms have no animals, and thus no muck to fertilise plants, so were entirely reliant [on artificial fertilisers] (Rebanks, 2020, p. 146).

We know that "environmental problems are also social problems" (Belchior Rocha, 2018, p. 1649) and the subsequent impact on the food which is then grown in that soil has a direct correlation with its nutrition value. In the case of the humble carrot evidence from the British Medical Research Council from 1940 to 1991 reveals that carrots lost 75% of their copper and magnesium content, 48% of their calcium and 46% of their iron (Harvey, 2006). From the perspective of the consumer paying an increasing price for goods in the supermarket, it is galling to realise that the quality of the products available is not what it had been previously. People trying to make good nutritional choices for their families face an increasing challenge, one which was not an issue in previous generations. Recent statistics, from a global study, suggest that a healthy diet costs five times more than one which is just sufficient in calories (FAO et al., 2020). While it is beyond the scope of this chapter, what cannot be ignored is the significant detriment to the natural environment, soils, rivers and oceans, that these farming systems are now inflicting (Monbiot, 2022). In our green social work agenda, it is important that we are able to pay attention to these issues and link them to the work that we are doing in practice. For further discussion on green social work, please see previous chapter.

It seems astonishing that food poverty can be prevalent in areas surrounded by food which is, quite literally, growing out of the ground. Despite this, food banks and charities working with those affected by these issues are not rare in rural areas and people's alienation from the food and farming systems around them are just as significant as they are in urban centres. The impact of welfare policies and state provision are, of course, significant players in these issues; as research from the Trussell Trust has demonstrated; "food cannot be the answer to people needing a food bank" (Thompson et al., 2020, p. 4).

The disconnect between people and the land could be argued to start right from childhood and commentators have suggested that the relationships that children develop with farming and food production is characterised by artificial experiences at farm parks, cartoon characters and picture books meaning that they are disconnected with reality, particularly that of meat production (Monbiot, 2022). Issues with food start right from the outset; the very first experience that human beings have, milk, either breastmilk or infant formula. The first is a bespoke, nutritionally complete substance which human beings have evolved to produce for their offspring. It is free, healthy, and loaded with everything the baby needs, it can play a role in helping mother and baby form a strong attachment and there is whole host of other health benefits for mother and baby alike. Various wide-ranging research on breastfeeding indicates health and wellbeing benefits; from a reduced likelihood of developing celiac disease to obesity, reduction in allergies, as well as an impact on neurodevelopment outcomes (Eidelman et al., 2012). Formula milk, comparatively, is a product to be marketed and sold, a human being's first experience of food and already there is familiarity in branding, marketing and profit; "for companies manufacturing infant formula, the mother's breast is simply a competitor to be neutralised" (Lang, 2021, p. 314). While it would always be important for social work to advocate for a mother's choice (and for babies to be fed!) there is little to no training for breastfeeding support aimed at social workers currently in the UK. As many social workers are in a position, alongside midwives and other health professionals, to support this kind of very early health and wellbeing food-based intervention it would seem like a logical place for future policy to give some support and focus.

Difficulties are compounded by cooking; quality of the raw materials is one thing but so is our ability to turn them into meals. The UK consumes the highest rate of ultra-processed foods in Europe (Lang, 2021) and it is easy to see why. High energy costs, busy lifestyles and appealing advertising make these products the simple option. Healthy, diverse, traditional meals cooked with fresh ingredients depend on the "near-servitude" of women (Monbiot, 2022, p. 206), and as social workers advocating for change, we would need to be careful not to reintroduce oppressive roles.

Despite these general trends, there are numerous excellent examples of communities and projects involving young people, forest schools, community gardens and farms including the British Beekeeping Association who aim to support schools to keep hives and enhance outdoor learning opportunities (BBKA, 2022). Rural communities and their access to space can and do lead the way in these initiatives, highlighting the importance of considering rural social work to learn about as well as to learn from (see Chap. 8).

For decades, supermarkets have been keeping the prices low to keep themselves competitive. They force down price at wholesale which keeps wages from rising too high anywhere in the food production industry. There is a huge food labour force in the UK of around 3.95 million people, making it the largest manufacturing sector in the country. Of this, only 11% work on farms, fishing boats and greenhouses, the rest in factories and distribution (Lang, 2021). The impact of supermarket pricing is felt throughout this sector and the consumer price index decides the level of benefit which is based on the prices of essentials from the supermarkets. "There is a well-established assertion that the corporate food sector destabilises food security and concentrates the accumulation of wealth" (Gordon, 2017, p. 153).

To improve their public image many supermarkets donate food waste to charities. However, they tend to over order from their suppliers with an agreement that any unsold food is not paid for. Thus, they use their exploitive relationship with their suppliers to improve their image by donating goods which they have not paid for (Bowman & O'Sullivan, 2018). Meanwhile said supermarkets have put baskets at the entrance to their shops for local food banks, encouraging philanthropic shoppers to spend even more (generating even more profit for the supermarkets) the very same food banks that are in existence because of this combination of market pressures and consecutive government's inability or unwillingness to step in and do anything about it.

And it affects everyone, because everyone has to eat.

People and Their Relationships with the Land

How to live is unavoidably linked with how to eat. Some members of society have freer choices in this regard than others but for us all, as human beings, we feel that there are "good" and "bad" ways to eat and fundamentally there is an ethical element to eating (Steel, 2020, p. 13). There can be some emotive feeling behind this and religions have shared opinion on what should be eaten for thousands of years. Moral, social and ethical thought go into many culinary choices as well as cultural tradition, province and habit. Food impacts on health, it impacts on wellbeing, it is, in a literal and philosophical sense who we are. There are numerous elements to food and eating which link into the emerging movement of green social work, as well as some of our more traditional values and ethics and consequently impacts on how we practice and educate future practitioners. Green social work is characterised by sustainability and challenges the exploitation of nature; issues which are becoming an increasing priority (Dominelli, 2012). Those with food choices limited by socio-economic status are likely to be those most familiar to social work practitioners in rural and urban areas alike. Struggles with stigma associated with food poverty are linked back to these ethical, cultural and even religious choices and social work practitioners need to be constantly mindful of their role in supporting people in an anti-oppressive way. In relation to food consumption, this involves recognising people's rights to eat as they choose.

According to Tim Lang the poor in society spend proportionately more of their income on food but get a worse diet (2021) and it is acknowledged by the Royal College of Physicians (2005) that individuals on a low income ate more processed foods and with less fruit and vegetables due to fear of food waste. According to research by the Trussell Trust the majority of food bank users (around 75%) report at least one health issue or live with someone who does (State of Hunger report, 2019) and other research indicates that children who live in food poverty are more likely to be overweight or obese (Samani-Radia & McCarthy, 2011). The longer-term effect on people's health is consequently unsurprising and this picture is probably familiar to experienced front line practitioners. It is the unfortunate truth that those in our society most in need of good food have the least access to it. The impact on our practice is significant, we work alongside food banks more than ever before and see referrals for families living in poverty on a repeated basis. Making assessments to support applications for financial assistance and food packages has become a regular staple in all areas of social work practice.

Deficiencies of certain vitamins and minerals can affect a person's physical and mental health, for instance good reserves of selenium found in Brazil nuts, meat, fish, seeds and wholemeal bread can help with feelings of depression and low mood. These are not products that a shopper on a tight budget would be able to prioritise nor are they the kind of foods that are often found in food parcels. Thinking back to the humble carrot, as previously discussed, even those shoppers able to benefit from the supermarkets driving down prices of necessities are not getting the benefits of a product packed with traditional goodness. Instead, they are spending their limited budget on something which, in terms of nutrition, would not be as valuable as the carrot their parents would have bought, or something that could be grown in a community garden. Referrals to social work about children's behaviours in school can sometimes be linked to poor nutrition at breakfast time, numerous studies have demonstrated the positive impact of eating breakfast, and the quality of that food on children's ability to concentrate and achieve in the classroom (Mahoney et al., 2005). As social workers apply this knowledge across society, the disadvantage to those living with limited and poor nutrient diets becomes an issue, or at least adds to other issues. Being called in to help support with behaviour in school, for one example, is addressing a symptom rather than the major cause.

Steel argues that we are at that crisis point again due to climate change, that the same need to make best use of the land are as important today for those reasons as it was during the Second World War (2020). Steel was writing pre-Covid, pre-Brexit, pre-cost of living crisis and pre-war in Ukraine, before there were supply issues triggered by shortages of workers, panic buying and before prices of gas, electric and food began to rise as a result of the domestic and international situations. Consequently, her argument becomes even more clear and urgent but our loss of relationship with the land and how our food is produced hinder people from recognising the issues and taking action. Panagiotaros et al. recognise the role of social work as now "critical" calling for practitioners to apply their existing skills, imagining the profession as essential to the development of a new system, promoting resilience and regeneration over capitalism (2022, p. 4781).

Rural Social Work

Maslow, presented human need in a pyramid, with basic needs such as food and shelter as the foundation blocks at the bottom, as if a person is starving they would not be able to pursue the needs from higher up the pyramid (such as status and recognition or self-actualisation). Despite these being the foundation layer that Maslow makes clear, they are not more important in terms of human need than any other: "it would not occur to anyone to question the statement that we 'need' iodine or vitamin C. I would remind you that the evidence that we need love is of exactly the same type" (Maslow, 1962, p. 27).

Stripped of the autonomy to make decisions in terms of their own food choices ("good" or "bad" in accordance with each individual's ethical decision making) then there is no argument to suggest that food banks and even the social and market pressures which present only certain types of products as affordable or accessible can possibly be meeting human need. Certainly not in accordance with Maslow anyway. It is for this reason alongside the background of loss of connection to the land, climate crisis and food supply issues that it leaves the vulnerable people with whom social workers are most likely to be in contact with being the most negatively impacted (Kemp, 2011).

As a result of land changes there are fewer and fewer jobs or working people left to make a stand for these unique landscapes, and the people who are left behind are often elderly, living in poverty, isolated from many services (or all of these) and social workers are asked to come up with creative solutions to meet this need. I visited an elderly gentleman with a colleague a few weeks ago. He had been waiting for a care package for over three months, living in his family home: a beautiful old house in the midst of the rural area in which I live and work. All around him were farm cottages which have been snatched up in a recent wave of enthusiasm for countryside second home ownership and lay empty on that cold January afternoon. I listened to my colleague explain that there had been no luck in trying to find carers who could visit him, the care agencies simply cannot recruit quickly enough and where they can they prioritise the towns. She spoke to him gently about the possibility that he could move to accommodation in one of the local towns and would likely have more luck getting the care he needed. It's a difficult conversation to have with a man in his 80s living in his childhood home and my colleague did a wonderful, compassionate job. Of course, he did not want to leave. Our only solution to meet his basic needs was to trade in his autonomy in terms of place and community, not because they could not be met there but because we lacked to resources to accommodate him. According to Androff et al. "concern for people's social environment has been long identified as a distinguishing element of social work practice" (2017) and in this example it can clearly be seen that our task as practitioners was not simply to process this gentleman to ensure that his physical needs we met but also to have care for his wider social environment.

I am aware that it is not just these very rural locations with staff short-ages and there are many people working tirelessly to address the issues across the UK, but here in the countryside there were once people work-ing the land, families working in all kinds of jobs where now stand smart second homes or blocks of forestry, and should a carer want to work in these remote locations they are unlikely to be able to; unable to afford housing as prices are artificially inflated (see above—second home owner-ship) and working for organisations on such tight budgets that are unable to provide any travel cost or time.

When I was working in a rural youth justice team as a student I was allocated a young man who had been, for a number of reasons, excluded from school. As part of his alternative education package, he was doing a couple of days a week of voluntary work with a group which was manag-ing a conservation area. On the whole, this was a really positive thing for him; he was building pro-social adult relationships, gaining a better understanding of the countryside and his local environment and funda-mentally having something productive to do with his time. Ideal, you might think. However, on one occasion I went along with him in the hope of being able to chat with him away from his family and build our relationship. While I was there, he was given a litter picking arm and a bin bag and sent to collect rubbish from the verge. At the time, I mucked in with him and we talked about the reasons for litter picking (not just about making the place look tidy) but it hadn't sat very comfortably with me. I had the opportunity, luckily as a student, to explore this with my team's senior. He agreed that this was problematic for the young person and we discussed how this may have felt like "practice" for the inevitable community service or unpaid work that was lurking in his future. I felt empowered to challenge the conservation team on the young person's behalf and after highlighting my concerns, they were embarrassed that they hadn't made the connection themselves; to them this was just a teen-age boy there to help out and they had not realised that there was any issue with this particular activity. Rural social work has unique opportu-nities, problems and challenges, yet our role as advocates for the people that we work with remains the same. Engaging with the land and build-ing a relationship with nature and the community is not without its pot-holes and it is our responsibility to see those and respond accordingly.

Much of what we can do as social workers is also what we can do as individuals. All the wonderful important work that we already do which is so often overlooked, listening to people, giving our time, knowledge, experience, advocating for them and their families. Many of the students I work with get frustrated if they cannot refer to the perfect service, find a care package or meet every need themselves and I encourage them to see the value in the therapeutic conversations that are had during the assessment (Milner & O'Byrne, 2009). In Japan there is a practice of "forest bathing," spending time in nature which has been shown to reduce stress and improve the immune system (Li, 2009). Encouraging people to engage with the natural world and the food systems around them can be helpful and inexpensive. We have all heard about using a car as a therapeutic space, similarly walking outside where people are able can have a similar effect—for a more in-depth example of this you may want to have a look at Chap. 8 of this book.

In terms of our green social work agenda, being involved in growing food has great potential to contribute to a model of practice (Gordon, 2017) and there are many benefits associated with growing food: physical exercise, relaxation, as well as exposure to nature (Kortright & Wakefield, 2011). While it may not be currently practicable to suggest that individuals in poverty should grow their own food as a solution, there is certainly scope for there to be a movement towards community gardens or the collaboration between social workers and projects already running. Evidence from university studies, particularly in America indicate that there are numerous significant positives in deprived communities due to the introduction of community gardening (Mama, 2018). A growing movement of allotment usage and community gardens in the UK has also been occurring for a number of years, and although the majority of literature around these focuses on their use in urban areas they are just as beneficial to rural communities as Pitt's study on therapeutic experiences in community gardens demonstrates; "even in a green, rural area participants described a sense of escape at Garden Three" (2014, p. 88).

In Scotland at the time of writing there was a bill progressing through the Scottish parliament mandating that Scotland be a "Good food nation." Although the exact wording has not been finalised, the bill requires the Scottish Ministers and certain public bodies to create Good

Food Nation Plans. These plans include consideration of child poverty, health and wellbeing, alongside animal welfare and sustainable agriculture (Scottish Government, 2022) There is extraordinary potential here for social workers to feed into plans and policies at a local and national level and will give a voice at the table for a green social work agenda, as Dominelli has long been advocating for (2012). As acknowledged by Gordon; "While there is a well-established collaboration between social care, education and health, other professions such as conservationists, agronomists and economists remain on the periphery and, as such, rarely become collaborators." (2017, p. 152), the Good Food Nation bill offers the opportunity to change this in Scotland. Green social work models relating to food security are locally and culturally specific; however, it is essential that interdependencies are highlighted and embedded into initiatives (Dominelli, 2012). Commentators and economists have been advocating for major and significant over-hall to agricultural and food policy for a number of years (Lang, 2021; Monbiot, 2022) and whether these changes be gradual, unexpected or innovative it is likely that there will be some changes to the way we shop and eat in the next decade. From our position as social workers, we have a responsibility to be mindful of the potential for challenges for the disadvantaged people with whom we are most familiar.

In recent years some successful food poverty campaigns have gained huge followings on social media and, with the support of celebrities like Marcus Rashford and Jack Monroe, they have helped to highlight and champion people living in poverty and have made real political change. Adding our individual voices, as well as encouraging others, to campaigns such as these can help to elevate the message and drive policy decisions. Kennedy advocates that a "key role that social work need to fill, both in practice and research, is to act as the bridge between the community and the local or upper levels of government, special interest groups and outside sources of knowledge technology and power" (Kennedy, 2018, p. 409). Understanding the specific challenges for rural communities over and above the general picture is also important, given consideration to the expense of food and transportation from the rise in fuel costs mean that the more rural the community the likelihood is that costs of goods and services will be higher. Particularly thinking about Scottish islands and the most remote highland communities there are frequently additional charges for transportation of goods to these communities, the cost of which is passed on to those living and working in the communities regardless of affordability (HIE, 2016).

Consequently, social work voices need to be heard in the media and within policy development (Dominelli, 2012) and this is so important for social workers living in rural areas. Farmers and landowners in rural areas are predominantly men over the age of 50, which is not representative of the people living there, so in terms of the farming, agricultural and countryside policy it is important that a conscious effort is made to provide fair representation of how the land is used where it impacts on everybody living on it. In order for social workers to provide meaningful contribution in these areas, however, there needs to be some input on environmental issues as part of social work education (Besthorn, 2012) and there have been numerous calls for green social work to feature on the taught curriculum (Androff et al., 2017). Rural social workers are in a unique position that, geographically, much of this is happening in their local area and, given the right tools and connections, could be in a strong position to help form connection and promote positive change. Social workers already possess the skills and values which mean that with creative application acting on environmental issues can become part of their repertoire (Ramsay & Boddy, 2016). Environmental issues refer here to the physical environment but also the social issues created by the changes to our rural communities, for example the lack of housing options and available care for older people as mentioned in the above example.

What we need to do for ourselves and for the people that we work with is connect these issues, thinking about recreating more balanced rural communities for the people living, working and eating in them. Supermarkets, technologies and government policy have changed our agricultural landscape and rural environment while at the same time driving poverty for many disadvantaged groups and communities. It is likely that these changes will continue to evolve over the next few years. "Despite the disillusionment and challenges facing societies, there is great scope to promote the integration of food into community-based social work practice in collaboration with social movements" (Gordon, 2017, pp. 157–158). In Scotland, it looks hopeful that this will soon be underpinned by legislation and there are many other initiatives and community-led groups who have recognised the threat of climate change, capitalism and pollution and have already been empowered to make changes.

Movements in green social work make similar arguments as Steel in terms of climate change and the impact that this should have on social work practice (Gordon, 2017). As a movement green social work is "a form of holistic professional social work practice that focuses on the interdependencies amongst people; the social organisation of relationships between people and the flora and fauna in their physical habitats;" (Dominelli, 2012, p. 25). What is apparent is that we need to apply this thinking to social work education and practice, alongside our personal and professional habits in a changing world. Food insecurity for disadvantaged people, lack of access to good nutritional food and rising prices for everyone characterise our work and need to be given appropriate consideration alongside debates on poverty and agricultural policy as well as health and wellbeing. Times of change are also times of opportunity and the already many positive movements set good examples and encourage hope that social work can be part of establishing a system that is fair and works for all our communities, rural or otherwise.

Conclusion

By engaging in environmental and agricultural issues, social work can find its voice in advocating for those affected by rural issues by remembering its role working at the macro societal level rather than always at the micro individual. Social workers are already familiar with the impact of years of neoliberal policies and the effect that this has had on communities across the rural environment and embodying green social work principles within our practice is one way to start to think about how we can mitigate the impact on those of greatest disadvantage. Of course, there are also many possibilities at the micro level if we can keep these principles in mind asking ourselves questions such as if this new mother needs some specialist breastfeeding support? Has this child who has been labelled as disruptive had a good breakfast? Fundamentally addressing those very basic of needs before we jump in with more complex strategies or plans for support. Added to that thinking about how we use a nearby outside space as a place to engage with individuals, turning assessment itself into a therapeutic environment with the help of the natural world.

References

Androff, D., Fike, C., & Rorke, J. (2017). Greening Social Work Education: Teaching Environmental Rights and Sustainability in Community Practice. *Journal of Social Work Education, 53*(3), 399–413.

Belchior Rocha, H. (2018). Social Work Practices and the Ecological Sustainability of Socially Vulnerable Communities. *Sustainability, 10*(5), 1312–1327.

Besthorn, F. (2012). Deep Ecology's Contributions to Social Work: A Ten-Year Retrospective. *International Journal of Social Welfare, 21*, 248–259.

Boetto, H. (2017). A Transformative Eco-Social Model: Challenging Modernist Assumptions in Social Work. *The British Journal of Social Work, 47*(1), 48–67.

Bowman, M., & O'Sullivan, C. (2018). *Farmers Talk Food Waste: Supermarkets' Role in Food Waste on UK Farms*. Feedback. Accessed July 14, 2022, from https://feedbackglobal.org/wp-content/uploads/2018/08/Farm_waste_report_.pdf#:~:text=FARMERS%20TALK%20FOOD%20WASTE%20Supermarkets%E2%80%99%20role%20in%20crop,and%20subsequent%20waste%20of%20food%20on%20UK%20Farms

British Beekeeping Associate. (2022). *Bees in Schools*. Accessed July 14, 2022, from https://www.bbka.org.uk/Pages/Category/bees-in-schools

Dallimer, M., Tinch, D., Acs, S., Hanley, N., Southall, H., Gaston, K., & Armsworth, P. (2009). 100 Years of Change: Examining Agricultural Trends, Habitat Change and Stakeholder Perceptions Through the 20th Century. *Journal of Applied Ecology, 46*, 334–343.

Dominelli, L. (2012). *Green Social Work – From Environmental Crises to Environmental Justice*. Polity Press.

Eidelman, A., Schanler, R., Johnston, M., Landers, S, Noble, L., Szucs, K., & Viehmann, L., (2012). Breastfeeding and the Use of Human Milk. *Pediatrics, 129*(3), e827–e841. Accessed May 06, 2022, from https://doi.org/10.1542/peds.2011-3552.

FAO (Food and Agriculture Organisation of the United Nations), IFAD (The International Fund for Agricultural Development), UNICEF (The United

Nations Children's Fund), WFP (World Food Programme) and WHO (World Health Organisation). (2020). *The State of Food Security and Nutrition in the World 2020. Transforming Food Systems for Affordable Healthy Diets*. FAO. Accessed July 14, 2022, from https://www.fao.org/documents/card/en/c/ca9692en

Gordon, H. (2017). Climate Change and Food: A Green Social Work Perspective. *Critical and Radical Social Work, 5*(2), 145–162.

Harvey, G. (2006). *We Want Real Food: Why Our Food Is Deficient in Minerals and Nutrients - And What We Can Do About It*. Constable.

Harvey, G. (2016). *Grass Fed Nation: Getting Back the Food We Deserve*. Icon.

Highlands and Islands Enterprise (HIE). (2016). *A Minimum Income Standard for Remote Rural Scotland: A Policy Update*. Accessed August 28, 2023, from https://www.hie.co.uk/media/6441/aplusminimumplusincomeplusstandard-plusforplusremoteplusruralplusscotlandplus-plusapluspolicyplusupdateplus2016.pdf

Jones, P. (2010). Responding to the Ecological Crisis: Transformative Pathways for Social Work Education. *Journal of Social Work Education, 46*, 67–84.

Kemp, S. (2011). Critical Commentary: Recentring Environment in Social Work Practice: Necessity, Opportunity, Challenge. *The British Journal of Social Work, 41*(6), 1198–1210.

Kennedy, E. (2018). Historical Trends in Calls to Action: Climate Change, Pro-environmental Behaviours and Green Social Work. In L. Dominelli, B. R. Nikku, & K. Hok Bun (Eds.), *The Routledge Handbook of Green Social Work*. Routledge.

Kortright, R., & Wakefield, S. (2011). Edible Backyards: A Qualitative Study of Household Food Growing and Its Contributions to Food Security. *Agriculture and Human Values, 28*(1), 39–53.

Lang, T. (2021). *Feeding Britain: Our Food Problems and How to Fix Them*. Pelican Books.

Li, Q. (2009). Effect of Forest Bathing Trip in Human Immune Function. *Environmental Health and Preventive Medicine, 15*, 9–17.

Mahoney, C., Taylor, H., Kanarek, R., & Samuel, P. (2005). Effect of Breakfast Composition on Cognitive Processes in Elementary School Children. *Physiology & Behavior, 85*, 635–645.

Malhi, Y. (2014). The Metabolism of a Human-Dominated Planet. In I. Goldin (Ed.), *Is the Planet Full?* Oxford University Press.

Mama, R. S. (2018). Community Gardening: The Nexus for Community, Social Work and University Collaboration. In L. Dominelli, B. R. Nikku, & K. Hok Bun (Eds.), *The Routledge Handbook of Green Social Work*. Routledge.

Maslow, A. H. (1962). *Toward a Psychology of Being*. Van Nostrand.

Milner, J., & O'Byrne, P. (2009). *Assessment in Social Work* (3rd ed.). Palgrave Macmillan.

Monbiot, G. (2022). *Regenesis: Feeding the World Without Devouring the Planet*. Penguin.

Panagiotaros, C., Boddy, J., Gray, T., & Ife, J. (2022). (Re-)Imagining Social Work in the Anthropocene. *The British Journal of Social Work, 52*(8), 4778–4794.

Pitt, H. (2014). Therapeutic Experiences of Community Gardens: Putting Flow in Its Place. *Health and Place, 27*, 84–91.

Ramsay, S., & Boddy, J. (2016). Environmental Social Work: A Concept Analysis. *British Journal of Social Work, 47*, 68–86.

Rebank, J. (2020). *English Pastoral: An Inheritance*. Penguin.

Samani-Radia, D., & McCarthy, H. D. (2011). Comparison of Children's Body Fatness Between Two Contrasting Income Groups: Contribution of Height Difference. *International Journal of Obesity, 35*(1), 128–133.

Scottish Government. (2022). *Good Food Nation Bill*. Accessed July 13, 2022, from https://www.parliament.scot/bills-and-laws/bills/good-food-nation-scotland-bill/

Steel, C. (2020). *Sitopia: How Food Can Save The World*. Chatto and Windus.

Stein, J. (2015, November 2). Food Programme. *Radio 4*.

The Trussel Trust. (2019). *State of Hunger Report*. Heriot-Watt University. Accessed August 23, 2022, from https://www.trusselltrust.org/2019/11/05/state-hunger-2019-whats-driving-hunger-uk/

Thompson, E., Spoor, E., & Weal, R. (2020). *Local Lifelines: Investing in Local Welfare During and Beyond Covid-19*. The Trussell Trust. Accessed July 14, 2022, from https://www.trusselltrust.org/wp-content/uploads/sites/2/2020/10/LWAS_1020_v3.pdf

Turbett, C. (2010). *Rural Social Work Practice in Scotland*. Venture Press.

7

Rurality and Technology

Jane Pye

Introduction

This third chapter of the environment section of this edited collection will explore digital technology and social work in rural and remote areas. The position taken here is that rural social workers are *travelling* practitioners by necessity. Travel in this context usually means by car, and whilst it is hard to imagine a situation where it would be appropriate or even possible for social work to happen without travel, the climate challenges that we all face require us all to explore ways to reduce our environmental impact (Engstrom, 2022). Digital technology may, over time, reduce the requirement for the extensive travel that rural social workers currently undertake as more aspects of practice become possible virtually. There are a range of digital, technological and electronic transformations already ongoing in our communities which have resulted in many interactions with services and society now being online or mediated through some

J. Pye (✉)
Bowland North, Lancaster University, Bailrigg, Lancaster, Lancashire, UK
e-mail: j.pye4@lancaster.ac.uk

© The Author(s), under exclusive license to Springer Nature Switzerland AG 2024   **165**
C. Turbett, J. Pye (eds.), *Rural Social Work in the UK*, Rethinking Rural,
https://doi.org/10.1007/978-3-031-52440-0_7

sort of technology, usually as a result of ease and convenience from the perspective of the organisations providing the service. In this sense many of us are already experiencing significant elements of our world virtually (Kellsey & Taylor-Beswick, 2017, p. 29). This shift towards the increasing use of digital technology is certainly not aimed solely at physically distanced communities; it is part of a wider societal trend. However, its specific relevance to rural social work is that digital technology could contribute to addressing some of the challenges of working across large geographical areas and the travel this requires. A reduction in travel could produce practical benefits for social workers in terms of time and workload and crucially, as referred to above, contribute to a reduction of car usage. That is not to say that there are no environmental impacts of using digital technology to connect with people, but environmental factors are a worthy consideration alongside the potential efficiencies and flexibilities a greater use of technology could bring to rural social work practice.

The Social Care Institute for Excellence and the British Association of Social Workers (SCIE and BASW, 2019) have produced a very helpful guide outlining what the term digital technology can include in social work. Their list covers electronic systems, online resources, assistive technologies, social media, informatics, data, information management, hardware, online learning and artificial intelligence and machine learning. This chapter will take an equally broad view of the definition of digital technology, but the focus here is on technology that aids communication rather than, for example, the development of specific assistive technologies or technologies that enable care, although it is recognised that these may also develop new and novel ways to communicate. Technology focused on communication in social work can be broadly categorised into two. Firstly, the use of technology to support the record keeping and management of information such as online case management systems. Such systems have increasingly replaced the paper social work file and in many ways are far more efficient, secure and easier to use than their predecessors. However, there is a robust critique of the way some such systems have contributed to the rational-technical, bureaucratic managerialism that characterises so much of social work in the present day. There has been much concern raised about how these systems have had the unintended consequence of removing the human aspect of social work with information technology systems seemingly making decisions and undermining professional decision making (Broadhurst et al., 2010). These debates continue and remain relevant to social work whether practised in urban or rural areas. The focus of this chapter, however, is the second broad category, that is the way digital technology can be used explicitly to support communication and create connections either with people who use services or between professional colleagues.

It is to the credit of health and social care practitioners that they were so rapidly able to embrace digital technology when physical contact became restricted because of the virulent nature of Covid-19 (Maguire et al., 2021; Taylor-Beswick, 2021). These circumstances accelerated the fairly tentative steps that had already been taken prior to the global pandemic in the potential role of digital practice (López Peláez et al., 2020). We therefore find ourselves with a timely opportunity to consolidate recent learning and actively and critically consider what digital technology can contribute to rural social work practice. There can be resistance to the idea that technology can provide ways to communicate with people who use services in ways that are effective and ethical. However, resistance to new ways of 'doing things' is not new (Kellsey & Taylor-Beswick, 2017) and whilst the purpose of this chapter is not to argue that social work should whole-heartedly embrace all technology in every sense, it would be equally inappropriate to refuse to explore what technology could bring to rural social work practice given our recent experiences. As noted by Westwood (2014, p. 3), there is evidence that student social workers have, for some time, considered the possibility that technology could be helpful in rural and remote locations to support communication in social work practice. The significance of this should not be underestimated—students are the social workers of the future, and this is perhaps an indication of how those who have experienced all their life surrounded by technology see its benefits and potential. This chapter aims to critically explore how digital technology could enhance and contribute to communication in social work practice positively, whilst attending to the associated challenges and problems that an over reliance on digital technology could create for ethical and effective practice. It concludes with a plea for careful consideration if claiming that technology can solve some of the challenges of work in a rural setting. This chapter will encourage a forward thinking lens to consider what the legacy of the pandemic in terms of professional practice could be, whilst also recognising that the influence of technology in professional settings was being felt well before the pandemic (Susskind & Susskind, 2015).

Access and Connectivity

The most fundamental issue to address when considering the use of digital technology to support or even replace in-person social work communication is whether people who rely on services have access to suitable technology. This includes a fast and reliable internet connection. There is clear evidence that this cannot be presumed to be the case, especially in rural areas (Glass et al., 2021). Even when internet infrastructure does exist, its capacity must be sufficient to be able to support all online activities including video-calling for people to have confidence in their connectivity (Ashmore et al., 2015) and therefore believe it could have a role in supporting communication. Added to general concerns about access to suitable internet connections in rural areas, we cannot assume that people have access to appropriate devices to connect to the internet. Older people, who are in the majority in rural areas, are less likely to own a smartphone. Maguire et al. (2021) draw on interesting data from Ofcom (2019) which indicates high rates of ownership of smartphones, but significantly, this reduces with age to rates of ownership being around 50% for people aged 55 and older. People with lower incomes, even if they have devices to enable digital communication, may be limited by the tariffs they can afford to pay (Honeyman et al., 2020, p. 1), and there is evidence that young people in particular feel stigmatised by this (Black et al., 2019). The disadvantages created by the so-called digital divide affect people with reduced means and older people (Clair et al., 2021) who are often those who are most in need of services. The term 'digital natives' has been used to describe people who are comfortable and familiar with digital technology being an embedded aspect of life and 'digital immigrants' to describe those that are not. These rather crass terms capture a very important distinction between those of us who did not grow up in a world that was surround by (or dominated by) digital technology and instead have had to learn to use it in ways that work for our personal circumstances. The differences in responses to digital technology across generations is enormously significant for social work practice in rural areas given that many rural and remote areas have a higher proportion of older residents or 'digital immigrants'. The concern is that by adapting to digitally dominated ways of practice, social workers could disadvantage and exclude people in ways that in-person practice would not. It is imperative that services and organisations keep a close eye on digital and technological infrastructure across communities so that opportunities are not lost for developing ways of working when the infrastructure is in place, but that urban-centric organisations recognise that many rural places will not be as digitally connected as urban centres. It has been suggested that we are entering a new age in relation to the use of digital connectivity, but much of this thinking is urban led and without action; rural areas risk being left behind again in the continued revolution that digital technologies are thought to provoke. Cowie et al. (2020) make the case for rural places being the starting point for thinking about the future of digital technology. As social workers, we need to position ourselves to contribute meaningfully to these debates.

The question of access to online methods of communication is not solely focused on people using services in rural areas, but also how much practitioners and organisations are willing to increase their availability to others through digital technology in rural practice. Services are generally designed around organisational needs and requirements rather than how someone who uses services might prefer a service to operate. The traditional model of practitioners being based in an office, doing home visits and/or meeting service users in other mutually convenient or appropriate settings has already begun to change with increased agile working in social work. However, agility in working arrangements seems to have developed around the needs of organisations rather than people who use services. The increased use of digital technology could further transform services to include greater array of opportunities for connection and communication utilising online methods. These could be enormously significant for people who want or need to access services and are comfortable with the online world but have difficulties with in-person communication. For example, disabled people or people experiencing anxiety could find it helpful to have alternative ways of contact available in rural settings which would otherwise involve significant travel which can be both difficult and expensive. Denying people who use services these sorts of options because social workers are not yet comfortable or competent in using technology to communicate does not align with the value base of the social work profession (Reamer, 2013). There is some evidence that young people from both rural and urban areas find online methods to seek help positive which perhaps hints further at a generational difference to which social workers need to be alert (Best et al., 2016; Davis & Marsh, 2022). Given the relative physical isolation that young people may experience in rural and remote places, practitioners must be willing to facilitate interactions in ways that work for young people, and this seems likely to include the use of online or digital methods. This also requires social workers to have access to the technology that enables digital communication (Ferguson et al., 2022).

Mobility and Technology

The lack of public transport infrastructure in rural settings has been highlighted by social workers (Pye et al., 2020). Whilst public transport infrastructure remains poor, the car will remain essential for communities and practitioners alike when it comes to facilitating physical contact (Miller, 2020). Remaining mobile by having access to appropriate methods for travel and transportation has been an essential element of wellbeing for individuals and communities (Dabelko-Schoeny et al., 2020). Social workers serving remote and rural communities have always been expected to travel to those communities in order to carry out social work. It is some time ago now that Ferguson (2006) argued for social work to be considered from a *mobilities* perspective, that is to surface the subtle ways in which social work practice has come to rely on or be about movement across both time and space. The reality of working as a social worker in the UK means the car is a central feature of practice (Ferguson, 2006). Indeed, a small-scale study of rural social workers' experiences in one English county indicated that travel by car was the most prevalent practical feature of their day-to-day work (Pye et al., 2020). This study indicates that the car serves as a site of social work practice both in terms of direct work with people and as a site of administration and containment for social workers (Ferguson, 2009a). Whilst the required level of travel was felt to be stressful because of the demands on time and some of the practical challenges about driving in rural places, time in the car was also seen as a positive and an opportunity for reflection and appreciation of the place. Rural social workers also felt that being able to travel to see people was an essential part of their role despite some of the challenges it creates. The car is therefore an important place of practice, and lack of access to this space will potentially impact negatively on practice (Ferguson, 2009b, 2010). In social work and other helping professions, the car is and should be seen as central to the success of the role (Ferguson, 2016) as a place for practice and a place of safety and containment (Smith, 2003). In this sense, the car has become much more than simply a vehicle for enabling movement from one place to another in social work practice; it is an important characteristic of working rurally albeit an often unacknowledged one. However, the increasing demands on social workers' time means that the time taken up by travelling by car has been seen as an inefficient burden and social workers are increasingly under pressure to remain at their desks focused on administrative and bureaucratic tasks (Disney et al., 2019). It is not difficult to see how a solution to this pressure is to consider how the use of technology could be used to mitigate travel challenges by using technology to 'visit' people in need of services. This appears to conflict with social workers' desire to carry out social work in communities and remain as travelling professionals because their physical presence in communities and travel by car is an important feature with wellbeing benefits attached. There is some evidence that social workers value the flexibility technology gives when it comes to record keeping and report writing (Jeyasingham, 2019). Opportunities to engage in more agile ways of working when completing such administration tasks can unshackle social workers from central offices. However, there is also evidence to indicate that so-called hot desking is not popular with social workers (McGregor, 2012) because of the feelings of isolation the disconnection from a team can create (Pye et al., 2020). There appears then to be mixed views about the potential use of technology to support a more agile completion of administration tasks, but there is evidence to indicate that social workers are reluctant to replace face-to-face interactions with people using services with communication via electronic devices (Jeyasingham, 2019).

Technologically Facilitated Communication

There have been concerns raised in the past about how interactions mediated through technology risk losing the essential relational aspects of effective and ethical social work practice (Broadhurst & Mason, 2014). Traditionally, social work has valued the physical proximity of people so that the social worker can be fully present with the person who is using the service as this has been seen as essential element of relational practice. However, the global pandemic resulted in communication through the use of a screen becoming common place creating '*a sense of connection and disconnection simultaneously*' (Boddy & Dominelli, 2017, p. 177). The relevance of physical proximity is worthy of further exploration here as there have been suggestions that when the communication is not taking place in the same location, empathy, a key aspect of relational practice, could be reduced (Dolby, 2014). Broadhurst and Mason (2014) write powerfully about the importance of 'corporeal copresence' in social work. In this paper, they recognise that the use of technology can and is used to communicate and that there could be efficiency gains as a result. Applying this view to social work in rural and remote settings where social workers are undertaking significant amounts of travel, it is not difficult to imagine the rationale for holding a 30-minute conversation via technology which avoids a car journey of at least that time at either end of the contact or visit. However, whilst these workload and associated time pressures should not be ignored, as Broadhurst and Mason (2014) articulate so clearly, social work as a profession would be well advised to draw back from a workload management approach to practice which prioritises surface level efficiency. The potential for positive working relationships to be built when people are together is powerful. The opportunity for more than just our verbal communication skills to be used is clear. Social workers can *sense* the atmosphere in the home, can *feel* the living conditions and can *perceive* emotional responses when in person in ways that are either impossible or extremely difficult when communicating via technology. This allows a far more holistic understanding of someone's circumstances, and whilst the initial visit and time taken is likely to be seen increasingly as a luxury, in a pragmatic response to time management, it is an investment in time that is more than worth it. In a time when social work as a profession appears to find it hard to retain social workers (Grant & Kinman, 2012), it is essential that it does not further distance those who were drawn to the profession because of its commitment to relationships with people and communities using services. Social workers working in rural settings are often drawn to these settings because of the opportunities they give for working in a community orientated way (Turbett, 2018). To reduce the opportunity for community-based practice as a result in a shift towards digital connections rather than in-person connections is likely to alienate large proportions of rural social workers. It is hard to see how this would not be a disaster for rural and remote places which rely on the skills, knowledge and expertise of social workers who are committed to practising with the nuances and subtleties that rural practise requires. It is significant that recent work has revealed that social workers are keen to explore the possibilities of digital technologies as a way of enhancing and contributing to relationship-based practice, not as a replacement for spending time with people who use services (SCIE and BASW, 2019).

Despite the concerns about the use of technology replacing in-person contact in social work, the global pandemic resulted in social workers having to adapt their practice and use technology in new ways. There is evidence that despite the worries about how this would be, social workers did find ways to adapt their practice to continue relationships and remain 'close' to families through hybrid ways of working (Ferguson et al., 2022). It is important to note here that the success in the use of digital technology does appear to have been premised on relationships already existing in the 'real' world. This indicates that a digital only method of practice could be at best ineffective and at worst disastrous. As stated above, there is evidence to suggest that social workers are interested more generally in how technology could be used to enhance and add to relational ways of working (SCIE and BASW, 2019). Writing in the context of children's social work, Pink et al. (2021) make a compelling case for considering the benefits of the use of digital technology to support social work practice. One of the striking aspects of this study includes the voices of people using services who share that in some situations, the use of digital technology enables a willingness to engage with services and attend meetings that would be difficult to do in the physical world. However, this research is clear in its conclusion that the use of digital technology should be part of a hybrid approach to practice, that it has its own distinct value but does not replace in-person contact with the uniqueness that brings. Establishing our presence with others involves thinking about the use of digital technologies and how we blend these with more traditional ways of being 'with' people who use services (LaMendola, 2010).

Research demonstrates that adults who use services do not feel that communication can be effective without a relationship being in place (Simpson, 2017), confirming the value of developing relationships whether that be in person or via technology. This research also indicated that people who use social work services felt that having options to communicate in a variety of ways is essential and that social workers being unable to offer more than the standard telephone was considered poor. Interestingly, from this study, it seems that a motivation for people using services wanting a variety of communication options to be available was they could avoid having to contact social workers through a bureaucratic switchboard. This is an important example demonstrating how some of the traditional ways that social work has sought to be efficiently available are experienced as barriers and create a sense of inaccessibility. The strength of voice about the centrality of relationships in practice from the perspective of people who use services is, in many ways, reassuring for social work practitioners who were drawn to social work for this very reason. However, social workers must be able to widen the scope of available communication methods to include technology to enable working relationships with service users, and this may, at times, mean lobbying their employing organisation to enable this. This would permit a greater sense of presence and connection with people using services and communication *on their terms*. There is developing evidence to indicate that for some people who use services, digital technology enables engagement in services by, for example, reducing the sense of intrusion that regular home visits create, or the cost and stress associated with having to attend in person planning meetings. Care must be taken in social work that we do not fail to appreciate the potential benefits of using digital technology in spite of fear of using it and a risk adverse attitude (Best et al., 2016). However, social workers must also be alert to the fact that some people may locate themselves in rural areas as a perceived way of avoiding a digital online world (Cowie et al., 2020), so no assumptions about how service users feel about using technology should ever be made.

Technological Potential

There are different ways that digital technology can be harnessed to support people (Reamer, 2013), and many of these ways are relevant for both urban and rural areas. There are practical advantages of social workers having laptops and tablets which enable them to work responsively and efficiently by, for example, recording information within meetings and visits and to access information immediately. However, social workers typing directly into a laptop whilst in a meeting or visit with a service users can be perceived as a barrier to relationships and communication (Jeyasingham, 2020), so care must be taken to balance the need for efficiency with the requirement for practice to be relational. The use of devices such as smartphones to enable a more flexible approach to communication via text messaging in its various forms and video calls means that people can communicate on the move and flexibly. However, there are disadvantages to agile working as mentioned above, and in rural and remote areas, use of laptops and smartphones to access information, record notes and aid communication usually rely on internet access. It is absolutely not the case that all areas that social workers work in will be reliably connected to the internet. This is a significant point which must continue to be highlighted to those who may see digital technology as a method of mitigating the challenges of working rurally.

Digital technology includes the use of web-based information sources such as websites set up to engage people and provide information. This is an important development as there is evidence to indicate that children and young people in some situations value such non-face-to-face support methods for reasons such as flexibility and being able to seek help on their own terms (Davis & Marsh, 2022). An aspect of this type of support is the potential for anonymity. Chat functions that can be embedded in such sites could provide an attractive option for people who are facing challenges but do not feel they want to reveal these in person (Best et al., 2016). The opportunity for anonymity could make services feel more accessible to people who want to seek support but are anxious about the stigma associated with being 'in need'. Whilst anonymous help giving and support is well developed in some well-known services, this has not been a model traditionally used or even tried in statutory services. The high threshold for statutory services may mean that ways of making these services more accessible are not avenues that statutory services want to promote at the current time. But, regardless, the principle of social services being as accessible as possible to all aligns with the professional value base of social work meaning that ideas and ways to improve the relevance of services to those who could benefit from them should never be discounted.

The urban-centric nature of the UK means that the voices of people living in rural and remote settings are often unheard and assumed to be homogenous. Connection and collaboration through the use of digital technology could mitigate some of this discrimination. The dominant model of social work in the UK is individualist casework, and whilst the potential for supportive and positive relationships to be formed between people using services and social workers should not be undermined, this model does not appreciate the potential for communities to be self-actualizing, self-organising and agentic. A critical perspective of the current dominant model of social work practice in the UK might conclude that the casework model exists by design to help prevent poverty-stricken and forgotten communities from being able to establish practices of solidarity to challenge policies and practices which continue to admonish their needs and rights (Brake & Bailey, 1980). This applies not only to physically related communities which are located some distance from urban centres but also to people who experience oppression and discrimination because of who they are and their personal characteristics. Any social worker who is committed to radical and critical practices can now, more than ever before, harness technology to support connection and collaboration amongst groups of people who have been isolated, ignored, discriminated and oppressed. There is some evidence to indicate that social media can be a 'portal' into participation in community action and lobbying work (Sitter & Curnew, 2016). Social workers working in a true community-based way will also recognise the possibilities for self-advocacy from within communities. The use of social media is not without a need for ethical and practical considerations in community work, but communities of people can be connected without the constraints of geography. As the profession begins to engage critically with the possibilities that digital technology brings, there are a number of issues to consider including the potential of technology but also the risks associated with it and the need for social workers to be skilled in using the technology, especially in relation to confidentiality, consent, boundaries and dual relationships (Reamer, 2013).

Risks

The use of digital technology within practice can create opportunities for everyone working and living in rural and remote settings as long as people have access to the technology, internet connections and have the skills to use these. One aspect of the growth of opportunity for connection is the use of social media as a way of communicating and connecting. The nature of social media invites users to share information about themselves, and whilst this can be carefully managed by those who know how to limit what they share, the potential for individual social workers to find themselves connecting online with people that they work with is not hard to imagine. It is therefore essential that social workers consider what the ramifications might be of sharing lots of personal information online (Boddy & Dominelli, 2017, p. 179). BASW (2018) state that social workers should avoid formal connections with people that they are working with in the online world, presumably to avoid the issues surrounding dual relationships discussed elsewhere in this collection. Whilst this most certainly gives a clear instruction which serves to avoid any difficult ethical dilemmas about online connections (Boddy & Dominelli, 2017), this does not go far enough in setting out how as a profession social work manages online encounters—social workers may still come across material relating to people they are working with without having them as 'friends' or 'followers'. Similarly, there are well-known risks for service users in using digital technology, especially social media. The potential for exploitation through the use of social media has been well reported. Another notable risk which does not appear to have been well considered yet is how the promotion of social media and other digital technology for help seeking could mean that people in search of information may stay away from statutory or government websites and instead be drawn towards sites that might not be as regulated (Best et al., 2016). So, whilst promoting the option of the use of digital technology as a way of engaging people who want to be communicated in this way, awareness must be created about how this could increase vulnerability if it results in people accessing inaccurate information.

Skills and Education

This chapter has so far focused on technology as a potential response to the specific challenge of distance faced by social workers, people using social work services and communities in remote and rural locations. Whilst this chapter urges a cautionary approach to whole-heartedly adopting a digital based approach to mitigate challenge of distance, it also recognizes that we cannot deny that the use of technology is becoming more and more embedded in our lives and communities. As explored above, there could be potential benefits to the use of technology in practice if, for example, there was fair and equitable access to broadband, hardware and skills needed to use technology which as we have seen is often seriously lacking in rural and remote areas. It is wise for us to then consider how social work practitioners (and others) should be appropriately ready and skilled to harness the benefits of digital technology in practice given the pressure that is likely to be on rural practitioners to use technology. In an extremely thought-provoking article, Taylor (2017) captures the picture in relation to social work education and digital skills highlighting how social work education in the UK has in no way adequately supported students to be ready for the use of digital technology in practice. In a point made in the introduction to this edited collection, the role of social work education in preparing social work students for practice is clearly extremely important. BASWs (2018) social media policy, whilst helpful in many respects, has a tone of caution and appears to reflect a profession not being fully committed and aware of the potential of social media in practice. Having said this, it does urge social workers to develop their own skills in using social media to support practice.

The relevance of digital technology for social work educators is twofold. Firstly, digital technology can provide important learning experiences for students especially in relation to simulated practice opportunities (Neden et al., 2021) and using social media to support effective pedagogical practices (Mugisha, 2018). It is essential that social work educators consider how to harness technology in their teaching and assessment practices to create rich and diverse learning opportunities for social work students. Secondly, social workers of the future must be given the chance to critically consider the use of digital technology in their future practice, especially students wishing to work in rural areas where there is likely to be a growing influence of technology for the reasons described above. Modules and courses that focus on communication and interpersonal skills are already in a strong position to explore and introduce how digital technology can enhance communication (Blakemore & Agllias, 2020) whilst remaining aware of the need for a critical application and consideration of them. The move to include digital communication methods needs to include an appreciation of the ethics of doing so and these should be at the forefront of both research and in teaching of these skills (Boddy & Dominelli, 2017). Social work students should also have the opportunity to critically consider how technology enables connection with colleagues and with knowledge and information to support and help their practice whilst being mobile (Turner et al., 2020) whilst again adhering to ethical practice principles especially in relation to confidentiality and boundaries. Practice placements provide an ideal place for students to put into practice the learning, guidance and policies around, for example, social media (Voshel & Wesala, 2015), and this also requires that those with responsibility for supervising student placements to be able and willing to support this area of practice development. One of the challenges that all of those involved with the education of social workers face is that many of the technological advances that surround us may be new to experienced educators so appropriate support for social workers at all stages of experience must be available (SCIE and BASW, 2019). Given that more and more of us are engaged in online lives via social media, it is imperative that social work educators include critical consideration of the implications of social media presence for individual social workers, particularly as many of those now entering the profession will never have known a time without social media. Educators could consider how to model the use of social media with students as part of an awareness raising and educational experience around what the challenges of the blurring of the personal and private space can mean by, for example, explaining they will not accept 'friend' or 'follower' requests and why (Duncan-Daston et al., 2013). It would appear that the inappropriate use of social media, whether that is due to unawareness or purposeful use, could increasingly be a reason for referral to social work regulatory bodies.

Future

As society moves towards more use and reliance on digital technologies, it is hard to see how rural social work can avoid the ever-increasing influence. Shifting to use technology effectively and ethically is complex and needs time and the will of those involved (Maguire et al., 2021). The connections between a growing use of technology and the issues of privacy and inappropriate use of data should not be ignored (Eubanks, 2018). The potential for personal information being harvested via technology exists (Shaw et al., 2022) with organisations turning data into valuable material about people and their habits (Sadowski, 2020). Companies and organisations leading the way in the use of digital technologies have benefited enormously from the shift to use such technologies because of the pandemic. We should remember that technology is not neutral; it is part of a neoliberal world which promotes profit and marketisation rather than equality of access and social justice. The push to close the 'digital divide' to recruit more and more citizens to be active users of technology will mean more personal data will be available to those who use this to exploit others and create discriminatory algorithmic responses in automated online systems (Clair et al., 2021) and potentially be subject to surveillance by technology giants (Garrett, 2022). Social work in the UK has already enabled the use of such algorithms in direct practice decision making in some areas (Vannier Ducasse, 2021). Hodgson et al. (2022) urge for serious and critical consideration to be given to the role that artificial intelligence may play in social work in the very near future, including in the education of student social workers.

The reliance on digital technology as a method to reduce physical travel in its extreme could lead to individual 'movements' being monitored in ways that will be an impingement on civil liberties (Urry, 2008). It is also a grave mistake to offer the use of technology as a non-environmental impactful alternative to travel by car. The use of technology is not entirely 'green'—it has an impact (Lucivero, 2020), and the more we use technologies, the greater this impact will be in terms of both the production of hardware to enable technology and the storage and use of data. There can be no doubt that social work must engage with these global challenges faced by society to be ready to continue to operate in the twenty-first century (Yadav, 2022).

Conclusion

No one can deny the transformatory impact that the development of digital technology and the online world has had on our societies and communities. However, it is important to recognise that despite its impact, digital technology is relatively new and many people, including social workers, are likely to identify with the idea of being a 'digital immigrant'. Many people do not feel equipped with the skills and knowledge to use digital technology safely and competently. In this chapter, the possibilities of digital technology to enhance rural social work practice have been considered along with a reminder of the need to contemplate any move to digital ways of working critically and with a clear understanding of how this will impact on the person or people using the services. It is completely unethical to assume that a digital response to working with people in rural and remote settings is the answer to the challenges caused by distance and travel. Social workers must be alert to the fact that the more we promote digital technology in practice, the more likely people are to inadvertently share their personal data with sophisticated technological organisations. Having said this, social work also must remain open to the fact that some people may find communicating via digital means preferable to in-person contact. However, the reality is that until we can be confident that all remote and rural areas can access appropriate broadband internet connections, wireless technology and afford the actual devices required for online communication whether than be simple video-calling or the use of social media, social work practice cannot rely on digital technology as a core tool to support practice. It is likely that progress towards a digitally well-connected world will continue, thus opening more opportunities for social work and technologically enhanced communication and contact. As this progress continues, as social workers we need to think about the ways that we can contribute to the debates about virtual and digital practice to ensure we position ourselves to tackle some of the ethical questions that the increasing use of digital technology provokes. As Rodriguez et al. (2021, p. 199) articulate so perfectly,

> The social work profession is at a critical crossroads where we can take a proactive role in influencing the ethical use of digital technologies to benefit social work and advance social change, rather than be reactive to the whims of technology companies and developers that thus far, have dictated the rules of digital engagement and participation.

This is one of the most significant challenges for the social work profession in current times.

References

Ashmore, F. H., Farrington, J. H., & Skerratt, S. (2015). Superfast Broadband and Rural Community Resilience: Examining the Rural Need for Speed. *Scottish Geographical Journal, 131*(3–4), 265–278.

BASW. (2018). *Social Media Policy.* [Online]. Accessed December 11, 2021, from https://www.basw.co.uk/resources/basws-social-media-policy

Best, P., Manktelow, R., & Taylor, B. J. (2016). Social Work and Social Media: Online Help-Seeking and the Mental Well-Being of Adolescent Males. *British Journal of Social Work, 46*(1), 257–276.

Black, N., Scott, K., & Shucksmith, M. (2019). Social Inequalities in Rural England: Impacts on Young People Post-2008. *Journal of Rural Studies, 68*, 264–275.

Blakemore, T., & Agllias, K. (2020). Social Media, Empathy and Interpersonal Skills: Social Work Students' Reflections in the Digital Era. *Social Work Education, 39*(2), 200–213.

Boddy, J., & Dominelli, L. (2017). Social Media and Social Work: The Challenges of a New Ethical Space. *Australian Social Work, 70*(2), 172–184.

Brake, M., & Bailey, R. V. (1980). *Radical Social Work and Practice.* Edward Arnold.

Broadhurst, K., & Mason, C. (2014). Social Work Beyond the VDU: Foregrounding Co-Presence in Situated Practice - Why Face-to-Face Practice Matters. *British Journal of Social Work, 44*(3), 578–595.

Broadhurst, K., Wastell, D., White, S., Hall, C., Peckover, S., Thompson, K., Pithouse, A., & Davey, D. (2010). Performing "Initial Assessment": Identifying the Latent Conditions for Error at the Front-Door of Local Authority Children's Services. *British Journal of Social Work, 40*(2), 352–370.

Clair, A., Fledderjohann, J., & Knowles, B. (2021). *A Watershed Moment for Social Policy and Human Rights?: Where Next for the UK Post-COVID.* Policy Press.

Cowie, P., Townsend, L., & Salemink, K. (2020). Smart Rural Futures: Will Rural Areas Be Left Behind in the 4th Industrial Revolution? *Journal of Rural Studies, 79*, 169–176.

Dabelko-Schoeny, H., Fields, N. L., White, K., et al. (2020). Using Community-Based Participatory Research Strategies in Age-Friendly Communities to Solve Mobility Challenges. *Journal of Gerontological Social Work, 63*(5), 447–463.

Davis, J., & Marsh, N. (2022). *When Children Seek Help in Non-Face-to-Face Settings: What Do We Know? A Review of the Literature.* [Online]. Accessed February 4, 2022, from https://learning.nspcc.org.uk/research-resources/2022/why-children-seek-help-in-non-face-to-face-settings-review

Disney, T., Warwick, L., Ferguson, H., Leigh, J., Cooner, T. S., Beddoe, L., Jones, P., & Osborne, T. (2019). "Isn't It Funny the Children that Are Further Away We Don't Think About as Much?": Using GPS to Explore the Mobilities and Geographies of Social Work and Child Protection Practice. *Children and Youth Services Review, 100*, 39–49.

Dolby, N. (2014). The Future of Empathy: Teaching the Millennial Generation. *Journal of College and Character, 15*(1), 39–44.

Duncan-Daston, R., Hunter-Sloan, M., & Fullmer, E. (2013). Considering the Ethical Implications of Social Media in Social Work Education. *Ethics and Information Technology, 15*(1), 35–43.

Engstrom, S. (2022). Can We Keep the Environment in Mind Whilst We Adjust to New Freedoms? In D. Turner & M. Fanner (Eds.), *Digital Connections in Health and Social Work: Perspectives from Covid-19*. Critical Publishing.

Eubanks, V. (2018). *Automating Inequality*. Picador.

Ferguson, H. (2006). Liquid Social Work: Welfare Interventions as Mobile Practices. *British Journal of Social Work, 38*(3), 561–579.

Ferguson, H. (2009a). Driven to Care: The Car, Automobility and Social Work. *Mobilities, 4*(2), 275–293.

Ferguson, H. (2009b). Performing Child Protection: Home Visiting, Movement and the Struggle to Reach the Abused Child. *Child & Family Social Work, 14*(4), 471–480.

Ferguson, H. (2010). Therapeutic Journeys: The Car as a Vehicle for Working with Children and Families and Theorising Practice. *Journal of Social Work Practice, 24*(2), 121–138.

Ferguson, H. (2016). Professional Helping as Negotiation in Motion: Social Work as Work on the Move. *Applied Mobilities, 1*(2), 193–206.

Ferguson, H., Kelly, L., & Pink, S. (2022). Social Work and Child Protection for a Post-Pandemic World: The Re-making of Practice During COVID-19 and Its Renewal Beyond It. *Journal of Social Work Practice, 36*(1), 5–24.

Garrett, P. M. (2022). Surveillance Capitalism, COVID-19 and Social Work: A Note on Uncertain Future(s). *The British Journal of Social Work, 52*(3), 1747–1764.

Glass, J., Shucksmith, M., Chapman, P., & Atterton, J. (2021) *Covid-19, Lockdowns and Financial Hardship in Rural Areas: Insights from the Rural Lives Project*. [Online]. Accessed January 23, 2022, from https://pure.sruc.ac.uk/ws/portalfiles/portal/35878199/Rural_Lives_Covid_19_and_financial_hardship_FINAL_05.05.21.pdf

Grant, L., & Kinman, G. (2012). Enhancing Wellbeing in Social Work Students: Building Resilience in the Next Generation. *Social Work Education, 31*(5), 605–621.

Hodgson, D., Goldingay, S., Boddy, J., Nipperess, S., & Watts, L. (2022). Problematising Artificial Intelligence in Social Work Education: Challenges, Issues and Possibilities. *The British Journal of Social Work, 52*(4), 1878–1895.

Honeyman, M., Maguire, D., Evans, H., & Davies, A. (2020). *Digital Technology and Health Inequalities: A Scoping Review*. Public Health Wales NHS Trust.

[Online]. Accessed December 19, 2021, from https://phw.nhs.wales/publications/publications1/digital-technology-and-health-inequalities-a-scoping-review/

Jeyasingham, D. (2019). Seeking Solitude and Distance from Others: Children's Social Workers' Agile Working Practices and Experiences Beyond the Office. *The British Journal of Social Work, 49*(3), 559–576.

Jeyasingham, D. (2020). Entanglements with Offices, Information Systems, Laptops and Phones: How Agile Working Is Influencing Social Workers' Interactions with Each Other and with Families. *Qualitative Social Work, 19*(3), 337–358.

Kellsey, D., & Taylor-Beswick, A. (2017). *The Learning Wheel - A Model of Digital Pedagogy*. Critical Publishing.

LaMendola, W. (2010). Social Work and Social Presence in an Online World. *Journal of Technology in Human Services, 28*(1–2), 108–119.

López Peláez, A., Erro-Garcés, A., & Gómez-Ciriano, E. J. (2020). Young People, Social Workers and Social Work Education: The Role of Digital Skills. *Social Work Education, 39*(6), 825–842.

Lucivero, F. (2020). Big Data, Big Waste? A Reflection on the Environmental Sustainability of Big Data Initiatives. *Science and Engineering Ethics, 26*(2), 1009–1030.

Maguire, D., Honeyman, M., Fenney, D., & Jabbal, J. (2021). *Shaping the Future of Digital Technology in Health and Social Care*. The Kings Fund. [Online]. Accessed December 16, 2021, from https://www.kingsfund.org.uk/publications/future-digital-technology-health-social-care

McGregor, K. (2012). *Nine out of 10 social workers believe hotdesking saps morale*. Community Care 6th November 2021 [online]. Accessed 14th March 2023. Available at https://www.communitycare.co.uk/2012/06/nine-out-of-10-social-workers-believe-hotdesking-saps-moral/

Miller, V. J. (2020). The Experience of Transportation to Visit a Nursing Home Resident: A Case Study. *Social Work in Health Care, 59*(5), 300–321.

Mugisha, D. C. (2018). Social Work in a Digital Age: The Need to Integrate Social media in Social Work Education in the UK. *Journal of Social Work Education and Practice, 3*(4), 1–10.

Neden, J., Boddy, J., & Ramsay, S. (2021) An Emerging Future for Work and Education: Implications for Integrative Learning in Social Work. *Social Work Education*. [Online]. Accessed September 3, 2022, from https://www.tandfonline.com/doi/full/10.1080/02615479.2021.1919072

Ofcom. (2019). *Communications market report 2018*. London; Ofcom [online] Available at https://www.ofcom.org.uk/_data/assets/pdf_file0022/117456/CMR-2018-narrative-report.pdf (Accessed 14th March 2023).

Pink, S., Ferguson, H., & Kelly, L. (2021). Digital Social Work: Conceptualising a Hybrid Anticipatory Practice. *Qualitative Social Work, 21*(2), 413–430.

Pye, J., Kaloudis, H., & Devlin, M. (2020). *Rural Social Work in Cumbria: An Exploratory Case Study*. [Online]. Accessed January 23, 2022, from https://www.cfj-lancaster.org.uk/files/pdfs/RSW%20report.pdf

Reamer, F. G. (2013). Social Work in a Digital Age: Ethical and Risk Management Challenges. *Social Work, 58*(2), 163–172.

Rodriguez, M., Storer, S., & Shelton, J. (2021). Organizing in the digital age: Digital macro practice is here...to say. *Journal of Community Practice, 29*(3), 199–202.

Sadowski, J. (2020). *To smart: How Digital Capitalism Is Extracting Data, Controlling Our Lives and Taking Over the World*. MIT.

SCIE and BASW. (2019). *Digital Capabilities for Social Workers: Stakeholders' Report*. [Online]. Accessed January 23, 2021, from https://www.scie.org.uk/social-work/digital-capabilities/stakeholders#:~:text=Social%20workers%20require%20good%20digital,to%20support%20their%20complex%20role.&text=The%20report%20aims%20to%20share,of%20the%20projects'%20future%20resources

Shaw, H., Taylor, P. J., Ellis, D. A., & Conchie, S. M. (2022). Behavioral Consistency in the Digital Age. *Psychological Science, 33*(3), 364–370.

Simpson, J. E. (2017). Staying in Touch in the Digital Era: New Social Work Practice. *Journal of Technology in Human Services, 35*(1), 86–98.

Sitter, K. C., & Curnew, A. H. (2016). The Application of Social Media in Social Work Community Practice. *Social Work Education, 35*(3), 271–283.

Smith, M. (2003). Gorgons, Cars and the Frightful Fiend: Representations of Fear in Social Work and Counselling. *Journal of Social Work Practice, 17*(2), 153–162.

Susskind, R., & Susskind, D. (2015). *The Future of the Professions: How Technology Will Transform the Work of Human Experts*. Oxford University Press.

Taylor, A. (2017). Social Work and Digitalisation: Bridging the Knowledge Gaps. *Social Work Education, 36*(8), 869–879.

Taylor-Beswick, A. (2021). Social Work, Technology and Covid-19. In D. Turner (Ed.), *Social Work and Covid-19 Lessons for Education and Practice*. Critical Publishing.

Turbett, C. (2018). *Community Social Work in Scotland.* [Online]. Accessed April 11, 2022, from https://www.iriss.org.uk/resources/reports/community-social-work-scotland

Turner, D., Landmann, M., & Kirkland, D. (2020). Making Ideas "App"-en: The Creation and Evolution of a Digital Mobile Resource to Teach Social Work Interviewing Skills. *Social Work Education, 39*(2), 188–199.

Urry, J. (2008). Climate Change, Travel and Complex Futures. *The British Journal of Sociology, 59*(2), 261–279.

Vannier Ducasse, H. (2021). Predictive Risk Modelling and the Mistaken Equation of Socio-Economic Disadvantage with Risk of Maltreatment. *The British Journal of Social Work, 51*(8), 3153–3171.

Voshel, E. H., & Wesala, A. (2015). Social Media & Social Work Ethics: Determining Best Practices in an Ambiguous Reality. *Journal of Social Work Values and Ethics, 12*(1), 67–76.

Westwood, J. (Ed.). (2014). *Social Media in Social Work Education.* Critical Publishing.

Yadav, R. (2022). Conversation with the Twenty-First Century Social Work: Some 'Post(s)' Perspectives. *The British Journal of Social Work, 52*(5), 2966–2983.

Part III

Community

8

The Trojan Mouse: The Benefits of Social Work Out of Doors

Carla McLaughlin and Karin Eyben

Preamble: Patterning Something Different

'When we speak of systemic change, we need to be fractal' (Brown, 2017, p. 59). Fractals are the patterns that shape all living beings, from the micro to the macro level; the common patterns that have evolved as life affirming, whether these are the branches of trees, animal circulatory systems, snowflakes, lightning and electricity, plants and leaves, geographic terrain and river systems, clouds, crystals. The same spirals on seashells can be found in the shape of galaxies. When we speak of change, it is about creating patterns that are life affirming and cycle upwards. How

C. McLaughlin (✉)
Garvagh Health Centre, Garvagh, County Derry/Londonderry,
Northern Ireland, UK
e-mail: Carla.McLaughlin@northerntrust.hscni.net

K. Eyben
Hare's Corner Cooperative, Garvagh, County Derry/Londonderry,
Northern Ireland, UK

191

and what we do at small scale can reverberate to the largest scale—this is where the Forest Families Project was located, as a small fractal or 'trojan' mouse offering a different way to do relationships.

> Tune in to the prevalence of spiral in the universe—the shape in the prints of our fingerprints echoes into geological patterns, all the way to the shape of the galaxies. Then notice that the planet is full of these fractals—cauliflower, yes, and broccoli, ferns, deltas, veins through our bodies, tributaries, etc.—all of these are echoes of themselves at the smallest and largest scales. Dandelions contain an entire community in each spore that gets blown on children's breath.
> (Brown, 2017, p. 51)

Building on our theme in this section of the book on *communities*, this chapter examines an example of the utilisation of space and natural assets to do social work with people, both individually and in groups, across the lifespan. It considers the interface between social work and the community sector with particular emphasis on working in a rural area. This includes consideration of the social work role, barriers, stigma and the difficulties getting away from the bureaucracy of what the role of social work has become. Within the chapter, we explore the way the role can engage with the community sector and provide early intervention and support to families before they reach a crisis. This can be done using the outdoors, and, in this chapter, we will be reflecting on the practice of social work in a forest and how it might contribute the changing the story about social work.

Introduction

Garvagh (from the Irish *Garbhach*, meaning 'rough place' or *Garbhachadh* meaning 'rough field') is a village in Co Derry, Northern Ireland. It was developed in its current lay out by an English family, the Cannings, in the seventeenth Century following the 1640s Irish Rebellion with land confiscated by the English Crown from the O'Cahans, a large Irish Clan. Garvagh Forest today is 600 acres in size and is a mix of broadleaf and conifer forest. From its more recent story as land ruled by different chieftains in Gaelic Ireland and managed through the Brehon laws to private ownership through the Canning family to state managed and owned from the 1950s as a commercial forest, this small piece of land has evolved through different forms of ownership, management and colonialism. Garvagh today is a small rural town of around 1500 inhabitants; it is a farming community with a number of small family-run engineering firms. The town itself is majority protestant/unionist surrounded by a catholic/nationalist hinterland. As with many places across Northern Ireland, the ethno-nationalist fractures and divisions dating back to the seventeenth century still shape community relationships. It is important to consider the unique position of social workers in Northern Ireland where what are commonly described by all sides as 'The Troubles', erupting in the late 1960s, had a significant impact on the role of social workers who were often dealing with the consequences of violence and intimidation (Heenan, 2004; Duffy et al., 2019). The Troubles ended formally with the Good Friday Agreement in 1998, but their legacy continues. The forest itself can be seen as a natural interface between different political traditions.

Just before the beginning of the pandemic, a new group of staff arrived in Garvagh Health Centre: a multi-disciplinary team (MDT) composed of social workers, a mental health practitioner, pharmacist and a physiotherapist. Initial relationships were established between the social workers and the Garvagh Development Trust's 'Garvagh People's Forest Project'. Then, the pandemic struck, and the relationships grew as both statutory agencies and communities worked together in finding ways forward in a place with no maps.

Out of this Covid formed relationship, where many turned their gaze outdoors, the idea of the *Forest Families Project* evolved as a partnership between the social workers at Garvagh Health Centre and the Garvagh People's Forest Project.

This chapter has been written with some of the families who participated in the Forest Families Project (described in detail in the chapter) to help us write this contribution. It will reflect on how they perceive and then experience the role of social work in standing beside them and supporting them to create the changes that they wish to see—and what can shift in a forest environment.

As Hilary Cottam says, the principles of our current welfare system are 'assess me, refer me, manage me' (Cottam, 2018 p. 197). This chapter explores how the forest can create space to prioritise relationships building with creative steps that are small and simple.

> At the heart of this new way of working is human connection. I have learnt that when people feel supported by strong human relationships, change happens. And when we design new systems that make this sort of collaboration and connection feel simple and easy, people want to join in.
> (Cottam, 2018, pp. 17–18)

Areas that emerged in conversation with the families include:

- Role/perception of a social worker and a new way of working.
- Working together/partnership working.
- Forest offering a space for reflection and fulfilment.
- Social pedagogy model and how it fits with the approaches adopted.
- The family's journey and how the forest and the project has improved things or opened up new possibilities.
- Learning for other social workers and community groups as to what is possible.

How these themes were shaped and developed form the basis of this chapter.

Our Roles and Relationship

Carla McLaughlin is a social worker who was previously located in a physical health and disability team before taking the newly developed post of primary care social worker in Garvagh Health Centre. She is now developing her new role as social worker within the Primary Care team: focused on the principle of working with people along the life

continuum, 'from the cradle to the grave'. Shortly after taking up her new post, Covid-19 happened, and this created additional challenges.

During the life of the project, Karin Eyben was a community development worker with the Garvagh People's Forest Project, funded by the National Lottery Community Fund and hosted by the local development agency, Garvagh Development Trust. The Garvagh People's Forest Project has been about noticing, valuing and growing the relationships people have with their Forest contributing to wellbeing, learning and relationship building. Our questions have been, how can we live in a way that sustains the interdependence of wellbeing between a forest and its town, and how do we begin to live and work in a way that recognises that 'our community' must include the rest of the natural world?

Karin was one of the first people Carla met in her new role. Karin has grown to understand the forest's contribution to the community's wellbeing and previously offered to work with the Health Centre to help patients benefit from the forest; she knew that research evidence showed how nature can improve physical and mental wellbeing (Weir, 2020), but staff at the time did not have the capacity to take advantage of the offer. Karin noticed a change when Carla came into post as she was able to employ a community development approach to open doors and think creatively about health and wellbeing and the benefits of the natural world for the GP patients and their families.

The growth of trust and mutual relationships between social workers and the Garvagh People's Forest Project have been central to our joint planning. This shaped a programme of work informed by four important understandings that have emerged from our collective work:

1. That the conditions we are born, grow, live, work and age in impact on our mental health; people on the edges of our economic system bear the brunt of its failures—poverty, gender, race, disability can all exacerbate mental ill health and illness;
2. That we cannot just connect to the natural world—we have to change how we relate to nature from one of use and extraction to one of care and stewardship;
3. That people are experts in their own lives and that this must always be the starting point to any conversation.
4. The importance of exploring and understanding *double suffering*, a term that speaks to the reality that 'those who are harmed and discriminated against are not ennobled in the process. Workers are too often engaging with those who are hurt and hurting, angry and suspicious, defensive and defended' (Featherstone et al., 2018, p. 9). ... 'It is a slow grind in the context of histories of fear and lack of trust' (Featherstone et al., 2018, p. 16).

Wellbeing and Relationships Flourish Outdoors

Alienation from the natural world is a factor in the mental health crisis in Western countries (New Economics Foundation, 2020). There has been mounting evidence over the last 30 years that spending time in nature is vital for our mental health, from relaxing our attention to maintaining our circadian rhythms, and triggering our 'rest and digest' system (Guy-Evans, 2021). Time interacting with the natural world is now being commonly used as a treatment for mental health problems. Being in nature also brings benefits for many children and adults with Autism Spectrum Disorder and other conditions. The Garvagh People's Project has, for example, heard from educators over the last four years that when children return to the classroom from the forest, they are more focused, open to learning and at ease.

Alienation from the natural world has also led to an economic system which is pushing us over a number of the earth's nine life support systems. We are using natural resources and creating waste at twice the amount that the Earth can produce and absorb. The *Five Ways to Wellbeing*, now used across the Northern Ireland health and wellbeing family, were developed by the New Economics Foundation in 2008 to specifically challenge an economic system based on endless growth deeply impacting on how we live, value and shape our lives (Aked et al., 2008). As Thomas-Smith (2020, p. 20 states):

> Faced with the enervating whirl of relentless privatisation, spiralling inequality, withdrawal of basic state support and benefits, ever-increasing and pointless work demands, fake news, unemployment and precarious work, it's perhaps unsurprising that so many of us are struggling.

Garvagh Forest is surrounded by small rural communities which naturally lends to placing our relationship with the natural world as centre stage to sustaining good mental health in those communities. Many families also work the land to contribute to family incomes. As the new Northern Ireland Mental Health Strategy notes:

> For certain sectors, for example, the rural and farming community, mental health is a particular concern. This can be due to physical isolation from communities, worries about livelihood, or anxiety regarding personal and family safety. Research by the Farm Safety Foundation revealed that 84% of farmers under the age of 40 believe that mental health is the biggest hidden problem facing farmers (up from 81% in 2018).
> (Health NI, 2021)

The pandemic has seen great creativity as we learned to respond within a new landscape. New relationships have formed in the Garvagh area between communities and with voluntary organisations as well as the pharmacist and Health Centre. The pandemic has exposed and amplified what has always been there: inequality, poor mental health, loneliness, family breakdown, domestic violence, low wages, air pollution, poor housing, our disconnect from the natural world, and racial inequalities (Buheji et al., 2020). We have seen those connections between health and wellbeing and these wider factors in the Garvagh area; particularly, relationship breakdown, mental health and addiction as well as increased pressure on the forest during the lockdowns. Our challenge is not to drop the veil down again as the crisis recedes but keep it lifted and that we continue to understand and act on the social and environmental factors that influence our health (Health NI, 2016).

It is important to also note that the Northern Ireland official multiple deprivation measure (National Research and Statistics Agency, 2017) recognised that the area was measured at 272 of 890 on the multiple deprivation measure. Income deprivation was rated the highest, particularly, income affecting children and older people. With this in mind, poverty and economic deprivation is having an impact on the local children, and we considered this when providing forest families sessions; there was no charge to the families and transport was not required as it was within walking distance.

Social Work and Community Development

Community membership derives from ideas around self-identity and a sense of belonging. Turbett (2018) acknowledges that community social work is an essential approach for social workers to work preventively alongside service users within the communities where they live. Prevention, early intervention and community working are key themes in relevant social policy documents and have been instrumental in developing the role of generic social workers in GP's surgeries (Health NI, 2016). However, it is important to acknowledge the marginalisation of community social work during the 1980s and 1990s. Social workers became 'influenced by the social mandate of the welfare state … under this framework of welfarism. … Social workers are used by the state to monitor and manage oppressed groups' (Das et al., 2016, p. 376).

Welfarism meant social work distanced itself from community work, and community workers often viewed social workers' relationship with community development as problematic. Carla previously worked as a social worker in a mainstream community care team and felt swamped by bureaucracy and managerialism. She started to feel burnt out and was spending less time with families as most of her week was spent behind a computer doing all the paperwork. She knew she had to find something that took her back to the grassroots of social work and the reason for entering the profession. She always thrived on interactions with individuals and their families. Relationship building, advocacy and empowering people are all important to her. The new post as a 'generic' social worker allowed her to do this while working with all ages and areas of need. She had the opportunity to engage in community work and that is how she came to use the forest to deliver a service to the families and children that need support. At the beginning, the community and voluntary agencies were unsure of this new role and mistrust was evident. It was imperative from the beginning to create alliances with the communities, by working respectfully while re-engaging in community social work practice. However, Das et al. (2016) recognise that mistrust has affected the working relationship and that the social work role has become 'skewed … providing top-down paternalistic, individual based services rather than community-orientated practices that call for social change' (Das et al., 2016, p. 379).

Community development is underpinned by a set of values, social justice and community empowerment. Recognising strengths, skills and assets as well as enabling communities to reorganise and build on their own strengths is key when engaging in a community development approach (NICHI Health Alliance, 2015). Considering this, social work in NI needs to continue to develop a professional agenda, which will champion for social justice that includes engaging with communities. However, working in statutory teams as agents of the state influenced by managerialism, bureaucracy and policies/protocols leaves social workers with limited time or capacity to challenge oppression. Community empowerment and collective action for change integrate a radical approach to practice. Social workers in all areas of service need to keep fighting for social justice and recognising the roots of inequality in the structures and processes of society not in the individual or the community (Ledwith, 2020).

Forest Families Programme

The Covid-19 pandemic has highlighted the sheer importance of the relationship between community work and social work and how it needs to reconnect; pre-existing problems have been under the spotlight particularly within the health and social care systems struggling to cope with increased demand. These difficulties are amplified in the current political and economic climate, where principles of economy, effectiveness and efficiency have been taken into the world of social care (Gilchrist, 2019). A few months into the first national lock down, it became clear that many families were struggling. Families were feeling overwhelmed, anxious and craving human connections. Many families lost their support networks as contact with people, friends and health professionals was limited. Research on the impacts of Covid-19 highlights that it is a particularly tough time for children and young people with existing mental health difficulties, with Young Minds finding that 83% had experienced worsening mental health during the pandemic (Young Minds, 2020).

The research supported what had been within our own Health Centre: that children with additional needs prior to Covid were impacted significantly. These were children and young people with existing mental health conditions—such as those with autism spectrum disorder, obsessive compulsive disorder (OCD), attention deficit hyperactivity disorder (ADHD), anxiety and depression.

The Forest Families Project emerged from this context, and the first programme was delivered just after the first serious lockdown with the authors and Paul Johnston (Assistant Social Worker) in the summer of 2020. We then ran the programme in the Autumn of 2020 and then again in the Summer of 2021.

Our focus was to initially take referrals from the Health Centre (GP, practice nurse, MDT and the health visitor). In fact, all referrals received at the beginning came from the practice health visitor who had a relationship with a lot of the local families; she was able to refer the families that would benefit the most. Families included children on the child protection register, children receiving social work support, children recently placed in foster care and a child who had been adopted. We had a child with a moderate learning disability, and quite a few of the children who attended had ASD. We also had a Syrian refugee family with support from the Education Authority. Our intention was about offering an experience in Garvagh Forest for families who have been finding it particularly tough under lockdown.

The objectives were to improve wellbeing in the natural world through offering opportunities to:

- move (as gently or as vigorously as we wish to),
- learn (learn about the natural world, ourselves and each other),
- connect (experience difference in relationships within the family, with the rest of the natural world and with social workers),
- give (through being open to the experiences of learning about our relationships with the rest of the natural world we can begin to explore the impact of our behaviours),
- notice (use of all our senses).

The approach we grew was to create opportunities for play in and curiosity about forest. Sessions began with an interactive walk with a number of short stops for a variety of activities and games. Each member of the family often had a 'forest name' of a plant growing in the forest which they also had to find. For example, herb robert, nettles, meadow sweet, red clover and foxgloves. Our destination was the beech wood where we had set up provision for refreshments, relaxation with a number of hammocks and different activities that members of the family could choose from. These included clay work, building dens, forest volleyball, painting, bug hunt, creating jewellery or just swinging in the hammocks.

This first programme went well, and all families appeared to relax, reconnect and receive some support as required. The adults and children all engaged in the sessions and benefited from increased knowledge regarding plants/trees/nature. Karin was able to share her experiences with everyone that attended, and the expansion of knowledge was reciprocated as Karin gained further insight into the role of the social worker. Both Carla and Paul also learnt a lot about the forest space and the benefits of outdoor engagement.

There was a family with a involvement from social services, who used the welcome time out to make positive changes. The children thoroughly enjoyed the session and the dad/stepdad engaged with Karin and later became a volunteer at the youth club. He had his own difficulties with confidence and self-esteem, so this was a remarkable outcome.

Another benefit was that all the families that we spent time with were made aware of the support available in their local Health Centre, and a few of them reconnected with the social work team for further support. This has educated parents and carers on what support is available in the Health Centre and assisted with breaking down barriers. For example, one eight-year-old boy with ASD attended and was very anxious about returning to school post Covid; help was given to his mum to assist with this transition.

All three workers were needed to enhance the involvement of one large family: mum, three children, grandad, his two step-children, the mum's sister, her partner and their own three children. We began to understand family dynamics and their impact. Paul was able to spend time with the grandfather, and he and a grandson were able to engage with the forest and agree on future daily walks together. This seemed to help the physical and mental health of all family members.

Some examples of feedback provided from the families (permission has been given to share):

> Hi Karin, the girls have spoken about their day in the forest. … The one thing they would change is more hammock time. … They had a great time, thank-you. (Foster mum of three)
>
> Hello Carla, we had the best day at the forest. Yourself and Karin were fantastic with the children and left every one of them with great memories of their day out. It was an enjoyable morning for the mummies too. … I would recommend it to all families and I would do it all over again in the morning. (Mum of three, one child with ASD)
>
> When the thunderstorm came it was fantastic. Particularly for (Child A)—she totally blossomed in the rain. (Child B) was nervous but we got that shelter built. It was a memorable finish for our family. (Mum of 4 children all with ASD)

In some situations, having the whole family participate was of real benefit as they were able to nourish their relationships through having a bit of down time and play outdoors. In other situations, perhaps not having the 'male caregiver' was also important in that there was space to grow relationships with the mum. The day we spent with the Syrian family and the interpreter was very special. It was a beautiful summer's day with life bursting across the forest, and we three workers were able to reflect on our own practice and relationship building. There was an important moment when the smell of a plant brought back memories of the flora and fauna in their home in Syria and they were able to freely share about the home they had left.

We used the natural space and assets around us to deliver social work with people individually and in groups using the forest as a method of building up relationships and fostering a true human connection with children and families. Many families initially felt nervous at the idea of a session in the forest with a social worker present, making the social worker feel quite stigmatised; as one child said that they used to call social workers 'witches'. Karin assisted with this dilemma as she was not attached to any statutory body and was able to demonstrate how she used the natural environment to build connections. This learning was critical for Carla feeling at ease in taking her practice outdoors, and more broadly in helping shape her practice in terms of community development. The families were also very nervous about being outdoors, and there was an instinctive aversion to nature at the beginning: bees will sting; soil is dirty; worms are horrible. Transforming that aversion into curiosity is a critical part of this story.

It is important to note that whilst Carla has developed community work skills in her present role, she still has a degree of statutory responsibility as a social worker. She has to maintain a balance between a supportive and empathetic role to one where onward referral might be required. This was necessary with one family she had been supporting for some time who were involved in the Forest Project, where referral to the local children and family team became necessary because of issues of neglect of the children's basic needs. This was difficult for Carla and the family, a somewhat ethical challenge where values and the nature of social work practice changed direction. However, Carla was aware that she has a duty of care for the children she works alongside, and reflecting on this difficult period for the family, our relationship and rapport helped ease the journey. She felt comfortable explaining her concerns and the referral process while reassuring the family that she would continue to provide support when needed. An investigation was completed by the statutory childcare team and the positive outcome was that the family were referred back to Carla to continue her supportive role. The relationship was not fractured, the openness and transparency displayed enabled the family to continue to trust her. This was mainly due to the beginnings of our connections that started through the Forest Families Project and continued a journey through many different pathways of support.

The Families' Stories as Case Studies

Feedback from two families involved with the Forest Families Project is instructive in several ways. In the first case study, the parent is looking back on her involvement with professionals including social workers during a challenging time in her son's life. She has engaged with activities in the forest as her son and his siblings really enjoy engaging with the outdoors. She has shared her challenges alongside some hopes of how services and social work can be delivered in the future in a rural area.

In the second case study, a young woman reflects on her journey as she went through cancer treatment for a long period of time. She is married with three young children. She reflects upon the community and the role of the Health Centre, the social worker and the community and voluntary support. She engaged with the forest sessions and received support in the Health Centre through the social work team for her and her eldest son.

We chose these two case studies as both families experienced the therapeutic benefits of growing a relationship of care with the natural world; these nestled within a wider ecosystem of informal and formal care support systems, some of which are visible (e.g. the social work relationship) and some less so (e.g. friends, neighbours and the relationship with the forest and rivers of the natural environment). Both case studies illustrate the importance of care networks and relationships that exist in communities, and how formal care systems need to notice, value and enhance these rather than engage in a practice that can feel like crashing in without noticing or caring. Permission has been gained to share these case studies.

Case Study 1: A Parent and Her Son's Journey

I will never forget when I realised that the system at the time did not support or nurture me. I was sat down with three social workers who said I wasn't coping. But I knew I was trying my best to cope; I wanted them to realise that and that what I needed was help to get the services I needed. I still remember ten years later being put down and made to feel so small. I was never going to get the support and services I needed if was being treated as if I couldn't cope. When you're exhausted as a mum and have tried all avenues that is when you pick up the phone to social workers and then you need them to see your strength, courage and resilience.

I often think that as a family we needed a little tugboat to help us navigate challenging waters of our care system this could be the role of the social worker in the Health Centre. There are so many people at each stage. The health visitors and GPs before primary school age; then when my son got to school we had to learn about educational psychologists, child development specialist, CAMHS, SENCO, occupational therapist, speech and language therapists, physiotherapists. There are so many routes and sometimes you feel you are going around, forward, backward and in all directions. This became too much for my son and he had a breakdown—there were so many professionals involved with him. We realised someone needed to back off. He was constantly being taken out of school for appointments which was so disruptive to his pattern.

You keep fighting to get diagnosis and then when diagnosed the support can take so long to arrive leaving you in limbo for many months. Living in a rural area, there are always challenges to accessing centralised services with little public transport and the costs of private transport. It has been good to see with the pandemic more and more training and services going online.

What I personally would love to see would be a peer parent support space where you wouldn't need a label to be part of group. It would reduce isolation and the feeling that I can't access support because I don't fit into a box. Each of us carries so much wisdom that might be useful to others. For example, I used to struggle to get my son to sit down to a proper meal as he would snack on crackers beforehand. I kept trying to stop him snacking with no joy. Then I took a step back to try and understand why he needed the crackers. I realised that by eating crackers he was meeting a sensory need that needed satisfied before he could sit down to dinner. That experience would be of such benefit potentially to other parents. We tend not to listen or hear to our own children; particularly when we are so worried. It's hard to step back when you are so entangled in the system and so much is pressing down on you.

My son's need to be in the outdoors has taught me how to listen and prioritise his voice. At 3 years old, I found him outdoors in the pouring rain. I didn't understand at that time that he needed to be outdoors. That it soothed and relaxed him and gave him comfort. He felt capable outside and allowed him to develop and grow skills. I have learned with him what being outdoors means and what he needs after being confined to the classroom for many hours during the day.

As Featherstone et al. (2018, p. 70) comment, this case study surfaces the entanglement of the care system and how difficult it is for people to find the route through it.

The backdrop to a complex and bewildering tapestry of services. Seeking help was often the start of a difficult and, at times, traumatic journey around and through services. Families that sought help (rather than those who had services imposed) rarely knew what was needed initially, but knew they were struggling and tried various services and agencies … also, because some people haven't got a clue and have not been in that situation before, so they don't understand where they need to go or what they need to ask.

The conditionality attached to receiving help proved a stumbling block for many families. They regularly described what were experienced as hurdles to accessing help: Were they living in the right place? Did they have the right referral? Had they got the right diagnosis? Rarely, if ever, were families able to describe initial points of contact that simply asked the family to talk about their needs and then dealt with any inter-agency matters 'behind the scenes' (Featherstone et al., 2018, p. 70).

Case Study 2: A Cancer Survivor

I have had such an experience of being loved over the last couple of years. Such beautiful people consistently and with love leaving stuff off at my door. And 'I'm not coming in' because of Covid despite me often beseeching them.

People looked after my kids and took them to school. A group was formed called 'Anne's Road Trips' to take me to radio and chemo appointments. I didn't want to be a patient—people had to tread a fine line with me—between caring too much and not caring at all. Such a balance between vulnerability and courage. I knew there were secret WhatsApp groups—strategizing and as a support for my carers. I felt carried like a queen.

Cancer affects so many families. There was a tricky time when another woman in the community died of cancer. I knew people were thinking 'will Anne be next?' That was tough. One friend has been such a quiet help—a non-hugger. She knew there is no magic to this and there are up and down days. She has picked up my son every morning at 8.00 am to give me space and time with the younger two children.

People have seen what my husband and I have been through. Things you do in life do come back at you. I would always make a point of dropping off eggs at people's gates. Got me out; gave me a purpose. My own family has come over every month. I have seen my sisters thank the community for looking after their sister. We're all stubborn girls—and we knew we could get through this.

This community, as with all communities, is complex. It comes with a past and history. I came in as an outsider—a blow in. Or as I told people, I was a hurricane. 'I'm not a blow in, I'm a hurricane'. People always want fresh meat and unless you challenge it you can get eaten up.

So many of the professional carers around me also went the extra mile. The receptionist at the Health Centre. My GP. My husband getting moved up the line for his Covid jab as he was asked, 'Are you Anne's husband?'

The forest was such a lovely family experience for us. From all the activities, the games, the map of the world. We were able to breathe and build a different kind of relationship with the social work team. I have told all my friends about our social workers. When my son had a melt down, it felt ok and normal to be scared. Knew there was a support system there.

The social worker role is so important—when families are overcome with anxiety, emotions that there is a direct line to seek support from and to help make sense of things. I learned not to expect too much from my son.

I was so lost when I came to you. It's the dance between the informal care network that carries a family in need and how the formal system supports, values and works with that.

Key Messages from the Case Examples

- Family's perception of the role of the social worker and a new way of working together—in Case Study 2, the growth of trust in the social worker extended to telling friends and neighbours about the supports offered and experienced.
- The strengths of working together in partnership—Case Study 1 offers a good example of the absence of direct interventions by the social worker.

- The Forest offering a space for reflection and fulfilment—both realised through the therapeutic benefits of the natural world.
- The use of a social pedagogy model and how this fitted with the approaches adopted. In Case Study 2, this involved an understanding of the significance of the history of the community, the land and the relationships that formed around it.
- Both case studies illustrate the journeys of the participants and how the Forest Project improved their situations and opened up new possibilities.

Conclusions: Ponderings and Reflections

Both authors believe the experience of the project underlines the importance of relationship-based practice in the very real sense described by Featherstone et al. (2018). This avoids an emphasis on the dynamics of the interpersonal relationships between worker and family, and instead focuses much wider: giving significance to 'increasing connections with neighbours, networks and communities' (ibid, p. 14).

Learning for the workers involved reflecting on some things that need further thought and consideration. These include:

- Aversion to nature: fear of getting wet, hands dirty, muddy shoes, etc.—issues for some children and their carers.
- Worker awareness of different sensory needs and capabilities within a family: outdoor experiences can be frightening for some.
- Gender dynamics either with or in the absence of a male care giver: does this offer opportunity for the mother, or impede a view of the whole family system?
- The sense that this was seen as a one-off experience for families with a beginning, middle and end. Opportunity for a longer programme would have been good for many families, as would the facility for further connection between participants.

Carla's Reflections Engaging with the community and voluntary sector and working with the families in such a different way than I had been used to has re-energised me completely. I feel I can build relationships with the 'whole' family' and I have learnt by changing my ways of working how much potential community social work has especially in a small rural area. It requires a sense of being brave and trying new things and as Ledwith (2020) highlights, the importance of continuing to challenge ideas, to question practice and to not settle for the status quo. In my new role as a MDT social worker, I have been given the platform to do this, and I feel privileged to be able to work with the local community where I am based. Recognising some of the challenges discussed above I am aware that I cannot make people better, but in my current role, I can open up possibilities of working towards an 'abundant community' where they can embrace their own humanness, come together and unite. As McKnight and Block (2012, p. 19) express: 'A competent community is one that takes advantage of its abundance, admits the realities of the human condition … variety, uniqueness and appreciation for the one-of-a-kind are at its essence'.

Karin's Reflections Brambles are often seen as the jokers of the forest; they catch you when you are least looking and try and trip you up. They can also be an important reminder that we are all entangled with each other and as the nineteenth-century conservationist John Muir is widely quoted as saying, 'when one tugs at a single thing in nature, we find that it is attached to the whole universe'. The fungi can teach us about death and when things break down there, then comes nourishment and growth. Creating curiosity about the life around us can still the mind with possibilities then around creating layers of connections and stories. As Bartholomew (2001) put it: 'It is a long journey from the head to the heart, and an even longer journey from the heart to the hands'.

Being outdoors can offer a small step in that journey in growing more life-affirming patterns and shapes. The forest was not just a different location for practising social work, but it offered the opportunity for a paradigm shift with regard to the definition of 'community' and what this might mean for community development practice. The opportunities for this kind of approach are not restricted to rural areas—the growth of wild spaces, city farms and imaginative use of park areas have opened up opportunities in urban locations, and they should be seized by our colleagues there. Our example here demonstrates its application in an area where rural people live and work. Its success (in our view) perhaps challenges one of the myths of the rural idyll mentioned frequently in other chapters—that rural people have ready access to experiences in wild places—often they do not, and they need support and encouragement to do so.

(Permission was given by the anonymised participants to use their stories in the case studies; all photographs are from the Garvagh People's Forest Library and none feature anyone involved in the chapter.)

References

Aked, J., Marks, N., Cordon C., & Thompson, S. (2008). *Five Ways to Well-Being*. NEF. Accessed November 2021, form https://neweconomics.org/uploads/files/five-ways-to-wellbeing-1.pdf

Bartholomew. (2001). *"Sacrifice: The Missing Dimension," Address at the Closing Ceremony of the Fourth International Environmental Symposium*. Accessed November 2021, from https://www.livedtheology.org/green-blues-climate-change-lament/

Brown, M. A. (2017). *Emergent Strategy*. AK Press.

Buheji, M., et al. (2020). *The Extent of COVID-19 Pandemic Socio-Economic Impact on Global Poverty – A Global Integrative Multi-Disciplinary*. Accessed June 2022, from https://www.researchgate.net/profile/Mohamed-Buheji/publication/341044016_The_Extent_of_COVID-19_Pandemic_Socio-Economic_Impact_on_Global_Poverty_A_Global_Integrative_Multidisciplinary_Review/links/5eaab2f045851592d6ac3165/The-Extent-of-COVID-19-Pandemic-Socio-Economic-Impact-on-Global-Poverty-A-Global-Integrative-Multidisciplinary-Review.pdf

Cottam, H. (2018). *Radical Help: How We Can Remake the Relationships Between Us and Revolutionize the Welfare State*. Virago.

Das, C., O'Neill, M., & Pinkerton, J. (2016). Re-engaging with Community Work as a Method of Practice in Social Work: A View from Northern Ireland. *Journal of Social Work, 16*(2), 196–215.

Duffy, J., Campbell, J., & Tosone, C. (2019). *Voices of Social Work Through the Troubles*. BASW.

Featherstone, B., Gupta, A., Morris, K., & White, S. (2018). *Protecting Children: A Social Model*. Policy Press, ProQuest Ebook Central.

Gilchrist, A. (2019). *The Well-Connected Community: A Networking Approach to Community Development* (3rd ed.). Policy Press.

Guy-Evans, O. (2021). *Parasympathetic Nervous System Function*. Accessed June 2022, from https://www.simplypsychology.org/parasympathetic-nervous-system.html

Health NI. (2016). *Health and Well Being 2026 – Delivering Together*. Accessed June 2022, from https://www.health-ni.gov.uk/sites/default/files/publications/health/health-and-wellbeing-2026-delivering-together.pdf

Health NI. (2021). *Mental Health Strategy 2021-31*. Accessed June 2022, from https://www.health-ni.gov.uk/publications/mental-health-strategy-2021-2031

Heenan, D. (2004). Learning Lessons from the Past or Re-visiting Old Mistakes: Social Work and Community Development in Northern Ireland. *British Journal of Social Work, 34*(6), 793–809.

Ledwith, M. (2020). *Community Development: A Critical and Radical Approach* (3rd ed.). Policy Press.

McKnight, J., & Block, P. (2012). *The Abundant Community: Awakening the Power of Families and Neighbourhoods*. Berrett-Koehler.

National Research and Statistics Agency. (2017). *Northern Ireland Multiple Deprivation Measure 2017*. Accessed November 2021, from https://www.nisra.gov.uk/sites/nisra.gov.uk/files/publications/NIMDM%202017_Technical%20Report.pdf

New Economics Foundation Zine. (2020). *Is Our Economy Making Us Sick?* Issue 2. Accessed November 2021, from https://neweconomics.org/2020/10/the-new-economics-zine-2

Northern Ireland NICHI. (2015). *Community Development National Occupational Standards*. Accessed August 2023, from https://healthallianceni.com/site/wp-content/uploads/2020/05/Tool-1-NICHI-CDNOS-Standards-2015.pdf

Thomas-Smith, A. (2020). *This Is Your Brain on Neoliberalism, Is Our Economy Making Us Sick*. New Economics Foundation Issue 2 Zine. Accessed November 2021, from https://neweconomics.org/uploads/files/NEFZINE-issue2-mental-health-and-the-economy-2.pdf

Turbett, C. (2018). *Community Social Work in Scotland: A Critical History, Fifty Years After the Social Work (Scotland) Act 1968.* Accessed October 2021, from https://www.iriss.org.uk/resources/reports/community-social-work-scotland

Weir, K. (2020). *Nurtured by Nature Psychological Research Is Advancing Our Understanding of How Time in Nature Can Improve Our Mental Health and Sharpen Our Cognition* (Vol. 51, No. 3). American Psychological Association. Accessed November 2021, from https://www.apa.org/monitor/2020/04/nurtured-nature

Young Minds. (2020). *Coronavirus: Impact on Young People with Mental Health Needs.* Accessed November 2021, from https://youngminds.org.uk/about-us/reports/coronavirus-impact-on-young-people-with-mental-health-needs

9

Patriarchy, Masculinities and Gender-Based Violence in Rural Communities

Colin Turbett

Masculinity and Its Significance in the Rural Context

Many years ago, I moved from an urban Scottish social work setting to a remote rural one and immediately met a range of issues that I had not expected. One concerned a prominent member of the community who, his teenage daughter disclosed, had been systematically sexually abusing family members. The other involved a quiet young man who had been goaded into reacting against bullying threats by producing his father's shotgun outside a hotel bar. The first individual became subject of very public ridicule and approbation and quickly moved away from the community: rural gossip thrives on such situations, and there can have been few who did not know a lot of detail about his alleged activities. The second, who had never been in trouble in his life, was given a deferred

C. Turbett (✉)
Shiskine, Isle of Arran, UK
e-mail: ctur282388@aol.com

sentence and retreated to his parental home and the steady life he had previously led. Both these concerned rural evocations of masculinity that I was to become familiar with over ensuing years: the sex offender, as might be expected, had transgressed commonly accepted codes and would be unable to recover his credibility and place in the community whatever the outcome of the legal process that was to follow. The young man with the shotgun, in an environment where crimes of violence were rare, but where firearms were far more common than had been the case in the Glasgow housing scheme where I had previously worked, was considered to have stood up for himself and suffered no such community recrimination. After this it became almost routine when responding to new referrals where confrontation might arise, to check with the police about the presence of licenced guns. That might have become less of an issue with the tightening of regulations after the 1996 Dunblane massacre of children in a quiet rural school, but the presence of a commonly held but nonetheless distorted sense of masculinity has moved on slightly, but still pervades.

So, what do we mean by *masculinity* and why should it matter in the rural context? Masculinity refers to the characteristics and qualities that are associated with the male gender. The premise of this chapter is the now broadly agreed premise that masculinity is based on social construction, culture (and therefore historic tradition), rather than biology and innate characteristics of men. The most accepted authority in the study of masculinities is the Australian R.W. Connell (2005). He draws on the Italian Marxist Gramsci's description of cultural hegemony—the means by which the dominant ideas in a society are reproduced through the manipulation of facts and perceptions by the ruling group whose interests they perpetuate (the clearest examples are popular newspapers owned by millionaires whose expressed opinions are accepted as fact by readers). Connell describes the concept of *hegemonic masculinity* which explains how legitimisation is given to men's dominant position in society (patriarchy), the physical traits of manhood that justify this (physical strength and other alpha-male features) and the subordination of less masculine men and all women. Through this means embedded masculinity requires an emphasis on manly attributes and their reproduction through child rearing practices within the home, and likewise the perpetuation of feminine qualities associated with women: from the positive ones of softness and kindness, nurturing and caring qualities, through to expectations about behaviour and personal presentation including clothing styles. Given the associations of gender stereotyping with marketing and advertising, these are clearly issues within wider UK society.

Feminism challenges the expression of masculinity through patriarchy and has made advances in recent decades (hooks, 2004; Ford, 2020). However, few would deny that equality of the sexes has a long way to go, and that other forms of self-identity (being transgender or non-binary) are only beginning to gain recognition and challenge prejudice based around masculinity. This is true generally although women are now far more likely to be found in formerly male occupational preserves than was the case in the last century. In rural areas, however, patriarchy and masculinity have survived better and still play a significant role (DeKeseredy, 2015; Shannon et al., 2016). This is no accident: it arises from traditional occupations in rural areas: farming, agriculture and forestry predominantly, and to a lesser extent fishing, mining and quarrying. All of these involve hard labour where physical strength has historically been an important quality and is celebrated through culture and custom. Men's physical strength is needed in the battle against nature and the harsh environment (Little, 2017). The typified rural man was the hairy-handed-son-of-toil found in literature—a rugged and self-reliant individualist who would work with others when the need arose, but took pride in not being the regimented and pasty-faced factory worker of urban industrial Britain. In as much as this idea of masculinity lent itself to pride and place in the rural community, we shall describe it as 'successful' masculinity.

The countryside is now easily accessible from the city in most cases and contrasts are not so obvious. Whilst the perception of rural masculinity might remain popular, the reality is that few occupations nowadays require male physical strength as a primary consideration due to technological progress; indeed, many male preserve occupations are actively promoting gender equality and diversity. This includes the Fire Service, a male bastion: in rural areas emergency response often relies on retained firefighters and volunteers and at least one English Brigade has tried to address recruitment issues through a targeted approach to women (Local

Government Association, 2018). Sporting activities popular in some rural areas, such as rugby, have clear associations with masculinity, and some of these are changing: girls and women now involve themselves directly in most sports, and some top male rugby players have declared their gay sexuality publicly—all chipping away at the traditional male toughness associations that stem from the worship of masculinity. Farming remains central to the popular conception of indigenous rural life, and masculinity holds its sway within that community due to the typically isolated nature of the work. Nowadays it is only labour intensive, if at all, at harvesting time, and for the rest of the year is often undertaken by the farmer on their own, or with another family member. There are positive challenges to the patriarchal social construct around farming, and Tina Laurie's chapter in this book demonstrates a move away from the traditional view of food production in the countryside. Agricultural colleges are now attracting women entrants in numbers—the FarmingUK website reported in October 2021b that a majority of students studying agriculture at Aberystwyth University in Wales were women. The Scottish Government launched a scheme in late 2021 to recruit women into agriculture, part of the aim of which was to ensure farm succession was not determined by gender (FarmingUK September 2021a).

Women in rural communities are associated traditionally with a support role to the male breadwinning one, principally that of housewife and family organiser. This role is especially important with farming: the farmer's wife performed (and still performs in some cases) essentially supportive work on the farm: not just traditional housework and child rearing, but some subordinate farm-related activity: feeding and caring for some categories of livestock (e.g. poultry), administrative work and meal provision to support the irregular and long working hours of the male farmer (Campbell et al., 2006).

Power and decision making in rural communities is said to reflect masculinity and male dominance (Little, 2002). This is exercised in myriad ways including quite intentionally and blatantly, an example being the role historically of Masonic Lodges in rural (and urban) UK communities: an all-male setting where business deals and much else were done within a secret society. The role of police officers and other public officials in Freemasonry may have declined with moves towards gender equality, but they nonetheless remain in existence and are not without influence; as recently as 2009 the Labour Government was forced to scrap a law it had introduced a few years previously that made new magistrates and judges declare Masonic membership (Sparrow, 2009). In small communities such patriarchal institutions played an important role in helping businesses and tradesmen support one another and membership was almost obligatory. Anecdotal evidence from the author's own rural community would suggest that their significance has waned with the diversification of rural economies away from traditional occupations, as well as moved towards gender equality. However, many rural institutions such as Parish Councils and Community Councils are dominated by men, often older men with business backgrounds, and women who try and participate can find themselves talked over and marginalised. The case of Jackie Weaver and the Handforth Parish Council in rural Cheshire was a well-publicised case in point in 2021: a woman daring to stand up to a group of men whose dominance was said to be causing problems (Pidd, 2021).

Patriarchal institutions exclude women whose need to meet together and share experiences has been exercised through their own rural associations: the *Women's Institute* (WI) in England and Wales, and the *Women's Rural* in Scotland. These organisations traditionally provided social connectivity and the sharing of skills around food preparation and homemaking. This has always proudly been inclusive and regardless of social class and marital status. Hughes (1997) studied some WIs in rural England and found that most women involved celebrated their domesticity and regretted the assimilation of women into the rural workforce; she noted that the acceptance of a homemaking role for women was one also readily adopted by incomers from the city—presumably well-heeled-ones as the need to work, even on a part-time basis, was an economic necessity for most families. The erosion of farming as the mainstay of rural economies and the growth of tourism will have changed these perceptions in the past few decades (Shucksmith et al., 2021). In keeping with such societal changes, the WIs have moved beyond 'Jam and Jerusalem' and have been vocal nationally around domestic abuse and violence against women.

Government equality policies may have reached the point where the idea of masculinity is questioned in a modern society, but the idea continues to be drawn upon when useful to men in power. Campbell et al. (2006) comment on how past American presidential candidates tap into the idea of rural masculinity that they clearly view as significant to win elections: they pose in cowboy hats on horses or in rural settings reminiscent of the old Marlboro cigarette advertisements that evoke the spirit of the tough frontiersman. This has been discarded in recent times, but its imagery has been taken up by some of the right-wing militias that threaten US democracy. In the UK, a recent prime minister responded to pressure by almost daily photo-opportunities wearing a hard hat and a high-viz jacket in a subliminal appeal to his white male working-class constituency. Marketing and advertising also draw on gender stereotypes, especially for children where toys and clothing for boys and girls are hard to avoid. In an urban environment, there are more likely to be factors that moderate their influence, but in the countryside, this is less likely to be the case.

In some respects, the predominance of masculinities in a rural community will reflect place on the rural/urban continuum referred to in Chap. 1. Cities with their density are more likely to have heterogeneous populations, reflecting the influence of feminism and LGBTQ+ awareness/acceptance, as well as their sheer diversity of race, ethnicity and class diversity. Rural settings may have less overall diversity and therefore challenge, from within and without, to masculine stereotypes. In the UK, which is smaller and where even the more remote places are increasingly accessible, this is changing in a way that might be slower in the Canadian Northern landscapes described by Tranter (2005) when discussing this subject.

Assuming acceptance of the social construct explanation of masculinity, it has to be viewed not as a quaint throwback to a rural past, but as an anachronism that has to be confronted and consigned to history. Its dangerous manifestation is of interest to social workers because of its association with family and personal dysfunction, and it follows that the profession has a public duty to understand and offer private solutions to the problem as well as supporting and promoting public ones. The next section of this chapter will review the consequences of masculinity on the basis of the evidence.

Negative Manifestations of Rural Masculinity

The National Rural Crime Network (NRCN) in England, an organisation funded by Police Forces and Crime Commissioners and supported by other organisations, published a report in 2019 that scoped domestic abuse in rural areas, based on research and victim feedback. Its findings were surprising to those who considered rurality was associated with a relatively crime-free and safe environment. It listed ten key findings that are significant enough to be summarised here. However, it gave primacy, not unnaturally given the policing emphasis of the report, to the manifestations of domestic abuse in rural areas before referring briefly to the cause (enduring patriarchy) and then looking at how the issues might be tackled. They are presented here in the order they originally appear:

1. Domestic abuse in rural areas last an average of 25% longer than in urban areas because the victims (mostly women) have few acceptable alternatives to enduring abuse (e.g. availability of housing, schools, family support).
2. Policing response is inadequate due to a dearth of female officers and officers with specialised training. A police presence might be at some distance and a response is likely to be highly visible, factors that reduce requests for help.
3. The more rural the setting the higher the risk of harm—an inevitable consequence of the first two factors.
4. Coercive control (financial, isolation from wider family and friends) are well documented aspects of abuse that are increased by rural location, with some abusers moving to remote locations deliberately to facilitate control of victims.
5. Close-knit rural communities facilitate abuse unconsciously through their very strengths: confidentiality can be difficult to maintain so that victims might not be able to share their experiences with neighbours and friends. Perpetrators can use this to their advantage by 'recruiting' communities to their viewpoint.
6. Research evidences that this last factor is furthered by the patriarchal nature of rural communities. Men are held in esteem and generally hold positions of influence and authority, whether through their

work, their social lives or political involvement. They are typically heads of household, landlords, landowners, employers and often police officers. These combine to maintain an environment where coercive control is easier to maintain than within the anonymity of a city.

7. Support services (Women's Aid, Rape Crisis etc) are scarce, hard to access and less effective because of other rural factors. They are also visible where they do exist and are not seen to offer the security and confidentiality of their urban equivalents.

8. Rural services in general are on the decline: from general health services like GP surgeries (and the centralisation of more specialised ones like mental health services) to bus services, shops, libraries and other public venues. Reliance on car ownership aids coercive control by abusers. Investment in public services per head of population in rural areas is less than in urban localities, with far-reaching implications.

9. Service provision is fragmented and commissioned support agencies are often having to focus effort on chasing funding rather than actual support. Their services can also be overlapping due to the various funding stream mechanisms.

10. Because rural victims are half as likely to report their abuse, there is an absence of crucial data based on their experiences to support investment in change and better services. This cycle is self-perpetuating in an austerity-driven environment of fierce competition for resources.

(NRCN, 2019)

An interesting aspect of these findings is that concerning coercive control and how it is exercised in rural areas. The idea that perpetrators can 'recruit' communities to support them resonates with the author's own experiences from 23 years spent in remote rural social work practice in Scotland (Carrington & Scott 2008; DeKeseredy, 2021). This varies as with the example of the sexual abuser in the introduction to this chapter: someone considered as an outsider because they have moved into a community where indigenous inhabitants are still the majority, will in most cases find themselves rejected. I can think of an example within one such community of two convicted sex offenders. One was born within and embedded in the local farming community and well respected: many of his neighbours rallied round in support of him and turned on his accusers to the extent that they were forced out of the community. The other had moved in a number of years before and was quickly turned upon—'paedo' sprayed on the wall of his home, and his family left the community. This aspect of rural division seems to be a phenomenon reported in the UK but not in the extensive rural literature from North America and Australia, and forms part of the background to the 1992 Orkney Child Abuse Report (Clyde, 1992).

The notion that moving into a remote location might afford some space to exercise coercive control is certainly familiar to rural social workers on islands and in other remote places. Such motives are not always obvious, especially given present trends of migration from urban to rural communities which now predominates across all age bands except 17–20-year-olds (Gov.UK, 2021). This might involve a desire to engage in a lifestyle outside the mainstream, but the idea that this will not attract attention in a small and traditionally conservative community is usually misplaced. Gossip may not lead to referral to agencies who will start asking questions, but if this is triggered for any reason, a move away to another rural community to avoid further scrutiny often follows. Male domination and control may not seem obviously coercive in such cases, including where religious belief is at the root of family lifestyles arising from non-mainstream belief or culture. The author also came across families whose inward migration motive to avoid scrutiny involved unusual family relationships that although not technically involving contravention of incest laws were such that negative public judgement might arise were details known. Attempts to hide from public approbation might be characterised by identity changes that would not be easily recognised. Another ploy to avoid engagement with authorities is that of home-schooling of children, a right that is notoriously under-regulated according to a Guardian Newspaper report quoting official figures in England (Weale, 2020). As commented already, the idea that a remote location might be a place to hide is often, however, misplaced. Gossip finds its way to public figures with a duty of care—often the headteacher of the local school and scrutiny might follow (my partner and I, both social workers in the same remote rural location, found that useful gossip often passed us by, perhaps because of our positions, perhaps because people assumed we knew anyway!).

Homophobia is an enduring facet of rural life. Recent research by Hoffelmeyer (2021) into the experience of gay farmers in the USA confirms the continued prevalence of the 'family farming model' (i.e. heteronormativity—the notion that heterosexual relationships are both normal and preferred) as a means of maintaining rural life. This presents immediate problems for those who challenge the norm, but also suggests the possibility that by doing so they are opening new potentials for rural development. Rural masculine narratives are therefore accompanied by other mechanisms to support their endurance, heteronormativity and the idea of the traditional family being central. In an academic study of personal experience after being 'outed' as a lesbian after many years of successful teaching in an English rural primary school, Thompson-Lee found herself victim of a course of events that caused her to give up her post. This ended with the establishment protecting the heteronormative discourse through a refusal to challenge the views of a parent whose motivation was clearly bigoted. This involved acceptance of a view that gay people are a threat to children, an idea that was central to the now discarded Clause 28 (a UK wide enactment that outlawed the promotion of homosexuality), and in her case, evidence was manufactured to prove the point (Thompson-Lee, 2019). Recent research into the lives of gay men in rural England and Northern Ireland found that gay men, whose active sexuality was illegal within living memory (decriminalised in England and Wales in 1967), remain stigmatised in rural communities and that some personal sacrifice is necessary in order to enjoy the benefits of rural life (e.g. tranquillity and a more relaxed pace of life). McKearney (2020) found that the availability of support networks in the locality or workplace for LGBTQ+ people made a difference and that without such supports the legislative changes of the 2000s (such as the right to Civil Partnerships) made little difference to prejudice and bigotry. Such groups and activities made proud public appearance possible: an example being the annual Gay Pride marches in strictly religious Stornoway in Scotland's Western Isles that started in 2018. This suggests change is happening, albeit slowly. Little (2002) notes research discussing the presence of a gay manifestation of rural masculinity in films and media that is actually at odds with the real lives of rural gay men and makes life harder for them.

From a social work child protection perspective, Featherstone et al. (2018) identify from research the link between masculinity and domestic violence. They discuss the concept of 'hyper-masculinity' amongst vulnerable young men experiencing poverty and alienation:

> Such hyper-masculinity can be defined as acts of aggression, violence, risk taking, substance misuse, drinking large amounts of alcohol, and overt heterosexuality and homophobic language and behaviour.
> (Featherstone et al., 2018, p. 140)

Rural women also suffer a subordinate position in relation to rural employment. The cost and dearth of childcare render limited choices for mothers. Changes in recent decades in rural economies from farming and forestry to tourism have not changed the seasonal, low paid and precarious nature of work options (Shucksmith et al., 2021). This is another factor that mitigates against escaping domestic violence.

Featherstone et al. also suggest that, although under-researched, there seems to be no authoritative link between masculinity and ethnicity but that international findings rather point to a link with poverty and social exclusion. This is important when confronting popular conceptions that might linger in rural areas concerning some ethnic minorities, a consideration discussed in Chap. 5 of this book.

Sarah Nelson (2016) describes one causation of sexual abuse within families: the male perpetrator may have learned through example that macho-masculinity justifies violence and abuse, that the victim is responsible not the perpetrator. Victimhood on the part of the male who goes onto abuse denotes weakness and questions heterosexual norms. It must be emphasised that only a very small number of male victims of abuse go on to become abusers. However, it is the absence of masculine characteristics, and the cultural behavioural expectations that go with them, that prevents the very vast majority of women victims from becoming abusers. We can conclude that the role of masculinity in abuse within the family, including sexual abuse, physical abuse of children and violence against women partners, is highly significant. If this is the case, then the recognition of this dominant narrative in rural areas has to be identified and addressed in treatment programmes. Feminist assumptions that challenge masculinity are fundamental to most women's support services and therefore might encounter a potentially hostile or sceptical reception when based in a rural location.

So far consideration has been given to the role of rural men who become abusers because of a combination of causal factors associated with masculinity. The pressures of performing expected roles are one of these factors, another is the toll on the mental health of many rural men that is turned inwardly rather (or as well) as towards others. This has been researched extensively in Australia and the USA in relation to the farming community but less rigorously in the UK, although widely recognised as a matter of concern (Jones-Bitton et al., 2019; Hagen et al., 2019, 2021). In February 2021 the Farm Safety Foundation (UK) website reported 102 suicides recorded in 2019 in England and Wales (Yellow Wellies, 2021). A Norfolk-based charity 'YANA' (*You Are Not Alone*) provides information and support to UK farmers on mental health and suicide prevention. None of these mention masculinity as a causal factor, but the link has been made in Australia (Bryant & Garnham, 2015): their findings suggest that modern farming practice in a highly competitive capitalist environment has eroded the self-worth of farmers based on proud rugged masculine identity, and replaced it with one of failure-induced shame and suicidal potential.

We have already noted that in many rural localities masculinity is expressed through sport—often team physical contact games like rugby, where strength and male bonding has traditionally been celebrated. The association of masculinity with sporting activity is being eroded by the increasing involvement of women in the formerly male preserves of football, rugby and others. However, for adolescents and young men not interested in sport or lacking the physical characteristics required, a feeling of exclusion by peers can be experienced. This is especially the case when some schools set store by team sports. Non-heterosexual identity can also exclude, just as it does for adults as noted above. Most adolescent boys manage this through their own peer associations and activities, and the better educated will be motivated to move away to an urban environment for university. For those who do not have this choice and who are socially isolated, this can result in depression and mental illness.

Young men and adolescents who feel excluded from those around them who buy into the masculine norm can develop seriously deviant behaviour in a small number of cases. The shotgun incident mentioned at the head of this chapter is thankfully rare in the UK, but in the USA, where firearms are easily available, High School shootings are all too frequent, and certainly linked with 'toxic masculinity'. This is a term used by Haider (2016) to describe the motives of Muslim male extremists who engage in acts of individual terrorism that have the same roots in the framework of masculinity. Farr (2018) studied 31 US High School shootings that took place between 1997 and 2015, committed by boys or young men in both rural and urban locations, often ones where there were no general associations with poverty and social exclusion. She considers the role of 'failing masculinity' in the psychological profiles of all of the perpetrators: common were experiences of bullying and social isolation from classmates, rejection by potential girlfriends and anger at how peers and teachers undermined their attempts to display masculinity. These attempts might involve showing off weapons at school and including violent themes in their class work and presentations: anger and violence being perceived as desired masculine traits. All of the cohort studied displayed at least one of three personal troubles: psychiatric disorder, family dysfunction and situational volatility. The combination of such factors and the availability of firearms create these catastrophes, and Farr suggests programmes of early identification and treatment.

Although such events are less likely in the UK, the 1996 Dunblane shootings of Primary School children in a rural school setting suggest this is not an impossibility. Thomas Hamilton, the perpetrator, was a 43-year-old failed youth leader angry at his rejection for the role due to stories about his inappropriate behaviour with scout and youth groups he led in rural Stirlingshire. In the aftermath of the murders, public attention not surprisingly focused on firearm laws, and less was written about Hamilton's profile, but he does seem to have had some characteristics of failed masculinity: adoption by his mother's adopted parents, believing his mother was his sister until he was 22 and, in all probability, concealed homosexuality. His birth father had no real involvement in his life, and his grandfather seems not to have had a close relationship with him and left him to get his own way. Hamilton was regarded as different by his peers at school, fascinated by guns, and his life was about as distant from the lives of his eventual innocent victims as might be possible for someone who lived in relative social isolation just a few miles away (Collier, 1997).

Other less dramatic manifestations of failed masculinity which I have observed frequently from growing up both in a rural place and in rural social work practice are the relationships that develop between such excluded young men in their late teens and much younger girls in the 13–15-year-old age group. Such teenage girls typically have issues themselves that exclude them too from peer relationships with girls of their own age. This can become especially problematic if the relationship becomes a sexual one—an obvious concern to parents and agencies, including police and justice services if coming into their orbit. Understanding of the location of this issue within the context of masculinity, and whatever the underlying issues might be for the female involved, is important.

Social Work Interventions in the Rural Context

The last section raised numerous issues, some of which are beyond the remit of social work and, as with other social ills, lie within the responsibility of social policy makers. However, given the evidence of harm that they produce, a neutral attitude towards masculinity and its manifestations cannot be acceptable on the basis of tradition. The fundamental tasks of social work, embodied in the International Federation of Social Work ethical values statement, are to uphold human rights, challenge injustice, seek equality, challenge discrimination and unjust policies and practices (IFSW, 2018). There is therefore a strong basis for therapeutic interventions aimed at addressing masculinity. This section can only offer pointers and detail can be learned from the general literature cited on domestic violence, child abuse and sexual abuse. Education of children clearly plays a crucial role—if poor modelling is learned at home and then reinforced at school, it is little surprise that it is regarded as a norm. The role of schools, where working class children are educated, in reinforcing gender stereotypes was found in two studies in England relating to progression to physics A Level, where only 20% were female students

(Institute of Physics, 2012, 2013). A recent study across Scotland concluded that sexual harassment in schools is commonplace, although personal experience-based reporting varied regarding what was considered acceptable, and what was not (Sweeting et al., 2022). There is clearly an enduring issue here that should be of concern to educationalists.

Social work practice has often been criticised because of its focus, in child protection, on the mother (Scourfield, 2003; Featherstone, 2009; Maxwell et al., 2012). This is said to happen for many reasons: from the absence or unwillingness to engage of the father figure (the term is used in the sense here of a caring role rather than just a biological relationship) to traditional assumptions about gender roles (Maxwell et al., 2012). Traditional masculinity will lend to this and if not challenged properly can lead to ineffective interventions experienced punitively and oppressively by the mother; she may even be viewed as an accomplice because of her relationship with the father. Fathers are often labelled as either a 'risk' or a 'resource' through dichotomous thinking that fails to understand the complex mix of both in many situations (Maxwell et al., 2012, p. 167). The former often leads to their exclusion when, according to Featherstone, many mothers who are engaging with services want the fathers to be involved too (2009).

When fathers have been identified as the source of abuse directed towards any family member, the question of treatment becomes imperative, even if the matter is so serious that they might be permanently excluded from family life. This covers a very wide area of practice, from the voluntary request for help to resolve family relationship issues to serious physical harm (including sexual violence) to women or children. Programmes vary widely depending on the source of referral: a programme imposed by a Court or agreed to as a diversion from prosecution will normally have been the result of a recommendation depending on the aptitude and attitude of the individual perpetrator. These might be delivered through Probation Services (Justice Services in Scotland), and a quick google search indicates a number of third sector and private organisations delivering such programmes throughout the UK, including in prisons.

When interventions are less formalised, models vary. Feminist gender-based approaches have been criticised in working with domestic violence and abuse perpetrators for failing to recognise dynamics other than patriarchy, and that this is an important factor when looking at small 'communities' (Hilder & Freeman, 2016). However, in the case of geographically rural small communities in the UK, the argument here is that patriarchy plays such an important role that masculinity is very likely to feature in presentations as either 'successful', 'failed' or 'toxic', in situations where harm is suffered. It is likely therefore to be key to interventions, whether they take a cognitive/behavioural approach, or one that is motivational interview based (the latter, according to Featherstone, 2009, working well when resistance is encountered).

Tranter, writing from a rural (Canadian) perspective, offers a series of general guidelines for social workers who want to work with men (Tranter, 2005, pp. 112–116). These offer a useful guide and are worth summarising here:

1. *See gender as a central organising schema*—as most men will be conditioned to be blind about masculinity and its impact, it is unlikely to feature in their agenda for change. However this perspective will help throw light on the issues and expose barriers to change.
2. *Assess the degree of traditional/non-traditional views*—there are assessment tools that can help determine this, e.g. Eisler's Gender Role Conflict Scale, but it can be ascertained by asking simple questions on perceptions of the differences between men and women. This may help determine how embedded views are, and therefore the approaches required.
3. *Consider other more appropriate treatment modalities*—rather than trying to change the men to fit the method or approach, use knowledge gained about the depth of masculine attitude to determine the method. Men unused to therapy but familiar with education may gain more from a group learning course that they feel might equip them with new skills. Preparation is important.
4. *Recognise signs of discomfort and address them directly*—avoidance and detachment (and impatience) can be expected but can be tackled by reframing a subject that is causing discomfort.

5. *Don't go too deep too soon*—men can get left behind in couple counselling by a woman's willingness to engage with personal and emotional content from an early stage.
6. *Deconstruct masculinity, acknowledge masculine stereotypes and challenge them directly*—two skills involved here: that of asking the right questions that can begin to help an understanding of masculinity e.g. 'What kind of man do you think you are expected to be?' The second involves helping though humour and dialogue, the male to recognise and understand their own unconscious masculine defined behaviours in everyday life: e.g. closing down a son's tearful emotion.
7. *Recognise the difficulty that men have attempting to make change*—it is important to recognise efforts, however small and superficial they may seem at first, and accept that the change being asked for threatens long held security and is asking a great deal. This acknowledgement of progress can be important in keeping men on board.
8. *Explicit empathy and acknowledgement for their feelings of loss and grief*—loss and an inability to deal with it effectively are common amongst men and so need recognition and response.
9. *Provide a positive interpretation of their intentions*—masculinity must not be portrayed as all negative and something to overcome. Most men's failed attempts to sustain relationships and family life are well-intentioned and should be recognised as such: feeling misunderstood and mistrusted is a common experience and the worker should avoid contributing to this pattern. Efforts and intentions should be positively acknowledged but encouragement given to seeking the best means to achieve agreed goals.
10. *Insist on their ability to change*—insist that the man works hard to make change and break away from traditional thinking: it is not enough to simply curb violent behaviour without addressing the perspectives and beliefs that perpetuate it within relationships. This focus will ensure more meaningful progress and more lasting and deeper change.

Taking This Forward: Discussion and Conclusion

The digital age has, with some exceptions where internet coverage is patchy or non-existent, negated some of the differences between urban and rural. The rural teenager is as likely to encounter inappropriate online sharing of images and abuse as their urban counterpart, although the culture within which this is experienced might be different. As Jane Pye explores in her chapter in this book, these technologies can also be used to connect positively, particularly between isolated workers. The Orkney and Eilean Siar reports both highlighted just how complex sexual abuse cases can be in rural and remote areas of Britain (Clyde, 1992; SWIA, 2005). Both reports pointed to a need for attention to be given to the delivery of expertise in such locations, suggesting, without offering much detail, the creation of a national resource. This has been partially addressed since and rural issues are referred to in the latest national child protection guidance in Scotland (Scottish Government, 2021). It should be much more possible and meaningful to offer support with use of the online video mediums that are now commonly used as a result of the Covid-19 pandemic. Social workers dealing with children and families in the rural context may, in the absence of accessible specialist workers, be asking themselves if work with fathers and male perpetrators should fall on them. The answer is a profound yes, and it is here that the rural generalism discussed in Chap. 1 lends itself to creative solutions. The writer has experience of a rural team where a worker, supportive of structured interventions with young male perpetrators of sexual and domestic violence, undertook programmed work with individuals. This involved the supply of materials and some mentoring from specialised workers located an inaccessible distance away. Such support would be more readily available using digital communications.

Rurally located social workers tasked with children and family work, and those who support individuals with mental health issues, need to be attuned to the strong presence of patriarchally based masculine identities within their communities. Such knowledge should be embodied in everyday practice: this is not to characterise all men and boys as abusers, but to recognise how culture and tradition might further other factors that render this possibility. Such recognition should result in working styles and models that challenge patriarchy and masculinity at all levels. Finally this should not overlook that fact that forms of oppression, including manifestations of patriarchy, often exist within our own and partner organisations, and not just amongst those who are on the receiving end of our services.

References

Bryant, L., & Garnham, B. (2015). The Fallen Hero: Masculinity, Shame and Farmer Suicide in Australia. *Gender, Place and Culture, 22*(1), 67–82.

Campbell, H., Mayerfield Bell, M., & Finney, M. (2006). *Country Boys: Masculinity and Rural Life*. PSUP.

Carrington, K., & Scott, J. (2008). Masculinity, Rurality and Violence. *British Journal of Criminology, 48*, 641–646.

Clyde, L. (1992). *The Report of the Inquiry into the Removal of Children from Orkney in February 1991*. HMSO.

Collier, R. (1997). After Dunblane: Crime Corporeality and the (Hetero-) Sexing of the Bodies of Men. *Journal of the Law Society, 24*(2), 177–198.

Connell, R. W. (2005). *Masculinities* (2nd ed.). Polity Press.

DeKeseredy, W. (2015). New Directions in Feminist Understandings of Rural Crime. *Journal of Rural Studies, 39*, 180–187.

DeKeseredy, W. (2021). Male to Female Sexual Violence in Rural Communities – A Sociological Review. *Dignity – A Journal of Exploitation and Violence, 6*(2), 1–19.

Farm Safety Organisation (2021, February). *Suicide – The Last Stigma of Mental Health*. Accessed February 2022, from https://www.yellowwellies.org/suicide-the-last-stigma-of-mental-health/

FarmingUK. (2021a, September 3). *New Scheme Aims to Boost Women in Scottish Agriculture*. Accessed February 2022, from https://www.farminguk.com/news/new-scheme-aims-to-boost-women-in-scottish-agriculture_58883.html

FarmingUK. (2021b, October 19) *Record Number of Women Studying Agriculture at University*. Accessed February 2022, from https://www.farminguk.com/news/record-number-of-women-studying-agriculture-at-university_59160.html

Farr, K. (2018). Adolescent Rampage School Shootings: Responses to Failed Masculinity Performances by Already Troubled Boys. *Gender Issues, 35*, 73–97.

Featherstone, B. (2009). *Contemporary Fathering: Theory, Policy and Practice.* Policy Press.

Featherstone, B., Gupta, A., Morris, K., & White, S. (2018). *Child Protection – A Social Model.* Policy Press.

Ford, C. (2020). *Boys Will Be Boys – Power, Patriarchy and Toxic Masculinity.* Oneworld.

Gov.UK. (2021). *Official Statistics – Rural Population and Migration Updated to October 2021.* Accessed February 2022, from https://www.gov.uk/government/statistics/rural-population-and-migration/rural-population-and-migration#

Hagen, B., Albright, A., Sargeant, J., Winder, C., Harper, S., O'Sullivan, T., & Jones-Bitton, A. (2019). Research Trends in Farmers' Mental Health – A Scoping Review of Mental Health Outcomes and Interventions Among Farming Populations Worldwide. *PLoS One Journal, 10*, 1–20.

Hagen, B., Sawatzky, A., Harper, S., O'Sullivan, T., & Jones-Bitton, A. (2021). What Impacts Perceived Stress Among Canadian Farmers – A Mixed Methods Analysis. *International Journal of Environmental Research and Public Health, 18*, 1–14.

Haider, S. (2016). The Shooting in Orlando, Terrorism or Toxic Masculinity (or Both?). *Men and Masculinities, 19*(5), 556–565.

Hilder, S., & Freeman, C. (2016). Working with Perpetrators of Domestic Violence, Chapter 13. In S. Hilder & V. Bettinson (Eds.), *Domestic Violence: Interdisciplinary Perspectives on Protection, Prevention and Intervention.* Palgrave Macmillan.

Hoffelmeyer, M. (2021). 'Out' on the Farm: Queer Farmers Maneuvering Heterosexism and Visibility. *Rural Sociology, 86*(4), 752–776.

hooks, b. (2004). *The Will to Change – Men, Masculinity and Love.* New York.

Hughes, A. (1997). Rurality and Cultures of Womanhood – Domestic Identities and Moral Order in Village Life. In P. Cloke & J. Little (Eds.), *Contested Countryside Cultures.* Routledge.

IFSW (International Federation of Social Work). (2018). *Statement of Ethical Principles.* Accessed February 2021, from https://www.ifsw.org/global-social-work-statement-of-ethical-principles/

Institute of Physics. (2012). *Its Different for Girls – The Influence of Schools.* Accessed December 2022, from https://www.iop.org/sites/default/files/2019-02/different-for-girls.pdf

Institute of Physics. (2013). *Closing Doors – Exploring Gender and Subject Choice in Schools*. Accessed December 2022, from https://www.iop.org/sites/default/files/2019-03/closing-doors.pdf

Jones-Bitton, A., Hagen, B., Fleming, S., & Hoy, S. (2019). Farmer Burnout in Canada. *International Journal of Environmental Research and Public Health, 16*, 1–15.

Little, J. (2002). Rural Geography: Rural Render Identity and the Performance of Masculinity and Femininity in the Countryside. *Progress in Human Geography, 26*(5), 665–670.

Little, J. (2017). *Gender and Rural Geographies – Identity, Sexuality and Power in the Countryside*. Routledge.

Local Government Association. (2018). *An Inclusive Fire Service: Recruitment and Inclusion*. Accessed February 2022, from https://www.local.gov.uk/sites/default/files/documents/10.19%20-%2he%20Twenty-first%20Century%20Fire%20Service_05.pdf

Maxwell, N., Scourfield, J., Featherstone, B., Holland, S., & Tolman, R. (2012). Engaging Fathers in Child Welfare Services: A Narrative Review of Recent Research Evidence. *Child and Family Social Work, 17*, 160–169.

McKearney, A. (2020). Changing Contexts: From Criminal to Citizen. *Journal of Organisational Change Management, 33*(3), 515–526.

Nelson, S. (2016). *Tackling Child Sexual Abuse*. Policy Press.

NRCN (National Rural Crime Network). (2019). *Captive and Controlled – Domestic Abuse in Rural Areas*. Accessed February 2022, from https://www.nationalruralcrimenetwork.net/news/captivecontrolled/

Pidd, H. (2021, February 5). Good on Her: How Jackie Weaver Became an Internet Star. *Guardian Newspaper*. Accessed February 2021, from https://www.theguardian.com/uk-news/2021/feb/05/handforth-parish-council-jackie-weaver-internet-star

Scottish Government. (2021). *National Guidance for Child Protection in Scotland 2021*. Accessed February 2022, from https://www.gov.scot/publications/national-guidance-child-protection-scotland-2021/

Scourfield, J. (2003). *Gender and Child Protection*. Palgrave.

Shannon, L., Nash, S., & Jackson, A. (2016). Examining Intimate Partner Violence and Health Factors Among Rural Pregnant Appalachian Women. *Journal of Interpersonal Violence, 31*(15), 2622–2640.

Shucksmith, M., Chapman, P, Glass, J, & Atterton, J. (2021). *Understanding Financial Hardship and Vulnerability in Rural Areas*. Accessed February 2022, from https://www.rurallives.co.uk/rural-lives-final-report.html

Sparrow, A. (2009, November 5). Jack Straw Scraps Rule Saying Judges Must Declare If They Are Masons. *Guardian Newspaper.* Accessed February 2022, from https://www.theguardian.com/politics/blog/2009/nov/05/jack-straw-judges-masons

Sweeting, H., Blake, C., Riddell, J., Barrett, S., & Mitchell, K.R. (2022). Sexual Harassment in Secondary School: Prevalence and Ambiguities. A Mixed Methods Study in Scottish Schools. *PLoS One, 17*(2). Accessed February 2022, from https://journals.plos.org/plosone/article?id=10.1371/journal.pone.0262248

SWIA (Social Work Inspection Agency). (2005). *An Inspection into the Care and Protection of Children in Eilean Siar.* Edinburgh.

Thompson-Lee, C. (2019). *Heteronormativity in a Rural School Community – An Autoethnography Rotterdam.* Sense Publishers.

Tranter, D. (2005). Breaking the Connection Between Traditional Masculinity and Violence. In *Violence in the Family: Social Work Readings and Research from Northern and Rural Canada.* CPSI.

Weale, S. (2020, February 24). Children Schooled at Home Up 13% Despite Fears Over Lack of Regulation. *Guardian Newspaper.* Accessed February 2022, from https://www.theguardian.com/education/2020/feb/24/children-schooled-at-home-up-13-despite-fears-over-lack-of-regulation

10

'A Life Worth Living: All My Days'— Rural Social Work with Older People

Becky Squires

Introduction

In rural areas of the United Kingdom (UK), the number and proportion of older people with care and support needs are increasing (ONS, 2021a, b; Centre for Ageing Better, 2022). Despite the significance and diversity of this population, there is a significant lacuna—a gap—in the literature about social work practice with rural dwelling older people. In this chapter I will critically examine the roots and implications of this absence. I will argue the urgent need for social work practice which is founded on the ethics of human rights and social justice—and challenges social constructions of older age that are discriminatory and homogenising (Tanner & Harris, 2008; Beresford, 2022), and notions of the countryside where older and disabled people are amongst the 'hidden others' (Cloke & Little, 1997). This chapter makes a contribution towards addressing this gap by starting a conversation about the critical role that social workers

B. Squires (✉)
Cumbria, UK
e-mail: becky.squires@westmorlandandfurness.gov.uk

© The Author(s), under exclusive license to Springer Nature Switzerland AG 2024
C. Turbett, J. Pye (eds.), *Rural Social Work in the UK*, Rethinking Rural,
https://doi.org/10.1007/978-3-031-52440-0_10

have in allyship alongside older people (Gibson, 2014); bringing a 'specialist knowledge combined with a relationship that is 'on their side" (Manthorpe et al., 2008a, b, p. 1133). Despite the paucity of older people's voices within user-led research (Manthorpe et al., 2008a, b), the available studies demonstrate older people's lived experience of marginalisation, and explicit asks of social workers that are congruent with such an approach (Stevenson & Age Concern, 1989; Joseph Rowntree Foundation and Older People's Steering Group, 2004; King & Farmer, 2009; Hoban et al., 2013; Age UK, 2021).

This chapter explores the particular challenges and opportunities that rural contexts present for rights-based and relational social work alongside older people. It proposes the development of a practice framework, grounded in the social model of disability (Oliver, 1990, 2013). This provides an ethical foundation for social work with older people who come into contact with social workers as a result of illness or impairment, whether life-long or acquired through ageing processes. In locating the source of disability squarely with society's response to impairment, rather than individualised pathology, this approach provides a framework for intersectional and inclusive social work across the life course (Oldman, 2002; Kattari et al., 2017).

In rural areas, social work is characterised by particular applications of skills, relational practice and respectful appreciation of each unique community (Locke & Winship, 2005; Pugh & Cheers, 2010). Creative, generalist approaches are required, 'founded on the reality of isolation and remoteness' (Turbett, 2010, p. 24), that often characterises rural communities. Within rural social work literature, there is an increasingly critical need for professional curiosity (Burton & Revell, 2018) about how social workers can apply their skills and 'practice wisdom' (Beresford, 2022, p. 168) when working alongside disabled older people.

Social work must be able to respond positively to the challenge that, 'Growing old in rural communities is diverse, different and changing' (Manthorpe et al., 2008a, b, p. 466). A critical understanding of the myriad ways in which ageism (Bytheway, 1995) and other intersecting oppressions (Barnard, 2021) affect the lives of older people, will underpin rights-based social work, and support development of the relational practice that is valued in social workers (Beresford et al., 2011; Black,

2022). Social work with older people is not simply a matter of responding to changing need; it is a matter of social justice (The College of Social Work, 2015).

Rural Social Work

Around the world, the vast majority of people with disabilities live in rural rather than urban locations (World Health Organisation and World Bank, 2011). The International Federation of Social Workers highlights the critical need for understanding 'The various social systems that people are embedded in and the natural, geographic environment, which has a profound influence on the lives of people' (IFSW, 2014).

Defining what constitutes a rural place however is a contested area (Cloke & Little, 1997; Pugh & Cheers 2010). Attempts to do so encounter the 'slipperiness' of an all-encompassing definition (Pugh, 2003, p. 70). Seeking to move beyond attempts to define rural, Martinez-Brawley (2000) has instead suggested a more inclusive concept of 'small communities' to describe the places in which rural social workers work. Application of statistical aggregation using basic rural/urban markers to determine rural funding has significant impacts for older people in rural communities (Manthorpe et al., 2008a, b). Such an approach misses the nuances, social context, and experience of rural life (Pugh & Cheers, 2010), and diverts energy away from developing a more critical understanding of what rural, and rural social work, might mean (Ginsberg, 1998).

Attempts to establish definitive differences between urban and rural settings perpetuate the notion that essential elements of 'rurality' are to be found in all rural communities. Furthermore, reductionist approaches such as these also serve to exclude and marginalise diversity within communities (Pugh & Cheers, 2010). Ideas about rurality are frequently laden with unconscious assumptions; 'Conventional representations and definitions of rural life may portray the countryside as if it were an integrated and organic entity in which conflict and diversity is absent or underplayed' (Pugh, 2003, p. 69). Despite rural scholarship that has contested stereotypes and highlighted the diversity of rural identity (Cloke et al., 1994; Cloke & Little, 1997), disabled people have remained largely hidden, and absent from the debate (Morgan, 2017). Cloke and Little (1997) suggest that much academic literature on rurality has revealed less about what we 'know', and rather more about what we have chosen to study. Highlighting the complexity and variety of rural experience, Fluharty (2002) has commented, 'If you've seen one rural community, you've seen…one rural community' (in Pugh & Cheers, 2010, p. vii).

What emerges from the pockets of writing on the rural that do give voice to disabled and older people is not a discourse concerned with how to define rurality. Rural lived experience has meanings that are unique and multi-dimensional. Rural community is not an incidental backdrop to people's lives, but integral to their rich and contextual perceptions of identity and place (King & Farmer, 2009; Soldatic & Johnson, 2017). Cheers (1998) suggests that this indivisibility of place from people's experience is mirrored in the dynamics of rural social work; 'Social care practice is not merely influenced by the rural context—practice and practitioners are integral parts of that context' (p. 220).

Lohmann and Lohmann suggest that 'Good rural social work practice is, first and foremost, good social work practice' (2005, p. 315). In doing so, they highlight that it is not a different set of values, skills and knowledge that the rural social worker will require; rather, that the rural context shapes and supports the nature of social work practice in small communities (Pugh, 2000; Pugh & Cheers, 2010; Turbett, 2010). The distinct themes within the literature on rural social work practice (Locke & Winship, 2005) reflect the reality of practice in rural areas that are located significant distances from urban centres of health and social care provision, whether statutory, charitable or voluntary organisations (Turbett, 2010). Rather than examining whether rural social work *is* different to urban practice, Pugh and Cheers (2010) suggest that a more meaningful discourse stems from examining how it *should* be different, in acknowledgement and response to the rural context.

Despite the aspirations of the Care Act (2014) on personalised support, rights and wellbeing long campaigned for by disability rights organisations, the pervasiveness of a managerialist culture (Trevithick, 2014) and market-based neoliberalism (Parton, 2014) continue to compromise the delivery of more creative, relational social work approaches (Ruch et al., 2018). Rural literature, however, suggests that features of the social context in which people live have particular and profound impacts upon their lives and the challenges they experience (Age UK, 2021; Centre for Ageing Better, 2022). Neglecting the social context of social work practice (Pugh, 2009) therefore has critical implications for people living in rural communities, where these elements are inextricably linked (Turbett, 2010, Pugh & Cheers, 2010). As Martinez-Brawley suggests: 'The practice of social work has always required unique responses because individuals live under unique, local conditions and communities are all different' (2003, p. 293).

Social workers in rural areas have frequently developed their approaches through experience (Pugh & Cheers 2010), and through the necessity of having the knowledge and skills to be able to ensure parity and access to services for everyone they work alongside; 'a bit of everything' (Ginsberg, 1998, p. 9). Allowing awareness of the rural and social context to saturate social work practice requires 'integrative thinking' (Martinez-Brawley, 2003), through which social workers will consciously consider the various cultural, historical and local perspectives relevant to the area in which they work. Cheers et al. (2005) develop this concept to suggest that rural social workers occupy a number of 'practice domains' that influence the approaches they take. Awareness of these intersecting domains will assist social workers in identifying where areas of conflict or ethical stress arise, for example between individual desired outcomes and practical possibilities, or statutory duty and community concerns (Fenton, 2016). When identifying the most appropriate form of practice intervention for a particular issue, rural social workers will consider their statutory responsibilities; the skills and resources available; analysis of the issue within its context; the wishes of the person(s) involved; the potential risks and outcomes (Pugh & Cheers, 2010). Decisions should be cognisant of Fook's assertion that situational analysis and purposeful intention, matter more than the chosen method of intervention (Fook, 1993).

The available literature on rural living (for example, Cloke et al., 1994; Pugh, 2000; Turbett, 2010; Age UK, 2021) acknowledges the reality for many rural dwelling people of a paucity in specialised or sufficient service provision. However, this apparent downside is only one—and arguably, an urban-centric—aspect of the multi-faceted living experience of people in rural communities. Narrative accounts from older and disabled people

(Hinck, 2004; King & Farmer, 2009; Soldatic & Johnson, 2017) emphasise the powerful meaning that rural life has within identities of self and of place, so that for example, conventional notions of loneliness are challenged by the profound and comforting sense of attachment and connection to home (Caldwell, 2017). One of the 'oldest-old' women interviewed about living alone in rural and remote areas said, 'Home is a precious place to be'; another said, 'I never, never feel lonely' (Hinck, 2004, p. 784).

Social work always takes place in both social contexts and physical spaces, and social workers need to be able to recognise these complexities and adapt their practice and approach accordingly (British Association of Social Workers, 2018, 2021). For social workers, there is evidence that the challenge of working in areas with different social care structures can bring opportunities for more creative, autonomous and innovative practice (see for example, Samuel, 2022: https://www.communitycare.co.uk/2022/05/16/solutions-cant-be-scripted-here-you-have-to-be-creative/) and indeed is frequently cited as one of the main attractions and benefits to rural practice (Ginsberg, 1998; Lonne, 2002). The ability to work creatively, flexibly and to improvise solutions out of necessity is well regarded in rural communities (Collier, 1984; Locke & Winship, 2005), and a sense of belonging and social integration within the community is greatly valued by many social workers (Zapf, 1985).

Practice in rural areas requires organisational structures that reflect and are supportive of rural social work delivery (Turbett, 2010). Professional connection with other social workers beyond the immediate locality is also increasingly possible through technology (Brownlee et al., 2009) opening up different opportunities for supervision, peer support and reflection (see for example, Morrison, 1988; Wonnacott, 2014) and Chap. 7 in this volume.

Gaps in the rural social work literature remain significant for older disabled people, however, despite research suggesting that place has 'enormous importance in the lives of older people.....reflected not only in length of residence and familiarity with the area, although that was part of it; it also related to the extent to which people's sense of identity was rooted in the physical and social landscape they inhabited' (Joseph Rowntree Foundation, 2004, p. 65).

Practice experience with older people in rural areas indicates a real need and potential for developing greater understanding of rural social work approaches (Locke & Winship, 2005). However, the absence of older people's voices in social work literature, particularly within rural perspectives remains significant—older people are amongst those rural dwellers whose existence and needs are invisible and neglected (Pugh & Cheers, 2010). These are the missing pieces of patchwork that are essential for co-creating the participatory social work that people value (Beresford, 2022).

Older People

Defining rural is a contested area, and understanding what it means to be older, or old, is similarly problematic (Tanner & Harris, 2008). Many definitions take an objective approach and locate older age with either a chronological starting point such as age 60 years (see, for example, Age UK, 2021), or in relation to retirement from paid employment and the age-based qualification for the State Pension (see, for example, Office for National Statistics, 2021a, b). Within the UK, older people of State Pension age may make up over a quarter of resident populations in rural areas (ONS, 2021a, b), with an increasing number living with disabilities (ONS, 2020).

Objective, numerically based approaches such as these however mask the reality that people in particular ethnic and socio-economic groups and learning disabled people experience poorer health and an earlier onset of physical ageing (Policy Research Institute on Ageing and Ethnicity, 2004; Centre for Ageing Better, 2022). Inequalities that are experienced earlier on in life, will widen, deepen and significantly impact not only the biological changes that accompany ageing, but lived experience, mental health, and wellbeing (BASW, 2018; Milne, 2020). The worldwide Coronavirus pandemic that began in late 2019 deepened many of the inequalities faced by older people in the UK, underlining the need to improve the experience of ageing for many older people (Centre for Ageing Better, 2022). Life course trajectories for people as they age are profoundly shaped not only by individual experience and place, but also by other global events such as climate change, austerity and conflict (World Health Organisation, 2021a, b).

Taking a different, more subjective approach to understanding older age involves curiosity and reflection about whether we, or the person we are working with, see themselves as older (Bytheway, 1995; Tanner & Harris, 2008). Dominelli (2002) highlights the importance of understanding that identities including older age are fluid, and subject to changing perception and negotiation over time. Within the literature on how older people define themselves there is a rich diversity and heterogeneity, described by Phillips et al. as a 'collage of circumstances and experience' (2006, p. 33). Older people attach limited credence to the notion of *being old*, to the point where even people of very advanced chronological age do not consider themselves to *be old* (Thompson et al., 1990). A report published by Age Concern, a UK based independent charity, entitled 'The Way We Are: Older People Talk About Themselves' included a quote from an older person responding to the researcher's questions:

> You ask me what old people need, they need the same as everybody else. They want to feel wanted. They want to feel when they wake up in the morning that it's going to matter to someone that they live another day. Nothing about being old that makes us special. I'm still the same person I always was (Age Concern England, 1980, in Stevenson & Age Concern, 1989).

This quote is itself decades old and an anti-ageist approach should make its message no less relevant (Bytheway, 1995). Indeed, the same messages are echoed consistently throughout the literature following it. Many older people attach much greater importance to having a sense of wellbeing through purposeful activities, social connectedness, and everyday routines in their lives, regardless of their biological age (Langan et al., 1996; Gabriel & Bowling, 2004; Joseph Rowntree Foundation, 2004; Steptoe & Fancourt, 2019). In the Shaping Our Age project on improving older people's wellbeing (Hoban et al., 2013) which crucially involved older people from the four nations of the UK in co-producing the outcomes, the most significant factor was found to be a sense of belonging and connection with family, friends and the wider community, regardless of age. Older people described the positive benefits of belonging and feeling valued, of not being 'done to' but being able to reciprocate within relationships. The significance of these findings is not that older age needs to be understood differently in terms of wellbeing but that the opposite is true. The key indicators for wellbeing (see for example, Mind, 2020) apply across the life course. 'Old age is not about 'them'; it is about all of us' (Blood, 2013).

Ageism means stereotyping and discrimination against people based on their age (Bytheway, 1995). Despite being unlawful in the UK under the Equality Act 2010, it manifests nevertheless through socio-economic structures, personal interactions, social policy and the diverse experiences of older people (Hughes, 1995). A predominantly negative social construction of older age:

> Confers a loss of status and a devalued identity on older people. It has consequences in terms of older people's self-perception, how they are perceived by others, their exclusion from some social activities and relationships and the approaches taken to policy and practice in health and social care services (Tanner & Harris, 2008, p. 13).

Bytheway (1995) argues that 'ageism generates and reinforces a fear and denigration of the ageing process, and stereotyping presumptions regarding competence and the need for protection' (p. 14). Ageism intersects with other forms of discrimination such as disablism, racism, transphobia, homophobia and sexism (Monahan et al., 2020) and is a significant contributory factor to poorer physical and mental health, as well as the quality of life of older people (World Health Organisation, 2021a, b). The WHO also points to the financial impact that ageism has on societies; suggesting that this runs to billions every year (World Health Organisation, 2021a, b). During the Coronavirus pandemic, Fraser et al. (2020) describe the dominant narrative around older people as misleading and undervaluing. Older people were not afforded the same health response and access to hospital treatment as younger people despite being overwhelmingly more affected (Amnesty International, 2020).

Social workers working with older people have a significant role to play in highlighting and challenging ageist attitudes and inequalities

(Meisner, 2021; British Association of Social Workers, 2018, 2021). An intersectional approach to the unique experience of differing forms of power and discrimination provides a robust foundation for anti-oppressive practice (Simpson, 2009; Mattsson, 2014). Barnard (2021) suggests that 'Because intersectionality eschews homogenising older adults, it forces social workers to engage in critical conversations to identify considerations for innovative approaches for interventions that can capture the heterogeneity within diverse groups of older adults' (p. 86). Intersectional understanding also supports social work practice with older people who have dementia, a progressive condition affecting thinking, planning and memory abilities in a variety of ways (World Health Organisation, 2021a, b). The impact of dementia on a person's ability to undertake daily living tasks and make informed decisions, as well as on their relationships and wellbeing, poses significant risks of marginalisation and discrimination (Innes & Manthorpe, 2012) which will intersect with individual experience of other forms of oppression manifest throughout their life course (Milne, 2020). Thomas and Milligan (2017) suggest that the social model of disability has a positive contribution to make in understanding and challenging the connections between discrimination, ageing and dementia.

In the UK, the proportion of older people relative to people of 'working age', in itself an ageist social construct (Bytheway, 1995) is increasing, and the average age and proportion of older people in rural areas is higher than in urban areas (Office for National Statistics, 2021a, b). There are a number of factors that combine to account for these changing demographics. Better healthcare has resulted in people—in general—living for longer, though inequality exists within groups including learning disabled adults, who have also been disproportionately affected by the Covid-19 pandemic (Mencap, 2021). For some people, internal migration from urban to rural areas, particularly related to retirement patterns, has also increased (Social Exclusion Task Force, 2009).

The number of people living into old and very old age, often used to describe people aged 85 and over, has not been portrayed as cause for celebration but instead significantly problematised. Media accounts describe an 'apocalyptic demography' that contrasts starkly with positive and optimistic portrayals of increasing younger age populations (Fealy et al., 2011). Ray et al (2007, p. 76) document a stigmatising ageism throughout the history of social care; including a Department of Health and Social Security discussion document from 1979, which contained the line 'The rise in the elderly population puts a strain on all our pockets'.

Beresford et al (2011) argue that the only adult social care issue to make national headlines is the funding of social care; specifically, how much it costs to provide care for older people and the implications for their relatives' inheritance. In rural areas, the additional costs associated with geography and sparse populations—the critical mass approach—may significantly disadvantage older people in receipt of social care (Smith & Horner, 2009). The option of receiving support through a direct payment is not always consistently made available, despite research suggesting that personalised and culturally appropriate support may offer considerable benefits to older people (Joseph Rowntree Foundation, 2004). Manthorpe and Stevens (2010) caution that care and further critical examination are required to ensure that older people in rural areas are able to enjoy access to the choice and control of a direct payment equitable with their counterparts in more urban areas.

Older people's individual and collective voices are rarely heard (Joseph Rowntree Foundation and Older People's Steering Group, 2004), and when it comes to developing services that have been 'rural-proofed' (The Countryside Agency, 2002), 'older people in rural areas are invisible, or at best, peripheral to policy development in England' (Milne et al, 2007, p. 484). Older people who represent the majority of adult social care service users, are also a hidden proportion of those self-funding their care and support needs (ONS, 2020). They are more likely to be 'signposted' away from Local Authority support (NIHR, 2014) and to pay up to 41% more in care home fees (ONS, 2021a, b). Standardised eligibility and commissioning arrangements commonly disregard the unique complexities and needs of individual lives in rural areas (Pugh, 2000). For rural dwelling older people, the lack of local care home availability may mean they have no choice but to move away not just from their own home but their community and social relationships. The growth in technology that has the power to sustain social connection has for many older people instead been a source of exclusion (ONS, 2019; TLAP, 2020). Beresford (2005) highlights the use of 'telecare' as a way to reduce more costly human services, despite consistent messages within the literature reaffirming the value that older people place on inter-dependence and social contact.

Tanner and Harris (2008) suggest that the 'essentialising' of older people lies at the heart of ageist attitudes and practices (p. 17). Reducing people to somehow all essentially the same—old—results in the loss of personal identity, narrative and voice; simply too many people to count (Harris, 2003). Such approaches frame notions of ageing through a singular normative lens which disregards diversity of experience (Westwood, 2019). Similarly, the Centre for Ageing Better (2017) highlights the under representation within research with older people who are gay, lesbian, bisexual and transgender; and with older people from Black, Asian and other minoritised backgrounds. Age UK notes in its report into 'Ageing in Rural and Coastal Communities' (2021) that 'the challenge to avoid a 'numbers game' in which smaller communities end up hidden and marginalised'; critical perspectives that pay deliberate attention to how people understand the places in which they live will instead offer more effective and personalised responses.

Phillips et al (2006) challenge social workers to practice positively and inclusively with diverse older communities, to deliberately rebut the myth that ageing is an inevitable period of decline. Social work practice has a role in challenging policy and decisions that are based on white, heteronormative and cisgender norms (BASW, 2018; Dunk-West & Hafford-Letchfield, 2018). The assertion by social psychologists Daatland and Biggs (2006) that an understanding of contemporary ageing can only be realised through recognising diversity, remains fundamental to how we approach and shape social work practice. The lives and life experiences of older people living in rural areas of the UK and beyond are varied, rich and diverse. As Pugh (2000) suggests, 'there is no simple picture of life in the British countryside; and complexity and variation are as evident in rural lives as in urban ones' (p. 50).

Social Work Practice with Older People in Rural Communities

Working alongside disabled older people is much of what rural social workers do. The available literature offers only partial theoretical approaches to rural social work with older people, within rural scholarship (Cloke & Little, 1997; Cloke et al., 1994; Soldatic & Johnson, 2017); rural social work practice (Martinez-Brawley, 1986; Ginsberg, 1998; Pugh & Cheers, 2010) and aspects of critical gerontology (Torres & Donnelly, 2022). More broadly, catastrophising media narratives about disabled older people's care needs (Fealy et al., 2011), and the challenges, financial cost and obstacles to providing social care in rural areas (SCIE, 2007; Rural England, 2017), dominate the debate.

Here, I propose that rural social work with older people living with physical and mental impairments, either arising or continuing into older age, requires critical synthesis of these different strands. Social work practice must have at its heart an embodied commitment to human rights and social justice for all people (International Federation of Social Workers, 2014; BASW, 2018). Providing a foundation for rights-based approaches to supporting older people, the social model of disability (Oliver, 1990, 2013) reframes the problematisation of older age, and provides for robust challenge and allyship against ageist and ableist discrimination (Oldman, 2002).

Social work with older people in rural communities provides opportunities for creative and relational practice which respect the person's social context and their impairments as intrinsic elements of their sense of self. Critically for rural social workers, being present in communities provides the opportunity for early intervention upstream of emerging issues, to be alongside people in a preventative and supportive role (Smale et al., 2000). Together with the creative, problem-solving approach of generalism (Collier, 1984), upstream practice is a necessary and distinguishing element of rural social work that can make best use of limited resources (Lipsky, 1980). Based on the development of an understanding and supportive relationship, social work practised in this way minimises the potential for disempowerment and instead offers opportunities for encounters that are life-enhancing (Ruch et al., 2018).

Thinking Differently About Ageing

> Disability is now regarded in policy circles as not simply a medical issue but also a human rights concern. A major catalyst for this development has been the social model emphasis on the material and structural causes of disabled people's disadvantages (Barnes, 2019, p. 26).

The social model of disability and its wider articulation and application by the disabled people's movement and their allies, makes a distinction between impairment and disability, and makes clear the disabling impact of society upon people with impairments (Oldman, 2002). Although many commonalities exist across experience and populations, social work education and ongoing professional development typically exclude older people from examination of disability (Kattari et al., 2017). Oldman (2002) suggests that the social model not only challenges 'tired and discredited' (p. 804) social policy towards older people, but also provides a framework for their solidarity and collective action against ageist discrimination.

Morgan (2012) describes the social model of disability as a threshold concept—one that moves us into a new place of understanding—for many social work students who enter their education with a desire to 'help'. Adopting social model principles may require a radical shift in reframing notions of power and empowerment as they are experienced and conceptualised by disabled people. Despite the facts surrounding the likelihood and diverse nature of impairment that people experience as they age (World Health Organisation, 2021a, b; Office for National Statistics, 2019), there has been limited research into how the social model of disability provides a framework for understanding older age (Oldman, 2002). Work on exploring the social model of disability in relation to people with dementia is emerging (Thomas & Milligan, 2017; Cahill, 2022) and has the potential to fundamentally challenge generally accepted societal responses and language around dementia (Shakespeare, 2006). Despite the principles of person-centred care (Kitwood, 1997) having been widely adopted by organisations that support people living with dementia (Manthorpe & Samsi, 2016), accounts of living with dementia confirm that barriers and challenges created by well-meaning professionals still remain (see for example, Mitchell, 2022).

Social workers must maintain a critical awareness and ability to challenge stigma and the impact of structural inequalities on individuals (British Association of Social Workers, 2018). Kattari et al. (2017) highlight many similarities between discrimination on the basis of disability and age: 'Like disability, aging is seen as a problem, a negative, depressing, and dreaded process that must be fought to prevent or be fixed' (p. 871). Both arise from ableist perspectives which posit a particular version of the body as whole and fully human. Bodies that are older and/or disabled are therefore projected as a diminished version of the ideal (Campbell, 2001). Both forms of discrimination exist through the language and behaviours of paternalism that exist to maintain unequal power relations and a superior moral authority (Jackman, 1994). A critical awareness of paternalism will enable social workers working with older people to challenge assumptions about the agency and autonomy of older people termed by Townsend as the 'structured dependency' created around older people (Townsend, 2022). As King and Farmer (2009) comment, 'Older people and their local service providers co-construct a paternalistic context where service providers are regarded as the experts in decision-making. Service providers' emphasis on efficiency is perceived to erode the personal contact associated with valuing older people; therefore, confidence as an older person may be eroded' (p. 10).

Paternalism also shapes the ways in which the concept of risk is applied to older people as a heterogenous group. Professionals asked to describe risk focused on physical harm sustained through falls; people using services however, talked about the risk of losing their independence (Faulkner, 2012). An anti-ageist approach will positively seek out an understanding of the strengths and resilience of older people in managing crises (Blood, 2016), and actively challenge professional preoccupation with risk avoidance (Fenton, 2016).

In Practice:

An older person has lived alone and independently in a rural community for many years. When they develop dementia, some of the ways in which they are living change. Relatives who live some distance away suggest that it might be better for the person to be cared for somewhere else. How could thinking differently about ageing develop the social worker's approach?

Ageism: critical exploration of the worries that might lie beneath the relatives' suggestion is essential to ensure that ageist and discriminatory assumptions about age and risk do not unconsciously determine the response. An understandable desire to prevent physical harm may reflect paternalist thinking about older age inevitably bringing diminishing abilities and a reduced quality of life. The social worker will also consider the impact of other oppressions on this particular older person—these might include gender, race, disability, sexuality....

Relationship-based approach: developing a trusting and purposeful relationship with the older person will be key for the social worker, in order for the person to feel confident to share their inner world thoughts and feelings. An empathic, affirming and congruent approach will create the conditions through which the social worker can better understand the person's unique strengths, characteristics and what is important to them. Alongside an awareness of actual risks to the person's health and safety, the social worker will want to draw out the person's sense of self and the importance to them of place—their home and their community.

Person-centred approach: The social worker will seek to understand the things that maintain and enhance the person's wellbeing and which have sustained them over the years. It will be vital to understand the person's unique experience of dementia and not assume that potential issues are actual ones. Rural social workers may well have intimate knowledge of the people and relationships within the person's community that can also play a part in responding to changing needs, understanding the importance of independence and inter-dependence in social relationships. A longer-term working relationship with both the person and their community is an opportunity to engage in meaningful conversations over time rather than in a crisis driven response to fear or risk aversion. It will enable the social worker to work alongside the person with small, incremental responses to change, maintaining dignity and wellbeing.

Applying the social model of disability: Rural social workers have a key role to play in allyship alongside older people where the 'problems' they face are attributed to the inevitability of ageing and the solutions are limited by negative, cost-driven assumptions. The social model clearly locates the 'problem' with society's responses to impairment, in this person's case, dementia. The social worker has a key role in reframing the narrative about the person's situation and in challenging the social and organisational structures around them to respond in socially just and inclusive ways.

Thinking Differently About Social Work

> There are no ideal communities comprising only supportive people, or open-minded people, or generous people, or benevolent people. Real communities will exhibit both positive and negative characteristics. It is how workers deal with those characteristics that matters (Martinez-Brawley, 2000, p. 242).

Managerialist approaches within social work that prioritise targets and procedures over professional values, have dominated social work practice in recent decades (Doel, 2012), in contrast to what people using services value in their social workers (Manthorpe et al., 2008a, b; Black, 2022). The time that social workers may have spent working alongside older people in participatory and relational ways, is now largely spent on processing assessments and brokering services (Torres & Donnelly, 2022), distancing social workers from purposeful relationship building and a deeper understanding of people's inner worlds, feelings and motivations (Fenton, 2016; Ruch et al, 2018). McMahon (2018) suggests however, that longer-term relational working offers 'the best hope of providing a quality of life which respects the humanity of all' (p. 164). The then College of Social Work (2015) developed a business case for social work with adults which also demonstrated the organisational and financial benefits of practice that held relationships to be central.

Relationship-based practice is not unique to rural social work, but its presence within all the defining features of rural practice (Locke & Winship, 2005), demonstrates its necessity and congruence with the social and community context of rural life. Relationships are the means through which social workers may gain a meaningful understanding of how 'structures of oppression are reproduced in the everyday lived reality of people' (Dalrymple & Burke, 2006, p. 18), and the unique strengths and qualities of those people. Relational work that embodies the core conditions of helping relationships; unconditional positive regard, empathy and congruence (Rogers, 1951), is in itself a demonstration of validation and respect for personhood, enhancing the other person's own capacity to develop positive relationships (Trevithick, 2014). Saleebey (2009) describes the importance of the strengths perspective in social work that deliberately takes a stand against deficit and pathology:

> Like social care taking and social work, the strengths perspective is about the revolutionary possibility of hope; hope realised through the strengthened sinew of social relationships in family, neighbourhood, community, culture, and country. That contextual sinew is fortified by the expression of the individual and communal capacities of all. The strength of that sinew is also significantly dependent on the opportunities and barriers afforded by social policies…that affect the quality of life and life chances for citizens (2009, p. 19).

The interconnectedness of relationship, hope and social action is intrinsic to social pedagogical approaches (Freire, 1966). Founded in the ethics of social justice and education, social pedagogy describes approaches to working alongside people that are humanising, developed through relationships and which believe in the value and potential of all people (ThemPra, 2017a, b). Social pedagogical ways of working are distinguished less by method and more by the creative actions that arise from this philosophy (Hämäläinen, 2003). Social pedagogy emphasises the empowering potential of lifelong learning (Charfe & Gardner, 2019). Despite a lower profile in the UK than in other European countries, there is growing interest in social pedagogy's potential to enhance social work practice across the lifecourse (Smith & Monteux, 2019; Squires, 2020).

In Practice:

> An older person with physical health and mobility issues cares for their adult son who has longstanding experience of mental ill-health. They live together in a remote rural area. Health professionals are concerned about the son's fluctuating mental health and the impact on the older person's wellbeing. Their limited contact with this family has included observations that the home is starting to look cluttered, but responses from the son have clearly indicated that help is not wanted. The older person has friends in

their local area who have expressed concern for their welfare. How could thinking differently about social work develop the social worker's approach?

Ageism: the social worker will want to critically reflect on not assuming that the older person's self-determination, choices and abilities are adversely affected by their age; other intersecting forms of oppression may also be significant. At the same time, without yet knowing and working alongside the older person, the social worker cannot be sure what their feelings and experiences are.

Upstream work: social work within rural communities has opportunities for creative practice that can get 'upstream' of crises before they happen, and prevent issues becoming entrenched. Early warning signs of potential concerns enable the timely building of relationships that will provide the foundation for long-term social work alongside this family.

Applying the social model of disability: for this family, consideration of the social model will highlight the disabling impact of society's treatment and exclusion of people experiencing both physical disability and mental ill-health. An intersectional approach to understanding the impact of oppressions including the stigma frequently associated with mental ill-health as well as the older person's caring role, will frame the social worker's practice positively. The social worker may, for example, need to work with the son and health professionals and services to ensure that appropriate support for his mental health is negotiated in ways that are meaningful and equitable. An approach that emphasises risk minimisation rather than elimination will be helpful in countering social constructions of how homes and family life 'should' look.

Relationship-based practice: relational work with this family will involve the social worker not just building a relationship with the older person and the son, but understanding the nature and importance of the relationship between the older person and their son. The relationship is an opportunity for the social worker to embody the ethics of social justice, care and dignity in their approach. In enabling the social worker to get to know the person and the son, it is also the way in which the social worker can most meaningfully consider concepts such as the relational universe within social pedagogy, the least restrictive options available to this family, and developing person-centred support.

Conclusion

Rural social work practice with disabled older people occupies something of a liminal space between social work, rurality and the voices of older people. In this chapter I have explored how ageism manifests through an absence of welcome and respect for the existence and needs of rural dwelling older people. I have argued the urgent need to address the gap that exists in rural scholarship, and affirmed that social work alongside older people in rural communities is incomplete without critical and contextual understanding of person and place.

Social workers have an ethical responsibility to practice in ways that challenge discrimination and oppression (IFSW, 2014; BASW, 2018). Despite the widespread adoption of the social model of disability (Barnes, 2019), disabled and older people continue to experience discrimination and exclusion across their lifecourse. The social model's relevance for older people and people living with dementia continues to be developed (Oldman, 2002; Kattari et al., 2017; Thomas & Milligan, 2017; Cahill, 2022), but much remains to be explored alongside older and disabled people to further challenge deeply entrenched views about age and disability within society and a neoliberal social work context.

Within social work education, there is a need for increased recognition of the World Health Organisation's assertion that social workers working alongside older people need to be able to apply their skills and values to understand individual experiences of life as well as ageing, in order that all people are enabled 'to be and do what they value throughout their lives' (WHO, 2021a, b, p. 4). To achieve this, social work students need to be enabled throughout their learning and development to embody social work values, and to embed their skills in relationship-based practice (Fenton & Walker, 2012; Preston-Shoot, 2011). Developing an explicit focus within social work education on rural social work practice is, as others have argued (Pugh & Cheers, 2010; Turbett, 2010), essential for positive experiences of both rural social workers and the people they work alongside. Rural social workers should be enabled by their organisations to access the benefits of peer support (Ingram, 2015) and to engage in critical thinking that acknowledges the complexity and messiness of practice (Morley & McFarlane, 2014), as well as reflective supervision that actively helps to contain and manage the healthy ontological anxiety (Taylor, 2007) that is an inevitable consequence of working with uncertainty (Fenton, 2016).

I have made the case for social work with older people in rural areas to be grounded in relational and empowering practice that challenges the creeping bureaucratisation and professionalising of social work to the extent that it loses sight of an ethic of care (Meagher & Parton, 2004). The challenge remains for rural practice to be able to listen, involve and respond to older people in ways that work for them, whether it be that 'little bit of help' (JRF, 2004), allyship in resisting negative assumptions or a commitment to ensuring social connection and meaning at all stages of a person's life journey. As Saleebey (2009, p. 21) reminds us:

> The central proposition of social work practice, as I see it, is to exploit the best in all of us; to work together to surmount adversity and trouble; to confront the appalling with all the tools available within us and around us; to wrestle distress and disillusionment to ground with determination and grit; to grab the hands of others and march unwaveringly….in the direction of hopes, dreams and possibilities.

References

Age UK. (2021). *Ageing in Rural and Coastal Communities.* Accessed March 8, 2022, from Ageing in Coastal and Rural Communities | Age UK

Amnesty International. (2020). *As If Expendable: The UK Government's Failure to Protect Older People in Care Homes During the Covid-19 Pandemic.* Accessed April 7, 2022, from Report (amnesty.org.uk)

Barnard, C. (2021). *Intersectionality for Social Workers: A Practical Introduction.* Routledge.

Barnes, C. (2019). Understanding the Social Model of Disability: Past, Present and Future. In N. Watson & S. Vehmas (Eds.), *Routledge Handbook of Disability Studies.* Taylor & Francis.

Beresford, P. (2005). *Gadgets Don't Care.* Community Care 18-24 August. Accessed May 30, 2022.

Beresford, P. (2022). User Involvement. In S. Torres & S. Donnelly (Eds.), *Critical Gerontology for Social Workers*. The Policy Press.

Beresford, P., Fleming, J., Glynn, M., Bewley, C., Croft, S., Branfield, F., & Postle, S. (2011). *Supporting People: Towards a Person-Centred Approach*. The Policy Press.

Black, R. (2022). *The Power of Small Gestures: Emotions and Relationships in Social Worker Practice*. Accessed June 15, 2022, from https://www.researchin-practice.org.uk/media/0rejjd05/smallgestures-9-1.pdf

Blood, I. (2013). *A Better Life: Valuing Our Later Years*. Joseph Rowntree Foundation.

Blood, I. (2016) E*nablement in Dementia: Practice Tool*. Research in Practice for Adults. Accessed May 29, 2022, from www.ripfa.org.uk/resources/publications/practice-tools-and-guides/enablement-in-dementia-practice-tool-2016

British Association of Social Workers. (2018). *Capabilities Statement for Social Workers Working with Older People*. Accessed April 27, 2022, from Capabilities Statement for Social Workers in England Who Work with Older People | www.basw.co.uk

British Association of Social Workers. (2021). *Code of Ethics*. Accessed April 27, 2022, from BASW Code of Ethics for Social Work | www.basw.co.uk

Brownlee, K., Graham, J., Doucette, E., Hotson, N., & Halverson, G. (2009). Have Communication Technologies Influenced Rural Social Work Practice? *British Journal of Social Work*, 1–16.

Burton, V., & Revell, L. (2018). Professional Curiosity in Child Protection: Thinking the Unthinkable in a Neo-liberal World. *British Journal of Social Work, 48*(6), 1508–1523.

Bytheway, B. (1995). *Ageism*. Open University Press.

Cahill, S. (2022). Dementia: A Disability and a Human Rights Concern. In S. Torres & S. Donnelly (Eds.), *Critical Gerontology for Social Workers*. Policy Press.

Caldwell, P. (2017). Belonging. In K. Soldatic & K. Johnson (Eds.), *Disability and Rurality: Identity, Gender and Belonging*. Routledge.

Campbell, F. A. K. (2001). Inciting Legal Fictions: Disability's Date with Ontology and the Ableist Body of the Law. *Griffith Law Review, 10*, 42–62.

Care Act. (2014). Available at: Care Act 2014. (legislation.gov.uk)

Centre for Ageing Better. (2017). Report: Inequalities in Later Life | Centre for Ageing Better (ageing-better.org.uk). Accessed April 7, 2022, from ageing-better.org.uk

Centre for Ageing Better. (2022). Summary | The State of Ageing 2022 | Centre for Ageing Better (ageing-better.org.uk). Accessed April 7, 2022.

Charfe, L., & Gardner, A. (2019). *Social Pedagogy and Social Work.* Sage.

Cheers, B. (1998). *Welfare Bushed: Social Care in Rural Australia.* Ashgate.

Cheers, B., Darracott, R., & Lonne, B. (2005). Domains of Rural Social Work Practice. *Rural Society, 15*(3), 234–251.

Cloke, P., & Little, J. (1997). *Contested Countryside Cultures: Otherness, Marginalisation and Rurality.* Routledge.

Cloke, P., Doel, M., Matless, D., Phillips, M., & Thrift, N. (1994). *Writing the Rural: Five Rural Geographies.* Paul Chapman.

Collier, K. (1984). *Social Work with Rural Peoples: Theory and Practice.* New Star Books.

Daatland, S., & Biggs, S. (2006). *Ageing and Diversity: Multiple Pathways and Cultural Migrations.* The Policy Press.

Dalrymple, J., & Burke, B. (2006). *Anti-Oppressive Practice: Social Care and the Law.* McGraw-Hill Education.

Doel, M. (2012). *Social Work: The Basics.* Routledge.

Dominelli, L. (2002). *Anti-Oppressive Social Work Theory and Practice.* Palgrave Macmillan.

Dunk-West, P., & Hafford-Letchfield, T. (2018). *Sexuality, Sexual and Gender Identities and Intimacy Research in Social Work and Social Care: A Lifecourse Epistemology.* Routledge.

Faulkner, A. (2012). *The Right to Take Risks: Service Users' Views of Risk in Adult Social Care.* Joseph Rowntree Foundation.

Fealy, G., McNamara, M., Treacey, M. P., & Lyons, I. (2011). Constructing Identities: A Case Study of Newspaper Discourses. *Ageing & Society, 32*(2012), 85–102.

Fenton, J. (2016). *Values in Social Work: Reconnecting with Social Justice.* Palgrave.

Fenton, J., & Walker, L. (2012). When Is a Personal Care Task Not Just a Task? *Journal of Practice Teaching and Learning, 11*(1), 19–36.

Fluharty, C. (2002). Keynote Speech at the 27th Annual National Rural Social Work Conference, Frostburg, MD, 17 July, cited in N. Lohmann and R. A. Lohmann (Eds), *Rural Social Work Practice* (pp. xi–xxvii). Columbia University Press.

Fook, J. (1993). *Radical Casework: A Theory of Practice.* Allen & Unwin.

Fraser, S., Lagacé, M., Bongué, B., Ndeye, N., Guyot, J., Bechard, L., Garcia, L., Taler, V., Adam, S., Beaulieu, M., Bergeron, C. D., Boudjemadi, V., Desmette, D., Donizzetti, A. R., Éthier, S., Garon, S., Gillis, M., Levasseur, M., Lortie-Lussier, M., & Wittich, W. (2020). Ageism and COVID-19: What Does Our Society's Response Say About Us? *Age and Ageing, 49*(5), 692–695.

Freire, P. (1966). *Pedagogy of Hope: Reliving Pedagogy of the Oppressed.* Continuum.

Gabriel, Z., & Bowling, A. (2004). Quality of Life in Old Age from the Perspectives of Older People. In A. Walker & C. Hagan Hennessy (Eds.), *Growing Older: Quality of Life in Old Age.* Open University Press.

Gibson, P. (2014). Extending the Ally Model of Social Justice to Social Work Pedagogy. *Journal of Teaching in Social Work, 34*(2), 199–214.

Ginsberg, L. H. (Ed.). (1998). *Social Work in Rural Communities.* Council on Social Work Education.

Hämäläinen, J. (2003). The Concept of Social Pedagogy in the Field of Social Work. *Journal of Social Work, 3*(1), 69–80.

Harris, J. (2003). *The Social Work Business.* Routledge.

Hinck, S. (July 2004). The Lived Experience of Oldest-Old Rural Adults. *Qualitative Health Research, 14*(6), 779–791.

Hoban, M., James, V., Beresford, P., & Fleming, J. (2013). *Shaping Our Age – Involving Older Age: The Route to Twenty-First Century Well-Being, Final Report.* Royal Voluntary Service.

Hughes, B. (1995). *Older People and Community Care: Critical Theory and Practice.* Open University Press.

Ingram, R. (2015). *Understanding Emotions in Social Work.* McGraw Hill.

Innes, A., & Manthorpe, J. (2012). Developing Theoretical Understandings of Dementia and Their Application to Dementia Care Policy in the UK. *Dementia, 12*(6), 682–696.

International Federation of Social Workers. (2014). *Global Definition of Social Work.* Accessed March 8, 2022, from Global Definition of Social Work – International Federation of Social Workers (ifsw.org)

Jackman, M. R. (1994). *The Velvet Glove: Paternalism and Conflict in Gender, Class, and Race Relations.* University of California Press.

Joseph Rowntree Foundation. (2004). *Building a Good Life for Older People in Rural Communities: The Experience of Ageing in Time and Place.* York Publishing.

Kattari, S., Lavery, A., & Hasche, L. (2017). Applying a Social Model of Disability Across the Lifespan. *Journal of Human Behavior in the Social Environment, 27*(8), 865–880.

King, G., & Farmer, J. (2009). What Older People Want: Evidence from a Study of Remote Scottish Communities. *Rural and Remote Health, 9*, 1–11.

Kitwood, T. (1997). *Dementia Reconsidered: The Person Comes First.* Open University Press.

Langan, J., Means, R., & Rolfe, S. (1996). *Maintaining Independence in Later Life: Older People Speaking*. Anchor Trust.

Lipsky, M. (1980). *Street-Level Bureaucracy: Dilemmas of the Individual in Public Services*. Russell Sage.

Locke, B. L., & Winship, J. (2005). Social Work in Rural America: Lessons from the Past and Trends for the Future. In N. Lohmann & R. A. Lohmann (Eds.), *Rural Social Work Practice*. Columbia University Press.

Lohmann, N., & Lohmann, R. A. (Eds.). (2005). *Rural Social Work Practice*. Columbia University Press.

Lonne, B. (2002). *Retention and Adjustment of Social Workers to Rural Positions in Australia: Implications for Recruitment, Supports and Professional Education*. Unpublished PhD Thesis, University of South Australia, Whyalla.

Manthorpe, J., & Samsi, K. (2016). Person-Centred Dementia Care: Current Perspectives. *Clinical Interventions in Ageing, 11*, 1733–1740.

Manthorpe, J., & Stevens, M. (2010). Increasing Care Options in the Countryside: Developing an Understanding of the Potential Impact of Personalization for Social Work with Rural Older People. *British Journal of Social Work, 40*, 1452–1469.

Manthorpe, J., Moriarty, J., Rapaport, J., Clough, R., Cornes, M., Bright, L., Iliffe, S., & OPRSI (Older People Researching Social Issues). (2008a). 'There Are Wonderful Social Workers but It's a Lottery': Older People's Views About Social Workers. *British Journal of Social Work, 32*, 1132–1150.

Manthorpe, J., Iliffe, S., Clough, R., Cornes, M., Bright, L., Moriarty, J., & OPRSI (Older People Researching Social Issues). (2008b). Older People's Perspectives on Health and Well-Being in Rural Communities in England: Findings from the Evaluation of the National Service Framework for Older People. *Health & Social Care in the Community, 16*(5), 460–468.

Martinez-Brawley, E. (1986). Community-Oriented Social Work in a Rural and Remote Hebridean Patch. *International Social Work, 29*(4), 349–372.

Martinez-Brawley, E. (2000). *Close to Home: Human Services and the Small Community*. NASW Press.

Martinez-Brawley, E. (2003). Putting 'Glamour' Back into Practice Thinking: Implications for Social and Community Development Work. *Australian Social Work, 55*(4), 292–302.

Mattsson, T. (2014). Intersectionality as a Useful Tool: Anti-Oppressive Social Work and Critical Reflection. *Journal of Women and Social Work, 29*(1), 8–17.

McMahon, L. (2018). Long-Term Complex Relationships. In G. Ruch, D. Turney, & A. Ward (Eds.), *Relationship-Based Social Work: Getting to the Heart of Practice*. Jessica Kingsley.

Meagher, G., & Parton, N. (2004). Modernising Social Work and the Ethics of Care. *Social Work and Society, 2*(1), 10–27.

Meisner, B. A. (2021). Are You OK, Boomer? Intensification of Ageism and Intergenerational Tensions on Social Media Amid COVID-19. *Leisure Sciences, 43*(1–2), 56–61.

Mencap. (2021). Press Release. Accessed April 23, 2022, from Eight in 10 Deaths of People with a Learning Disability Are COVID Related as Inequality Soars | Mencap

Milne, A. (2020). *Mental Health in Later Life: Taking a Life Course Approach.* Policy Press.

Milne, A., Hatzidimitriadou, E., & Wiseman, J. (2007). Health and Quality of Life Among Older People in Rural England: Exploring the Impact and Efficacy of Policy. *Journal of Social Policy, 36*(3), 477–495.

MIND. (2020). *Wellbeing.* Wellbeing - Mind. Accessed March 8, 2022

Mitchell, W. (2022). *What I Wish People Knew About Dementia.* Bloomsbury.

Monahan, C., Macdonald, J., Lytle, A., Apriceno, M. B., & Levy, S. R. (2020). COVID-19 and Ageism: How Positive and Negative Responses Impact Older Adults and Society. *American Psychologist, 75*(7), 887–896.

Morgan, H. (2012). The Social Model of Disability as a Threshold Concept: Troublesome Knowledge and Liminal Spaces in Social Work Education. *Social Work Education: The International Journal, 31*(2), 215–226.

Morgan, H. (2017). Hiding, Isolation and Solace: Rural Disabled Women and Neoliberal Welfare Reform. In K. Soldatic & K. Johnson (Eds.), *Disability and Rurality: Identity, Gender and Belonging.* Routledge.

Morley, C., & McFarlane, S. (2014). Critical Social Work as Ethical Social Work: Using Critical Reflection to Research Students' Resistance to Neoliberalism. *Critical and Radical Social Work, 2*(3), 337–355.

Morrison, T. (1988). *Staff Supervision in Social Care: Making a Real Difference.* Pavilion Publishing.

National Institute for Health Research. (2014). *People Who Fund Their Own Social Care.* Self-funders | NIHR SSCR. Accessed March 7, 2022.

Office for National Statistics. (2019). *Exploring the UK's Digital Divide - Office for National Statistics (ons.gov.uk).* Accessed May 14, 2022.

Office for National Statistics. (2020). *Shining a Light on What We Know About Adult Social Care | National Statistical (ons.gov.uk).* Accessed May 14, 2022.

Office for National Statistics. (2021a). *Demand for Adult Social Care Across Counties and Unitary Authorities in England - Office for National Statistics.* Accessed June 7, 2022, from ons.gov.uk

Office for National Statistics. (2021b). *Social Care: Estimating the Size of the Self-Funding Population | National Statistical.* Accessed May 9, 2022, from ons.gov.uk

Oldman, C. (2002). Later Life and the Social Model of Disability: A Comfortable Partnership? *Ageing and Society, 22,* 791–806.

Oliver, M. (1990). *The Politics of Disablement.* Macmillan. Accessed May 13, 2022, from www.leeds.ac.uk/disability-studies/archiveuk/index.html

Oliver, M. (2013). The Social Model of Disability: Thirty Years On. *Disability & Society, 28*(7), 1024–1026.

Parton, N. (2014). *The Politics of Child Protection: Contemporary Developments and Future Directions.* Palgrave Macmillan.

Patel, N. (2004). *Minority Health and Social Care in Europe: Summary Findings of the Minority Elderly Care (MEC) Project.* Policy Research Institute on Ageing and Ethnicity.

Phillips, J., Ray, M., & Marshall, M. (2006). *Social Work with Older People.* Palgrave.

Preston-Shoot, M. (2011). On Administrative Evil-Doing Within Social Work Policy and Services: Law, Ethics and Practice. *European Journal of Social Work, 14*(2), 177–194.

Pugh, R. (2000). *Rural Social Work.* Russell House.

Pugh, R. (2003). Considering the Countryside: Is There a Case for Rural Social Work? *British Journal of Social Work, 33,* 67–85.

Pugh, R. (2009, October). A Very Big Job in the Country. *Professional Social Work.*

Pugh, R., & Cheers, B. (2010). *Rural Social Work: An International Perspective.* The Policy Press.

Pugh, R., Scharf, T., Williams, C., & Roberts, D. (2007). *SCIE Research Briefing 22: Obstacles to Using and Providing Rural Social Care.* Accessed March 9, 2022, from SCIE Research Briefing 22: Obstacles to Using and Providing Rural Social Care

Ray, M., Bernard, M., & Phillips, J. (2007). *Critical Issues in Social Work with Older People.* Red Globe Press.

Rogers, C. (1951). *Client Centred Therapy.* Houghton Mifflin.

Ruch, G., Turney, D., & Ward, A. (2018). *Relationship-Based Social Work: Getting to the Heart of Practice.* Jessica Kingsley.

Rural England. (2017). *Issues Facing Providers of Social Care at Home to Older Residents in Rural England.* Accessed March 9, 2022, from Launch-Report-Issues-Facing-Providers-Social-Care-in-Rural-England.pdf (rural-england.org)

Saleebey, D. (2009). *The Strengths Perspective in Social Work Practice*. Pearson.

Samuel, M. (2022). *Solutions Can't Be Scripted Here: You Have to Be Creative.* Accessed June 30, 2022, from 'Solutions Can't Be scripted Here – You Have to be Creative' - Community Care

Shakespeare, T. (2006). The Social Model of Disability. In L. Davis (Ed.), *The Disability Studies Reader* (4th ed.). Routledge.

Simpson, J. (2009). *Everyone Belongs: A Toolkit for Applying Intersectionality.* CRIAW/ICREF.

Smale, G., Tuson, G., & Statham, D. (2000). *Social Work and Social Problems: Working Towards Social Inclusion and Social Change.* Macmillan.

Smith, M., & Horner, T. (2009). *A Review of Service Development and Innovation in the Delivery of Joint Health and Social Care and Support Services in Rural and Remote Areas.* Health Scotland Joint Improvement Team, Remote and Rural Implementation Group.

Smith, M., & Monteux, S. (2019) *Social Pedagogy and Its Relevance for Scottish Social Welfare.* Accessed April 11, 2022, from Social Pedagogy and Its Relevance for Scottish social Welfare (iriss.org.uk)

Social Exclusion Task Force. (2009). *Working Together for Older People in Rural Areas.* Cabinet Office.

Soldatic, K., & Johnson, K. (2017). *Disability and Rurality: Identity, Gender and Belonging.* Routledge.

Squires, B. (2020). *Social Pedagogy and Relationship-Based Social Work with Adults.* MA Innovation Project, Unpublished.

Steptoe, A., & Fancourt, D. (2019). Leading a Meaningful Life at Older Ages and Its Relationship with Social Engagement, Prosperity, Health, Biology, and Time Use. *Proceedings of the National Academy of Sciences of the United States of America, 116*(4), 1207–1212.

Stevenson, O., & Age Concern. (1989). *Age and Vulnerability: A Guide to Better Care.* Edward Arnold.

Tanner, D., & Harris, J. (2008). *Working with Older People.* Routledge.

Taylor, M. (2007). Professional Dissonance: A Promising Concept for Clinical Social Work. *Smith College Studies in Social Work, 77*, 89–99.

The College of Social Work. (2015). *Excellent Social Work with Older People: A Discussion Paper.* The College of Social Work.

The Countryside Agency. (2002). *Rural Proofing: Policy Makers' Checklist.* The Countryside Agency.

ThemPra. (2017a). *Social Pedagogy.* Accessed March 18, 2022, from Social Pedagogy - ThemPra Social Pedagogy

ThemPra. (2017b). *The Relational Universe.* Accessed March 18, 2022, from Relational Universe - ThemPra Social Pedagogy

Think Local Act Personal. (2020). TIG Report - TLAP Insight Group - Covid-19 Information - Think Local Act Personal. Accessed June 21, 2022.

Thomas, C., & Milligan, C. (2017). *Dementia, Disability Rights and Disablism: Understanding the Social Position of People with Dementia*. Lancaster University, Division of Health Research.

Thompson, P., Itzin, C., & Abendstern, M. (1990). *I Don't Feel Old: The Experience of Later Life*. Oxford University Press.

Torres, S., & Donnelly, S. (2022). *Critical Gerontology for Social Workers*. Policy Press.

Trevithick, P. (2014). *Social Work Skills: A Practice Handbook*. Open University Press.

Turbett, C. (2010). *Rural Social Work Practice in Scotland*. British Association of Social Workers.

Westwood, S. (Ed.). (2019). *Ageing, Diversity and Equality: Social Justice Perspectives*. Routledge.

Wonnacott, J. (2014). *Developing and Supporting Effective Staff Supervision*. Pavilion.

World Health Organisation. (2021a). *Ageing and Health*. Accessed March 26, 2022, from Ageing and Health (who.int)

World Health Organisation. (2021b). *Dementia*. Accessed March 26, 2022, from Dementia (who.int)

World Health Organisation and World Bank. (2011). *World Report on Disability*. Accessed March 26, 2022, from World report on disability (who.int)

Zapf, M. K. (1985). Home Is Where the Heart Is: Role Conflicts Facing an Urban-Trained Worker in a Remote Northern Community. In W. Whitaker (Ed.), *Social Work in Rural Areas: A Celebration of Rural People, Place and Struggle*. Proceedings of the Ninth National and Second International Institute on Social Work in Rural Areas, Orono, ME, University of Maine, 28–31 July 1984.

11

Protecting Rural Young People from Sexual Abuse and Exploitation

Sarah Nelson

Introduction

This chapter explores an important issue for rural child protection: sexual abuse of children and young people, both within their families and beyond them.

It first considers risks and problems which exist in rural and remote areas, especially in comparison with urban settings. It contends that difficulties are greater in rural and remote areas and that these outweigh the benefits. At a minimum, young people's access to safety and support should be as good as in urban areas—a 'level playing field' wherever they live. Yet that in itself is a limited ambition if children still remain under-protected from sexual crime in every kind of area. We should rather, I believe, aim for excellence and innovation wherever we work.

Secondly, this chapter proposes some ways in which the challenges and problems described can be addressed, and the inherent strengths of rural

S. Nelson (✉)
CRFR University of Edinburgh, Scotland, UK
e-mail: Sarah.Nelson@ed.ac.uk

© The Author(s), under exclusive license to Springer Nature Switzerland AG 2024
C. Turbett, J. Pye (eds.), *Rural Social Work in the UK*, Rethinking Rural,
https://doi.org/10.1007/978-3-031-52440-0_11

and remote areas harnessed and increased. The neighbourhood mapping for children's safety schema of Sarah Nelson and Norma Baldwin, the contextual safeguarding (CS) principles pioneered by Carlene Firmin, and existing best practice against child sexual exploitation and 'county lines' (discussed below) can all play a valuable part. Fundamentally, provision cannot be based on current known demand, but rather on need established through proactive investigation.

These measures can enable protective work to adapt to local features within a national framework; to engage all strengths and supports which exist there; to utilise modern technologies imaginatively; to work proactively against perpetrators; and to involve young people and adults collaboratively with social workers and other statutory and third sector staff. Imaginative, challenging collaboration is also likely to increase social workers' morale and sense of efficacy.

Child protection strategies, principles and policies in the UK and its devolved governments would thus be informed and strengthened. While the chapter's focus is on protection against sexual crime, these initiatives are likely to prove more widely protective: in narrowing the scope for violence, exploitation and maltreatment against young people, and in making such behaviour much harder to conceal.

Contrasting Perceptions...

One challenge to accurate assessment of sexual crime in rural and remote areas has been a legacy of contrasting stereotypes of rural life. On the first, parents and others see rural areas as *safe* places to raise children, including safety from sexual assault, in contrast to cities with their risks of crime, temptation and other dangers to young people. Children and unsafe people are more easily watched, everyone is supposed to know everyone, while parents, teachers, doctors and clergy can supposedly judge if families or respected community stalwarts would do 'something like that'. These comforting stereotypes may lead to a dangerous complacency and a lack of professional curiosity.

Criteria used in compiling 'the best places in the UK to raise children' do not prioritise safety from sexual crime (even were its prevalence accurately known). Remote and island areas figure highly. Orkney, for instance, has been named the second-best place in Britain to raise children, due to its high employment, low burglary rate and high educational spending per child (Sayid, 2017).

On a contrasting traditional stereotype or caricature, the countryside is a hotbed of incest and unusual sexual practices with humans or animals. Educationally challenged people on remote farms supposedly perpetuate these practices, which will be difficult to challenge. While writing *Incest Fact & Myth* (Nelson, 1987), I was flooded with 'hotbed' claims from professionals about the Fens, rural Aberdeenshire, the Antrim Glens, Pembroke and the Outer Hebrides. When intergenerational child sexual abuse (CSA) is believed 'part of that culture', the impetus to intervene can be dangerously reduced.

Can moving beyond such stereotypes reveal more accurately both the risks and supports young people experience in rural and remote areas of the UK?

Definitions

Definitions of rurality vary slightly among the UK central and devolved governments, although all foreground population and accessibility to services. For instance, the Scottish Government Urban Rural Classification (Scottish Government, 2016) defines most of Scotland's land mass as rural, with 18 local authorities having significant such populations. 'Rural' areas have populations below 3000 people, while 'accessible rural' areas are within 30 minutes' drive time of a 10,000-plus settlement. 'Remote' or 'very remote' areas are more than a 30-minute or a 60-minute drive to 10,000-plus settlements.

(Such calculations appear to take little account of tortuous or single-track roads in huge swathes of rural Scotland—or must be based on sports cars and speedboats!)

These are rigid, doubtfully useful classifications. One key to improving children's safety will be *accessibility in realistic journey time t*o services and support in towns or cities. There's no comparison between accessibility for rural Auchnagatt, 25 miles from Aberdeen city, and Poolewe, 50 tortuous road miles from Ullapool or 76 from Inverness. Public transport, good internet connectivity and the existence of outreach workers may also prove more significant than physical distance. That emphasises the need to develop safeguards which address particular *local* risks, needs and strengths.

Part 1: Current Problems and Disadvantages

Research has shown that problems for children and young people can encompass a wide range of rural and remote areas when safety from sexual or physical assault is especially considered.

Poverty and Deprivation

Greater vulnerability to poverty and unemployment (Black et al., 2019; Turbett, 2009) impacts their safety in many ways, such as inability to afford expensive public transport for seeking help or escape; increased dependence on parents (Fabiansson, 2015); and inability to afford scarce housing alternatives if their home is abusive; inability to afford scarce childcare if they become pregnant. The most vulnerable young people have also been disproportionately disadvantaged by welfare reform (National Audit Office, 2015). In this way political decisions by local or central governments, including about the availability of housing options for rural young people, may directly impact on their safety.

Provision by government, local authorities, health boards and other key services is based on known demand, affecting prediction of future needs: This is a major issue for rural child protection as well as being highlighted for domestic abuse provision, where there are similar issues with shame, secrecy and male entitlement (National Rural Crime Network, 2019). When crucial data is absent to support investment in more and better services, this cycle self-perpetuates in an austerity-driven environment of fierce competition for resources.

Accurate assessment of the prevalence of such a secretive, deliberately concealed and shame-inducing crime, as child sexual abuse has always been difficult, and rates from adult recall in all types of areas are often much higher than current estimates (Nelson, 2016a). While CSA reporting in rural and remote areas appears lower than in urban areas (Averill et al., 2007; Lewis, 2003), some researchers (Menard & Ruback, 2003; Annan, 2006) propose that, due to unique social norms within rural settings, greater poverty and unemployment, and more informal means of social control and silencing, rural regions may in fact experience *greater* levels of child sexual abuse. Rural sexual abuse survivors face specific barriers including fear of social stigma, self-blaming, caution about sharing information with outsiders, fear of gossip, long waits for mental health counselling and shortages of professionals knowledgeable about, or trained and supervised in, sexual abuse in their area (Logan et al., 2005; Kenyon-George, 2017; Turbett, 2009).

Nelson (2016a) shows in detail an additional problem for the exposure of CSA in both urban and rural areas. Child protection statistics about referrals, registrations, child protection case conferences and protective action taken reveal how professional concerns about child sexual abuse have been consistently falling throughout the UK in proportion to other concerns, despite increasing police reports of online and offline sexual crime against children and young people, and despite increased awareness about the realities of child sexual exploitation. These factors and these 'unknowns' make it especially important that the prevalence of CSA in rural areas and the resultant need for protection and provision are assessed not by currently known demand but by *proactive investigation*. That is discussed later in this chapter.

Other Relevant Issues

- **Resource and funding cuts:** Years of austerity have eroded local services, such as bus services, shops, libraries and other public venues, with increased centralisation of police, GP and mental health services. In particular are cuts to early years and youth work, so important for safeguarding and supporting children and young people. Stretched social workers may reduce their interventions to the statutory minimum. Cuts are proportionally harder if services were never extensive.

Cumulatively these measures redistribute social and societal risk, with young people, people with disabilities and overwhelmingly female lone parents particularly disadvantaged (May et al., 2020; Poinasamy, 2013).

- **Poor, non-existent or unreliable public transport:** This is another major issue. This can literally prevent escape, help-seeking, refuge or direct personal contact with services and increases safety risks from hitch-hiking, for example, by teenagers to work on fish farms.
- **'Ghost' villages:** In popular tourist areas, villages with numerous holiday homes and rentals can be virtually unoccupied for months. This is startlingly noticeable in some Lake District, Cotswold and Welsh villages. There may be no one around to report concerns or to call on for help. Abusers may use certain properties unnoticed. When in season villages are busy, there can be frequent turnover of unknown people, but also families who deserve a safe environment.

Scanty Mental Health Services

Mental health and counselling services are important, not just for recovery after known sexual assault but for prevention, by strengthening young people's confidence to report a perpetrator. Yet such services are much scantier in rural and remote areas, as studies showed (Allwood, 2020; Evans-Thompson et al., 2017). These revealed how children living in remote areas face isolation and struggle to get mental health support due to poor transport, lack of confidential spaces for meetings, distance to health services and poor digital connectivity. Allwood's extensive report calls for action and investment in digital infrastructure, mobile support services, peer support networks and the use of existing community spaces.

Limited Broadband and Mobile Coverage: Increasing Loss of Public Telephones

These are major problems for safeguarding, in remote areas of the UK especially. Yet their links to young people's ability to report, access help, share experiences and seek safety are rarely discussed—in comparison, for instance, to problems in gaining urgent medical or dental help.

Lack of Confidentiality, Stigma and Silencing

Studies have found rural survivors of CSA are less likely to report abuse through the close-knit culture of rural communities, networks of familiarity among residents, lower population hence greater visibility, lack of confidentiality and widespread failure to prosecute powerful perpetrators (National Rural Crime Network, 2019; Evans-Thompson et al., 2017; Pugh & Cheers, 2010; Pugh, 2007). Specialist support workers are easily identifiable, so survivors risk being 'outed' by neighbours who see them with an outreach worker.

Turbett (Chap. 9) highlights in valuable detail ways in which the patriarchal nature of rural communities can facilitate coercive control: men are typically heads of household, landlords, landowners, employers and often police officers. Thus, rural communities can be oppressive, socially excluding, racist and reactionary, as well as embracing and protective. There may be less tolerant, even discriminatory, attitudes towards children from different ethnic, religious and other marginalised communities and children whose gender or sexual identity is different to most others.

Particular fears are that prominent, powerful men within local communities would influence action and criminal justice: that they would not be prosecuted or if so would not be convicted. In Evans-Thompson et al.'s (2017) study, of perpetrators not well known in the community, more than half were prosecuted. Of those well known, not one was prosecuted.

The National Rural Crime Network (2019) demonstrated significant differences in admission to the shame and stigma involved in domestic abuse between rural and urban areas, suggestive that this may also be so in related crimes with similar shame, secrecy, coercion and patriarchal entitlement. The Welsh Women's Aid report (2020) noted difficulties in help-seeking because women didn't trust local professionals to keep confidentiality, especially if the abuser was also known locally or was a police officer or GP.

Thus, many problems exist for rural staff in maintaining boundaries and confidentiality. However, generalisations about rural values and prejudice may fail to detect differences which can be harnessed positively (see Neighbourhood Mapping for Children's Safety [NMCS] later in this chapter).

Some people attempting to avoid the law may move to remote areas from distant parts of the UK or abroad. Previous criminal and social work records may not efficiently be passed on to rural agencies.

New Risks of County Lines Activity

Rural areas of the UK are no longer safe from criminal exploitation with the growth of County Lines: indeed such areas are often deliberately targeted, opening a new field of concern (discussed below). This sees children and vulnerable adults groomed and manipulated to act as runners to transport drugs and cash all over the country. It is often associated with other child criminal exploitation (CCE), child sexual exploitation (CSE), violence, money laundering, modern slavery and human trafficking (The Children's Society, 2022; National Crime Agency, 2019; SCCYP, 2011). Yet many young people involved in gangs and criminal exploitation do not reach the high thresholds of statutory interventions, with few cases categorised as 'child protection', creating dilemmas around effective information-sharing which might safeguard them.

Part 2: What Can Be Done? The Basics…

Such daunting lists of rural problems can bring a sense of helplessness to social workers and other agencies. Yet identifying problems is the key to thinking imaginatively about how to address them, viewed here through the lens of their impact on sexual safety.

There is very limited research in the UK on improved ways of identifying and addressing sexual abuse specifically in rural areas. For example, two major reports on publicised sexual abuse cases in Scotland, Lord Clyde's Orkney Inquiry report (Clyde, 1992) and the Eilean Siar (Western

Isles) report (Social Work Inspection Agency, 2005), had many recommendations for improved practice (nearly 200, in Clyde's case). Yet there was a dearth of recommendations for tackling issues for rural or island areas. The Clyde report in particular led to legislative, procedural and organisational changes, yet the specifics of remote rural settings were somehow lost.

Getting the Basics Right

(a) Reducing Fears About Working with CSA

It may seem surprising to begin this discussion of positive action with two issues which are far from simply rural. Yet they underpin what staff and communities require to work confidently and effectively against CSA.

Research coupled with long experience by anyone working in this field suggests very many social workers, mental health and other staff find personal difficulty in working with CSA, especially in 'opening the can of worms' even to explore with young people or adults a possible abuse history (Hughes et al., 2019; Nelson, 2016b; Hepworth & McGowan, 2013). This can create even more difficulties in rural and remote areas where social work and mental health teams are more thinly staffed and where there is both necessity and strength in their having *generalist* skills (see Turbett, 2009, and introduction of this book). So, it will be important to have at least one team member who is knowledgeable and comfortable in working with the issue; to ensure access to online or in-person support and supervision; and to include routine training for all staff which is not heavily instructional and procedural, but discursive and confidence-building, sympathetically addressing fears about working with sexual assault.

In social work, policing, nursing and mental health, there must also be no prejudice about perceived weakness or untrustworthiness when staff themselves have a sexual assault history or seek therapeutic support. Such unjustified assumptions silence people. Long experience by trainers such as Safe to Say (Edinburgh) (https://safetosay.co.uk/training/) is that when caring staff during discursive training can disclose and address any issues they have, they can become particularly confident and effective in identifying child and adult survivors, in asking sensitively and in working positively with them.

(b) Ensuring that Sexual Abuse Survivor Agencies Exist

Support systems for adult victims of sexual crime—often headed by the third sector—also need establishing or strengthening in rural areas before many adults can address these issues for children and young people. When we ask local communities to become informed and to consider children's sexual safety, adults struggling with their own past need first to find the strength and confidence to do so through accessible support. A combination of outreach personal support and imaginative online support may be the realistic rural option. One positive outcome of Covid-19 is that means of online communication like Zoom are now widely familiar, enabling more personal dialogue than phonelines or email, while proving easier to 'manage' for those who find it hard to speak about their trauma to someone in the same space. More numerous support services also greatly help professionals who lack confidence themselves to address the issue—having knowledgeable services for referral if survivor(s) would welcome this.

Thinking Positively About Rural Working

How might everything possible be utilised to reduce rural inequalities and deficits and create best practice? I suggest the following:

- In low-population areas, people become the greatest potential asset. It is more important (and logistically much easier) to assess their skills, knowledge, experience and resources for keeping young people safe.
- Community cohesion can be oppressive but can also have positive aspects for safeguarding. Together, communities can pressurise governments and authorities to resource facilities.

- Reducing rural inequalities means scrutinising all facilities, services and buildings—however scanty—which do exist. What might each contribute?
- Existing strengths of local communities including traditions in music, the arts and digital skills need to be harnessed.
- Values and beliefs in rural communities, which might be barriers to safeguarding, need respectfully to be challenged.
- New technologies and online contacts, services and support need strengthening as far as possible: a crucial way to reduce current urban-rural disparities.
- Outreach work and multi-agency safeguarding hubs (MASH) should be widely utilised. Many rural areas are in fact reasonably close to size-able towns or cities, from which base the outreach staff can permeate.
- Drawing on existing examples of best practice includes work against child sexual exploitation, contextual safeguarding and 'county lines'. That avoids trying to 'reinvent the wheel'.
- Rural and remote needs must be assessed through proactive research into prevalence: not based on low known (or assumed) demand.

Part 3: Neighbourhood Mapping for Children's Safety

Mapping techniques are widely used in contextual safeguarding and in work against CSE, child trafficking and county lines. These are generally used to plot negative and damaging interconnections: but mapping can equally plot positive ones, highlighting *both* risks and supports.

Neighbourhood Mapping for Children's Safety (NMCS) is a schema by Sarah Nelson and Professor Norma Baldwin, who was a pioneer in mapping techniques for children's wellbeing (Baldwin & Carruthers, 2000; Atkar et al., 2000). It suggests how a time-limited research project involving statutory-voluntary collaboration, assisted by adults and school students in a chosen local area, can address a range of problems. Results will also valuably inform the wider child protection system.

What Is NMCS? A Summary

NMCS is rooted in the conviction that an over-arching view of the needs of communities and neighbourhoods, based on detailed local information and understanding of the links between different harms to children and young people, is crucial for developing child protection strategies (Baldwin & Carruthers, 1998, 2000; Atkar et al., 2000). It uses coordinated mapping exercises to gather and interpret relevant information, involving agencies and communities in partnership in identifying problems and seeking solutions through exploring *both* risk and support points.

It reduces opportunities for abuse both outside the home—hence fits well with expanding contextual safeguarding (CS) initiatives, whose principles it predated—and inside the home. This is because when sexual crime is named and openly discussed, when people become aware, informed and supported, they are empowered to begin talking about their own families and themselves and become more knowledgeable about signs of distress in their children or relatives.

NMCS undertakes four kinds of area mapping: demography, physical features and amenities, strengths of the community, and 'cultural' barriers to children's safety.

The chosen pilot or pathfinder areas can be parts of a city, small towns or remote/rural areas. The lead agency, which could be social services as in most CS initiatives, coordinates the project, using an independent university or college researcher backed by a multi-disciplinary support team. This time-limited NMCS project can usefully become part of a wider CS initiative, and its findings incorporated into planning.

There is only space for a summary here: there are detailed accounts of NMCS (Nelson, 2016c; Nelson & Baldwin, 2004).

Demographic mapping, aided by council planners and social geographers, asks: **'Who lives here?'**

Who especially might need, or give, extra support? Secondary school pupils can help contribute to this exploration.

In the deprived urban area where NMCS was pioneered, high percentages of the population were under 16. Many were vulnerable carers of addicted or disabled parents or had lost a parent to addiction or suicide.

A rural or remote area in contrast might contain retired people with useful skills; teenagers and young migrant workers doing poorly paid residential or day work in hotels, farms or fish farms; long-standing extended families; a marginalised community such as Gypsies and Travellers; seasonal tourists; a small 'utopian' religious or secular community, such as Scoraig in the West Highlands. Children may need to travel far to school, with safety en route a possible issue. In remote areas, unsafe people may have moved there to avoid criminal justice or difficult issues from their past.

This demographic mapping exercise greatly helps establish where help may be needed: online support systems for non-English-speaking seasonal workers would be only one example.

Physical features and amenities: '**What exists here?**' Secondary and primary pupils, again, can assist with this mapping.

A rural or remote area might contain some of these: a primary school; a boarding school or teenagers' residential outdoor centre; a marina, amusement arcade, caravan or chalet park; a beach where teenagers gather; a small health centre; a church hall or village hall, part of the extensive village halls network; a mobile library; pubs; remote farms; closed school buildings or derelict farm buildings; and 'ghost villages' of holiday homes. There is often little or no public transport, with poor broadband and mobile phone reception, and few if any remaining public telephones.

These form a mix of potential risk and support points for young people. Caravan and chalet parks and marinas can be idyllic for holidays but can also enable abuse networks to assault young people unseen unless they are made safer, inspected regularly and subject to periodic police surveillance.

Beaches and amusement arcades can feature abusive behaviour of some teenagers on others and recruitment by unsafe adults: the sort of gathering points familiar in contextual safeguarding initiatives across the UK.

Boarding schools and residential outdoor centres need scrutinising that their child protection policies are informed and their leaders carefully checked, with genuinely independent sources of student support. Children in 'utopian' communities need those too. Halls, school buildings and health centres can offer support, meetings, publicity and learning opportunities. Mobile libraries can publicise safety information and activities. Some small rural towns are even getting their cinemas back—such as Aberfeldy in Perthshire—enabling thought-provoking films and discussions. Closed schools might be used for community activities and after-school clubs, especially valuable where parents may work early evenings in hotels and pubs.

Poor public transport can be supplemented by community minibuses, for instance, to take teenagers to and from work on fish farms. Volunteers might travel on school buses to ensure children are safe with adults and each other.

Limited Broadband and Mobile Coverage; Increasing Loss of Public Telephones

Once inadequate broadband and mobile phone reception and closure of rural phone boxes are seen as safeguarding issues, communities, local councillors and their national politicians can campaign for improvements together. A public phone could be placed in a discreet booth in a village hall or local hotel. Zones and buildings with good mobile phone reception could be publicised.

These are major problems, in remote areas especially, yet are rarely seen as sexual safety issues.

Villages full of holiday homes and self-catering often have a pub, sometimes a church. These, along with public notice boards, could display contacts for a range of supports and to publicise safety information; suggest hotspots for good mobile reception or broadband reliability; and again, locate a public phone. Scattered local communities might also organise periodic use of community wardens.

NMCS Maps Traditions and Strengths to Build Upon

In NMCS in deprived Craigmillar, there happened to be a strong arts and drama tradition through its annual festival (https://craigmillarfestival.org/). In a rural area there may be talented community leaders, a lively church sector and voluntary sector, and many human resources and skills. There may have been campaigns for community land ownership, for better transport, or against measures like fracking, so that community cohesion for united action already exists. There may be a tradition of arts, traditional music and singing, or major rural events which have already drawn adults and young people to organise and publicise issues.

Events during tourist seasons, folk festivals or Highland games could show visitors the safety work of the community—and be a warning to any unsafe visitors. A travelling roadshow could prompt discussion on children and young people's safety issues at village halls. Travelling banks or food vans could carry safety publicity leaflets and posters in more than one language for, for example, migrant seasonal workers. In a primary school and a secondary, if one exists, work on safety, gender equality and respect can be prominent, given an aware school leadership. There can be workshops, online and printed flyers and brochures, self-report surveys and school- or health centre-based presentations. These are valuable preventative approaches, to increase public knowledge and awareness about CSA and child exploitation.

'Cultural' Issues: Barriers to a Safer Environment?

NMCS also maps what local people think about issues such as sexual violence, speaking out about shameful things and reporting suspicions to authorities.

For example, in urban Craigmillar, many people in poverty were deeply suspicious of police and social workers. They also felt both loyalty and fear towards often violent members of long-standing extended families. Thus, other ways had to be considered to persuade people to report: anonymously or through trusted third sector agencies.

Rural Areas May Vary, as Mapping Will Reveal

As noted earlier, it is too easy to brand rural and remote areas simplistically as single units, where local people all believe and react in similar ways. Yet there can be many differences. There might be a strongly puritanical, patriarchal religious tradition, where talk about sex or domestic abuse is discouraged. Long-established extended families can silence, especially through dominant males who are traditional community leaders. There may be liberal-minded, non-religious incomers, but these can under-estimate risks to local children and young people.

Yet many of these same young people—through their daily use of online technologies and social media—may now share many values with their young urban counterparts: both positive (tolerance to different lifestyles, disabilities, ethnicities, sexualities and gender identities) and negative (boys' ability to access 'hardcore' pornography with abusive attitudes to women and girls).

Some rural schoolteachers may believe respectable families 'round here' do not abuse. An isolated utopian community may idealistically dismiss that unsafe people may exist there, so think little about the need to 'notice' and protect. A Gypsy Traveller site may contain disadvantaged families who are discriminated against, but who also through tradition severely limit independent agency in teenage girls. Likewise, some other minority ethnic communities will face discrimination, but sexual violence is difficult to discuss openly. Where any beliefs and traditions within a rural ethnic or religious minority make protection more difficult, it will be important to work closely with them and not just with traditional male community leaders (Atkar et al., 2000; Jay, 2014).

Identifying the range of beliefs in an area can greatly assist in thinking about how to challenge respectfully—for instance, during community consultations about safety—values which make identifying, disclosing and addressing sexual crime difficult.

Where patriarchal attitudes are strong, project work with boys and young men to challenge these attitudes (see Turbett Chap. 9; Tranter, 2005) will be important—not just seen as suitable for deprived urban areas with high youth violence.

Sometimes a person influential against prejudice has emerged and can work with or beside the authorities. In one West Highland village where the Church of Scotland presbytery was strongly anti-gay, an outspoken local guest-house landlady kept challenging the church minister about attitudes which she felt were un-Christian.

Positive Use of Differences?

Relations between 'natives' and 'incomers' in rural and remote areas can be difficult. But sometimes incomers can find greater trust. Rural people can be silenced through fear of breached confidentiality by staff who are neighbours or relatives (Welsh Women's Aid, 2020). On one Scottish island where the Women's Aid team whom I interviewed all happened to be English 'incomers', vulnerable women told them repeatedly that it was a great relief and source of trust that they were *not* connected to their relatives or fellow villagers.

'Values and attitudes' mapping is harder and more challenging than other mapping and requires a range of community consultations, discussions and background research. However, the picture gained may make it possible to develop several helpful routes to disclosure and reporting.

The Money Problem....

During austerity councils, agencies and communities—as they well know—need to use their imaginations about funding opportunities. Better integration of child protection with CSE and CCE work enables the full use of policing and criminal justice funds, while NMCS projects could utilise, for instance, community safety and environmental funding. Looking imaginatively at how to use legislation can be useful. For instance, the Community Empowerment (Scotland) Act 2015 (The Scottish Government, 2015) is usually assumed to be about land issues and considers public involvement in the planning and delivery of local services. The Islands (Scotland) Act 2018 (The Scottish Government, 2018) further enhances opportunities for island communities. Yet their wide-ranging provisions do not exclude public participation in community planning issues about *social* provision.

Thoughts on Focused Imagination

Child protection (at least until contextual safeguarding) was becoming more narrowly professionalised and procedural. But this discussion of NMCS shows how *imagination and flexibility* among a wide range of people who ask the right questions are vital. How might this be a barrier or a support? Who could help? How could we use that building? Is there alternative protection to something we lack? Using focused imagination is also liberating and morale-boosting—to social workers, to other staff and to communities.

People then start thinking about their own working environment, even if connections with safeguarding are not immediately apparent. Thought-provoking examples include Action with Communities in Rural England gaining Lottery funding to promote good safeguarding practice for village and community halls (ACRE, 2021). Again, one prominent legal firm asks landowners and country house owners to consider safeguarding issues when under-18s work or volunteer there; when they host family public events; and when they organise educational visits or rent space for others on their estate (Farrer & Co, 2019).

Other Positive Issues for Rural Communities

New Technologies: One crucial way to create a more level playing field for rural and remote children is to expand online and telephone support as far as possible. Hence broadband and mobile connection are very important for child safety (https://www.childline.org.uk/get-support/). NMCS studies can map particular deficits, helping communities and their politicians to campaign for improvements.

A range of innovative technologies could enable access to protection and support for young people, especially in remote areas; within utopian groups; for resident hotel workers; where strict cultures act against speaking out on abuse; and to give migrant workers a link with speakers of other languages.

These can considerably reduce rural inequalities. Research projects need to be established which actively utilise young people's own skills and knowledge. Their support agencies—especially on topics like mental health—have often developed innovative means of contact, support and sharing. These agencies should be encouraged to contribute their innovations to research and to building best practice in areas where in-person contact and provision is difficult.

One example of innovation is 18 and Under in Dundee, a third sector agency where young people routinely contribute to its work (https://www.18u.org.uk/). Despite being city-based, they are contacted by many rural young people. 18 and Under has an online forum where young people can confidentially gain information, talk privately to a support worker, join a group of survivors, gain peer support and so on. They can find support via Snapchat, Instagram, Messenger or whichever social media they prefer. 18 and Under also informs them about a range of helpful apps, for example, MeeToo (https://www.meetoo.help/).

The confidential nature of many online supports responds to youngsters' huge concern about that issue while helping them build strength and confidence eventually to break that confidentiality.

However, online technologies should always be valuable components, not simply convenient, cost-saving, 'self-help' *replacements* for proper resourcing of personal contact and wider service provision (see Chap. 7 of this collection).

Contextual Safeguarding

It is apparent how NMCS schemes might sit well within, and strengthen, wider **Contextual Safeguarding** projects in a larger administrative area.

This constantly growing field of contextual safeguarding, initially developed by Professor Carlene Firmin, responds to young people's experiences of significant harm *beyond* their families. It recognises that relationships young people (especially teenagers) form in their neighbourhoods, schools and online can feature violence and abuse. Parents and carers can little influence these contexts, and young people's experiences can undermine parent-child relationships.

This means their physical and social spaces beyond the family are crucial to engage in keeping them safe. Thus, CS engages staff from much wider professions and occupations than traditionally, people who work, for instance, in parks, beach facilities or shopping centres, or in the night economy. In primarily considering family and home for risk or intervention, traditional approaches inadequately safeguarded vulnerable adolescents, whose influence by school and peer groups was greater than that of parents. The CS websites (https://www.contextualsafeguarding.org.uk/ and https://www.youtube.com/watch?v=mAIrlaEA-Vw) have a wide range of practitioner resources to explore the concepts further, as well as many tools for assessment and partnership, and many examples of good practice. Contextual safeguarding projects how now expanded right across the UK (Orr, 2021).

NMCS schemes can add to and strengthen contextual safeguarding in several ways. They aid learning by highlighting in greater detail local points of *support* as well as points of *risk*, the main focus for CS. NMCS can foreground rural areas, as well as urban and coastal areas. It can educate and inform more young people and parents within areas by involving them more widely and directly in mapping than CS currently does. It aids revelation of any interconnections between extrafamilial and intrafamilial abuse.

Outreach and the Use of Hubs

Particularly where a rural area is within reasonable travelling distance of a town or city, as many are, opportunities exist for **outreach work**, especially youth work. To repeat, rural areas can vary greatly in physical accessibility and should not be conflated nor subject to a single practice model. A central base with outreach opens many opportunities. All should be explored.

For example, **Multi-Agency Safeguarding Hubs (MASH)** and **Hub and Spoke** schemes against child sexual exploitation could function well. MASH hubs (https://www.gov.uk/government/news/working-together-to-safeguard-children-multi-agency-safeguarding-hubs), which now operate widely, especially across England and Wales, bring together agencies (and their information) in a single office receiving all concerns, to identify risks to children and young people early and to respond effectively. Such collaboration, especially between social workers and police, incidentally reflects good practice against CSA in the 1980s and 1990s which was discontinued (Nelson, 2016a). Social workers play a major role in the MASH. Information is shared securely, gathered from teachers, GPs, health visitors, school nurses or police officers, and the public.

In my own interviews in 2021 with MASHs in towns with a rural hinterland, staff appeared to concentrate on their urban areas. But this reflected professionals' own expectations of where risks were, along with low referrals from the rural areas, rather than intrinsic failings of MASHs. An information campaign in rural hinterlands, more professional awareness of potential rural risks and a team member with specialist rural knowledge could challenge this discrepancy.

Hub and Spoke schemes against CSE have involved an established third sector CSE service (the 'hub'), locating experienced project workers ('spokes') in new service delivery areas. These improve CSE work locally, including individual casework and awareness-raising with young people, along with consultancy, training and awareness-raising with professionals.

Evaluations suggest that placing of spoke workers within the host authority has been important to their visibility to potential referrers. These evaluations have suggested that voluntary sector involvement improves young people's engagement in services. Through relationship-based approaches, workers enable young people to develop control and self-efficacy, helping them to disclose abuse, leave unsafe relationships and begin recovery from exploitation. Location in a community or third sector resource has extended reach to those who don't meet the usual high threshold criteria of statutory authorities (Alexi Project, 2017).

Innovation in County Lines Work

Understanding links across child exploitation, modern slavery, county lines and trafficking will help all agencies respond more effectively to support children, but especially to identify perpetrators.

'County lines' refers to gangs using vulnerable children and adults to transport and sell Class A drugs, primarily from urban areas into coastal towns or rural areas to establish new drug markets or take over existing ones.

Since criminals have targeted rural areas, social workers, police and others have no choice but to consider how they might act effectively in rural and remote parts of the UK. It will be important to examine and learn from all examples of best practice in such rural areas.

The social worker Tilia Lenz, for example, outlines innovative work in rural Dorset and Wiltshire, noting a lack of early intervention and public education for rural communities. Funding had previously been targeted to urban localities *perceived* as 'gang areas' without the evidence, and knife crime was perceived as black and urban. Scoping, mapping and asking the right questions enabled her team to target surveillance and support. Lenz has also ensured that training and teaching receive high priority (Lenz, 2019).

Needs-Led, Not Demand-Led, Study of Sexual Crime

Finally, but essentially, needs assessment for support, protection and provision for rural and remote young people against sexual crime cannot now be based on the present low levels of reporting. It requires proactive investigation to unearth more realistic figures. There are several, complementary ways in which this might be achieved.

Detection of intrafamilial CSA can be perhaps the hardest and most secretive to identify. Yet it needs to be increased, as it so often triggers children's vulnerability to later CSE and CCE, to victimisation and other distressing problems in adulthood. Conversely, identifying children involved in CSE and CCE will at times lead back to discovering intrafamilial sexual abuse. Those interconnections make it even more necessary that work against different kinds of abuse and exploitation is not kept separate.

Measures already discussed in this chapter will increase knowledge of how many young people suffer sexual crime, yet a well-known circular problem faces agencies and communities who seek change. High-level political impetus and urgency to carry these changes through and fund them remains difficult, so long as known prevalence remains low (and can be quoted by funders as the reason to keep resourcing low).

Here are a few examples of proactive exploration.

1. Utilise mapping and identification methods which have already been shown to be successful in addressing CSE. The work of Daljeet Dagon and Barnardos, working closely with police in Renfrewshire, is only one example (Moodie & Vaswani, 2016) as are techniques used by the committed Oxford police officer Simon Morton (Race, 2020).

2. Examine successful identifications of CSA in institutions, professions and local communities in the past. Much innovative CSA work, even in the 1980s and 1990s, was discontinued (Nelson, 2016a).

3. Numerous barriers to disclosure by children remain the greatest continuing form of silencing, and they obscure CSA prevalence. This is of course not just a rural issue. One urgent need is for third sector organisations offering a higher degree of confidentiality to young people until they feel strong enough to report, to be integrated into child protection systems.

4. Routinely involve adult CSA survivors and support agencies for adults and children on area child protection committees and similar multi-agency safeguarding bodies.

5. Remove all 'silo' working against sexual crime against children inside and outside the family, and correlate the information gained. Abusers regularly assault children in both settings.

6. Study proactive investigation of under-reported domestic abuse, a similarly shameful and secretive crime, to learn of any valuable adaptations for sexual crime in rural areas. For instance, Lincolnshire council took over responsibility for domestic abuse support and began looking at areas which had very low incidence for no apparent reason. 'White spaces' on the map showed where reports would be expected but had not been recorded. This allowed for targeted outreach activity to be coordinated (Lincolnshire PCC, 2019).

Conclusion

Rural Proofing

Including, Not Excluding or Forgetting

The changes and improvements described in this chapter demand commitment and political will. Social workers can and will be very important in exerting pressure to achieve these changes, but commitment and influence also need to come from other major agencies involved in safeguarding young people: central governments, devolved governments, health boards, police services, schools and local authorities. One significant means towards achieving and speeding up change will come from routine insistence that policy and practice need to be 'rural-proofed' in all aspects of the safeguarding of children and young people.

Parliamentary proposals, policies and continuing political developments designed to 'rural-proof' legislation and policy in the UK, in many different policy areas, do not currently appear to do this (ACRE, 2020). Surely, the time is overdue that they did.

References

Action for Communities in Rural England. (2020). *Report Reveals How Government Is Failing to Adequately Address Rural Needs*. Accessed July 28, 2022, from https://acre.org.uk/report-reveals-how-government-is-failing-to-adequately-address-rural-needs/

Action for Communities in Rural England (ACRE). (2021). *Safeguarding: Information Sheet 5*. Accessed July 28, 2022, from https://acre.org.uk/wp-content/uploads/safeguarding.jpg

Allwood, L. (2020). *The Space Between Us: Children's Mental Health and Wellbeing in Isolated Areas*. Centre for Mental Health.

Annan, S. (2006). Sexual Violence in Rural Areas: A Review of the Literature. *Family & Community Health, 29*(3), 164–168.

Atkar, S., Baldwin, N., Ghataora, R., & Thanki, V. (2000). Promoting Effective Family Support and Child Protection for Asian Children, Chapter 21. In N. Baldwin (Ed.), *Protecting Children: Promoting Their Rights*. Whiting & Birch.

Averill, J. B., Padilla, A. O., & Clements, P. T. (2007). Frightened in Isolation: Unique Considerations for Research of Sexual Assault and Interpersonal Violence in Rural Areas. *Journal of Forensic Nursing, 3*(1), 42–46.

Baldwin, N., & Carruthers, L. (1998). *Developing Neighbourhood Support and Child Protection Strategies: The Henley Safe Children Project* (Routledge Revivals). 1st Edition

Baldwin, N., & Carruthers, L. (2000). Family Support Strategies: The Henley Project. In N. Baldwin (Ed.), *Protecting Children: Promoting Their Rights*. Whiting & Birch.

Black, N., Scott, K., & Shucksmith, M. (2019). Social Inequalities in Rural England: Impacts on Young People Post-2008. *Journal of Rural Studies, 68*, 264–275.

Clyde, J. (1992). *The Report of the Inquiry into the Removal of Children from Orkney in February 1991*. HMSO.

Evans-Thompson, C., Brooks, M., & Green, S. (2017). *Child Sexual Abuse and Rural Areas*. American Counselling Association.

Fabiansson, C. (2015). Young People's Societal Belonging and Perception of Social Status Within Networks. *Rural Society, 24*(1), 85–105.

Farrer & Co. (2019). *Children on the Rural Estate*. Accessed July 27, 2022, from https://www.farrer.co.uk/news-and-insights/children-on-the-rural-estate/

Hepworth, I., & McGowan, L. (2013). Do Mental Health Professionals Enquire About Childhood Sexual Abuse During Routine Mental Health Assessment in Acute Mental Health Settings? A Substantive Literature Review. *Journal of Psychiatric and Mental Health Nursing, 20*(6), 473–483.

Hughes, E., Lucock, M., & Brooker, C. (2019). Sexual Violence and Mental Health Services: A Call to Action. *Epidemiology and Psychiatric Sciences, 28*(6), 594–597.

Jay, A. (2014). *Independent Inquiry into Child Sexual Exploitation in Rotherham (1997-2013)*. Rotherham Metropolitan Borough Council.

Kenyon-George, L. G. (2017). Treating Child Sexual Abuse in Rural Communities. In *Information Resources Management Association, Gaming and Technology Addiction: Breakthroughs in Research and Practice*. ICI.

Lenz, T. (2019, June 26). The Challenges of Tackling County Lines in a Rural Area. *Community Care*. Accessed July 28, 2022, from https://www.communitycare.co.uk/2019/06/26/challenges-tackling-county-lines-rural-area/

Lewis, S. (2003). *Sexual Abuse in Rural Communities*. Accessed July 29, 2022, from http://vawnet.org/sites/default/files/materials/files/2016-09/AR_RuralSA.pdf

Lincolnshire PCC. (2019) *Lincolnshire Has Been Highlighted as the "Leading Edge"*. Accessed July 28, 2022, from https://lincolnshire-pcc.gov.uk/news-archive/2019/lincolnshire-has-been-highlighted-as-the-leading-edge-in-a-national-domestic-abuse-in-rural-areas-report/

Logan, T., Evans, L., Stevenson, E., & Jordan, C. (2005). Barriers to Services for Rural and Urban Survivors of Rape. *Journal of Interpersonal Violence, 20*(5), 591–616.

May, J., Williams, A., Cloke, P., & Cherry, L. (2020). Still Bleeding: The Variegated Geographies of Austerity and Food Banking in Rural England and Wales. *Journal of Rural Studies, 79*, 409–424.

Menard, K., & Ruback, B. (2003). Prevalence and Processing of Child Sexual Abuse: A Multi-Data-Set Analysis of Urban and Rural Counties. *Law and Human Behavior, 27*(4), 385–402.

Moodie, K., & Vaswani, N. (2016). *Evaluation of Safer Choices Missing Service*. CYCJ. Accessed July 28, 2022, from https://cycj.org.uk/wp-content/uploads/2016/10/Safer-Choices-Evaluation.pdf

National Audit Office. (2015). *Welfare Reform - Lessons Learned*. Accessed July 27, 2022, from https://www.nao.org.uk/report/welfare-reform-lessons-learned/

National Crime Agency. (2019). *County lines Drug Supply Vulnerability and Harm 2018*. NCA. Accessed from https://www.nationalcrimeagency.gov.uk/who-we-are/publications/257-county-lines-drug-supply-vulnerability-and-harm-2018/file

National Rural Crime Network. (2019). *Captive & Controlled – Domestic Abuse in Rural Areas*. Accessed July 28, 2022, from https://www.nationalrural-crimenetwork.net/news/captivecontrolled/

Nelson, S. (1987). *Incest Fact and Myth*. Stramullion.

Nelson, S. (2016a). From Rediscovery to Suppression? In *Tackling Child Sexual Abuse: Radical Approaches to Prevention, Protection and Support*, Chapter 1 (pp. 41–42). Policy Press.

Nelson, S. (2016b). Producing Radical Change in Mental Health. In *Tackling Child Sexual Abuse: Radical Approaches to Prevention, Protection and Support*, Chapter 8. Policy Press.

Nelson, S. (2016c). Community Prevention of CSA. In *Tackling Child Sexual Abuse: Radical Approaches to Prevention, Protection and Support, Chapter 6*. Policy Press.

Nelson, S., & Baldwin, N. (2004). The Craigmillar Project: Neighbourhood Mapping to Improve Children's Safety from Sexual Crime. *Child Abuse Review, 13*(6), 415–425.

Orr, D. (2021). *Child Protection in the 21st Century: A Role for Contextual Safeguarding*. IRISS Insight 60. Accessed July 28, 2022, from https://www.iriss.org.uk/resources/insights/child-protection-21st-century-role-contextual-safeguarding

Poinasamy, K. (2013). *The True Cost of Austerity and Inequality: UK Case Study*. Oxfam. Accessed July 29, 2022, from https://www-cdn.oxfam.org/s3fs-public/file_attachments/cs-true-cost-austerity-inequality-uk-120913-en_0.pdf

Pugh, R. (2007). Dual Relationships: Personal and Professional Boundaries in Rural Social Work. *British Journal of Social Work, 37*(8), 1405–1423.

Pugh, R., & Cheers, B. (2010). The Social Dynamics of Small Communities. In R. Pugh & B. Cheers (Eds.), *Rural Social Work: International Perspectives*. Policy Press.

Race. (2020). *How the Net Closed on Oxford's Grooming Gang*. BBC News, 13 March. Accessed July 28, 2022, from https://www.bbc.co.uk/news/uk-england-oxfordshire-51467518

Sayid, K. (2017). *The Top 20 Best Places to Bring Up Kids in Britain According to Quality of Life Survey*. Mirror, 14 October. Accessed July 27, 2022, from https://www.mirror.co.uk/news/uk-news/top-20-best-places-bring-11339572

Scotland's Commissioner for Children and Young People (SCCYP). (2011). *Scotland: A Safe Place for Child Traffickers? A Scoping Study*. SCCYP& UHI. Accessed July 28, 2022, from https://childhub.org/sites/default/files/library/attachments/1214_sccyp_child_trafficking_report_original.pdf

Social Work Inspection Agency. (2005). *An Inspection into the Care and Protection of Children in Eilean Siar (Western Isles)*. Scottish Executive.

The Alexi Project. (2017). *Evaluation of the Alexi Project 'Hub and Spoke' Programme of CSE Service Development: Final Report*. Accessed July 27, 2022, from https://www.beds.ac.uk/media/87236/final-report-alexi-project-evaluation.pdf

The Children's Society. (2022). *County Lines in the Countryside*. The Children's Society.

The Scottish Government. (2015). *Community Empowerment (Scotland) Act 2015, Parts 2 & 3*. Accessed July 27, 2022, from https://www.legislation.gov.uk/asp/2015/6/contents/enacted

The Scottish Government. (2016). *Scottish Government Urban Rural Classification 2016*. Accessed July 28, 2022, from https://www.gov.scot/publications/scottish-government-urban-rural-classification-2016/pages/2/#:~:text=(1)%20Large%20Urban%20Areas%20%2D,Areas%20%2D%20populations%20less%20than%203%2C000

The Scottish Government. (2018). *Islands (Scotland) Act 2018*. Accessed July 27, 2022, from https://www.legislation.gov.uk/asp/2018/12/enacted

Tranter, D. (2005). Breaking the Connection Between Traditional Masculinity and Violence: Toward a Context and Gender-Sensitive Approach to Counselling Males. In K. Brownlee & J. R. Graham (Eds.), *Violence in the Family: Social Work Readings and Research from Northern and Rural Canada* (pp. 105–118). Canadian Scholars Press.

Turbett, C. (2009). Tensions in the Delivery of Social Work Services in Rural and Remote Scotland. *British Journal of Social Work, 39*(3), 506–521.

Welsh Women's Aid. (2020). *Briefing: Rurality and VAWDASV*. Welsh Women's Aid. Accessed July 28, 2022, from https://www.welshwomensaid.org.uk/wp-content/uploads/2020/05/Rurality-and-VAWDASV.pdf

12

Final Words: Social Work and Rural Communities—Reflections and Ways Forward

Jane Pye and Colin Turbett

Introduction

We hope readers with a rural interest and engagement have been stimulated by the chapters in these pages. We believe these offer not just a fresh perspective on themes covered in previous rural social work literature, but some new ones that are original and innovative. These, we believe, are crucial given concerns about climate change, sustainability and the post-COVID world we share. In this final chapter we highlight emerging themes from the book and outline some challenges for the future of social work in rural communities and finally some possibilities for consideration.

Whilst rural social work in the UK has been characterised generally by an absence of formal recognition, some of the problematic issues that

J. Pye (✉)
Bowland North, Lancaster University, Bailrigg, Lancaster, Lancashire, UK
e-mail: j.pye4@lancaster.ac.uk

C. Turbett
Shiskine, Isle of Arran, UK
e-mail: ctur282388@aol.com

297

emerge through the various chapters are reflective of a neoliberal managerial driven centralisation and emphasis on procedure that has pervaded the profession for more than twenty years. It should be no surprise that in the UK such trends were bound to be universal—the uniformity that accompanied them ensured that different approaches to social work would be subsumed by ones considered tried and tested, that fitted prevailing agendas. These included the reduction of social work to a prime concern with the assessment of risk, a move away from generally supportive and preventative practice, and growing invisibility within communities.

Some of this, which was embedded in social work education, was welcomed by a beleaguered profession such as the move towards specialised practice. This turn away from the generic models that were celebrated in the international rural social work literature in the past did not sit well with many rural practitioners (Turbett, 2010). However, that ship has sailed, and specialised practice is now almost universal, although its application varies, and opportunity for approaches that are closer to communities will always be there, hence the focus throughout this book. Perhaps the tide is now turning: dissatisfaction with social work as practised within statutory settings seems now to feature in most change agendas: there is a recognition that the profession is quite demoralised with a high turnover of staff, poor public image and a failure to stem the growing weight of intractable caseloads (Miller & Barrie, 2022). Never-ending austerity means that workers and their managers are expected to keep costs as low as possible. These factors are as applicable in rural settings as in urban ones in the UK. Our final chapter will focus on the major currents of the book and offer some thoughts on the future of rural social work.

Emerging Themes

The chapters in this book have all demonstrated in diverse ways, the original hypothesis in Chap. 1 that social work in rural communities is different, and in our view constitutes a specialism worthy of more recognition than it currently receives. We broke this book up into thematic chapters so a review of emergent themes should follow that pathway.

Stigma

Chapters 2, 3 and 4 focus respectively on the worker's experience in settings where invisibility and anonymity are significant issues, the impact of problematic drug and alcohol use, and the experience of being a member of a marginalised and commonly discriminated against community. These chapters are varied in content: from issues for workers and their families, to experiences arising from a society that creates pressures that might lead to harmful dependency for those who have simply been born into adversity. The commonality here is that in a small community, relationships are difficult to avoid, and judgements are made by one person about another that can be harmful. As we will see in other chapters the closeness and mutual dependency of a rural community can also be an asset.

For the worker, stigma and its effects in the sense described by Gillian Ritch (Chap. 2) may not be an issue for a model of practice delivered from outside (as seems increasingly to be the case whether or not this is due to distance and remoteness), but our contention is that real understanding of the dynamics of rurality should be based on community knowledge and networking that are best developed from within. This does not mean that the worker has to live in the community being looked after (a dispersed patch would make this an impossibility anyway), but it does mean they need to be immersed enough inside it to be a known source of support. The word *stigma* has negative associations, and many social workers will feel that this is something they carry wherever they work because of their role, or the role usually expected of them in statutory settings (as commented upon elsewhere in this chapter).

In a rural community the immersion described should work alongside a building of personal respect, a process that takes time and care (Pugh, 2000; Turbett, 2010). The outcome sought is one of a breakdown of stigmatic association and the building of positive relationships not just with individuals but with communities that are associated with care and support. This certainly resonates with the chapters in this book concerning actual practice on the ground (well exemplified in Chap. 8 on working with people in outdoor spaces). That is an outcome we would want to emerge from this book—the development of practice styles and approaches that break down the undoubted stigma of social work.

Heather Still's Chap. 3 on addiction issues in rural Scotland discusses the experience of individuals who suffer and those who care for them: one beset with stigma that takes shape in denial and the consequent absence of support. She also refers to 'gossip' as a particularly negative feature of communities where there is little invisibility, a contributory factor to stigma. This is a theme discussed in the rural social work literature past and present (Cheers, 1998; Pugh & Cheers, 2010; Daley, 2021). Harmful gossip based on misinformation can be challenged if undertaken carefully without breaching confidentiality—a possibility if not a duty, requiring consent and negotiation (Martinez-Brawley, 2000). The aim here, as in good social work generally, is to reduce stigma through systematic relationship-based interventions agreed with the person (or persons) at the centre.

Chapter 4, authored by Allison Hulmes and Peter Unwin, focuses on some of the most maligned and mistreated communities in rural Britain—Travellers and Romanies. This is full of the impact of unwarranted stigma but based on long-standing and, at least in the past, institutional prejudice and discrimination. The authors start by suggesting that these prejudices will almost certainly exist amongst social workers and those others in officialdom who encounter these communities. As with the chapter on addiction issues, the authors highlight how idealised perceptions of rurality both conceal and reinforce stigma. Again, the role of the social worker in the rural community should be to support efforts to end the marginalisation that threatens different cultures generally and the way in which prejudice is manifested in the treatment of individuals. This, as the authors insist in both Chaps. 3 and 4, should be based on awareness and understanding. The long-standing role of social work to be anti-discriminatory requires special attention in the rural setting.

Environment

COP26 in Glasgow in November 2021 highlighted issues that urgently confront humanity. Sustainability is now a concept most people will have heard of even if its practice seems patchy on both an individual and an institutional basis. This underlies Chaps. 5, 6 and 7.

Lena Dominelli's Chap. 5 provides a globally inspired account of what she describes as *rurbanisation*—the introduction of urban land and housing practices into rural spaces that have eroded the landscape and damaged the natural environment. She argues passionately (and in tune with the environmentalists and environmental disaster=victims whose voices were heard at COP26) that rural landscapes should be far more than playgrounds or escape avenues for urban dwellers. Social workers, she argues, have a role in advocating for the environment as they support those who fall foul of rurbanisation—she offers a model of green social work practice. Genericism suits such approaches and she contends, in keeping with the premise of this book, that such broadening of skills is found more readily in rural practice.

Writing from the perspective of a social worker living on a farm, Tina Laurie continues the green social work theme in Chap. 6. As with other authors in the book, she separates the rural idyll from the actuality of living in a landscape, managed, for better or worse, by human beings. This touches on alcohol, food production, food poverty and the themes described in the previous chapter as rurbanisation. With a focus on practice, she examines how the landscape is full of possibilities for innovative strategies that tackle such issues alongside those who are left behind by agendas driven by the wealth and requirements of urban dwellers.

In contrast, Jane Pye's contribution in Chap. 7 to this section looks at the digital revolution in communication and how this can both help and hinder rural practice (a theme so significant in this book that we discuss it separately). Such new ways of working involve a reframing of how we relate to the environment and how we might use digital technology to overcome issues of geography and distance. As mentioned in the two previous chapters, such innovation has allowed wealthy individuals with second homes to work in urban environments whilst enjoying rural beauty—pushing up house prices, gentrifying the countryside and further marginalising the elderly, the young and others who are poor. The author focuses on the needs and requirements of the 'travelling practitioner' and how unfamiliar mediums might enhance practice and save on the wasteful use of resources. However, she is clear that we are still at a stage where inequalities of access and control prevent universal use and that critical debates are yet to take place around the extension of digital technology. She contends, in line with themes running throughout the book, that relationships remain central to good social work and that these are based on real rather than virtual contacts between people.

Chapter 8 offers a practitioner's take on a project designed to use a natural rural environment to work with individuals and families in an imaginative way, using some of the community social work approaches discussed in Chap. 1. Karin Eyben, a community worker, and Carla McLaughlin, a social worker, provide a very personal account that describes their learning, as well as some first-hand witness from the people who were subject of their interventions. These examples are the sort of rural social work stories, rich in content, that offer a worthy substitute for the lack of formal research we, and other contributors, have identified elsewhere in the book (see further discussion on this cross-cutting theme).

Community

The final themed section of the book brings together very real practice issues for social work that are affected by rurality and which we have grouped in Chaps. 9, 10 and 11 under the umbrella term 'community'.

The first of these, by Colin Turbett (Chap. 9), concerns masculinity and patriarchy and their place in the shaping of rural communities. As with other content this is set against a background of the idealised rural idyll, a mask often for oppressive family relationships. These create a variety of adverse experiences, from domestic violence to mental health problems, that social workers may be required to address. Ingrained attitudes lead also to racism and homophobia—matters discussed in Chaps. 1 and 4. Whilst such issues are not unique to rural communities, they have been sustained by employment patterns and cultural traditions. As with other chapters, the generalist skills of the rural social worker are discussed in relation to tackling such issues. The personal behaviours of the worker might also be significant in settings where there is increased community scrutiny, again a theme echoed in Chap. 2 and elsewhere in the book.

Chapter 10, by Becky Squires, takes a broad and considered look at how services are provided to disabled elderly people in rural communities, offering useful practice examples. Her view of the components of good relationship-based rural practice contains elements found elsewhere in the book and is based on a thorough understanding of the dynamics and possibilities within rural communities: local knowledge, social action and cultural prejudice (in this case ageism). Becky Squires also confronts issues of professional misjudgement and avoidance, themes echoed in the other two chapters in this section. Becky also introduces the idea of social pedagogy as an approach that fits rural settings—indeed one of the principal practical theorists she quotes, Paulo Freire, undertook much of his work in rural areas of Brazil. She also discusses the social model of disability, a notion discussed in other chapters: contending that many of the issues social workers deal with are constructed from an interchange between society and the environment.

Chapter 11, looking at sexual abuse in the rural context, continues the theme of harmful relationships that are often accepted as part of rural culture, and their potential to ruin lives. Sarah Nelson brings to this her long experience of examining this subject in detail, including her scrutiny of the remote rural Orkney events of the early 1990s. She (as with Chap. 9) contends that the generalist skills found amongst rural social workers should help them overcome the fears of working in this difficult area. She also, and very usefully, details support and methods grounded in research and experience, including facing up to the challenge of invisibility and denial of the issue—again a theme that resonates with other chapters. One subject not evident in Sarah Nelson's previous principal literature is that of the impact of digital technology on children and new risks to their welfare and safety—a matter of significance separately discussed in the next section.

Key Cross-Cutting Themes

Three themes are repeated across chapters and are worthy of key theme status in this book. The first of these concerns the refrain of absence of interest in rural social work in the UK sufficient to produce research—the significance of **Stories as Data**. This is not a new theme and mention is made of the implications of missing out on the richness of rural life through narratives in Chap. 10, quoting the work of Ginsberg (1998) and Pugh and Cheers (2010). The work of Cheers describing practice in rural Australia is full of such accounts that provide background and context to his practice suggestions (Cheers, 1998). Other chapters offer strong evidence that rural practitioners have stories to tell that should be regarded as an evidence base for a rethink about service design and practice. Indeed this book arose, as explained in Chap. 1, from the sharing of such stories amongst a group that came together in Scotland to create a current on rural social work. The idea that stories as data are of significance is a matter apparently unexplored in UK social work literature but does appear in a medical journal article (Bleakely, 2005) and more general accounts of narrative methods in social research (Goodson et al., 2012). Chapter 2 provides strong material about the experience of working and living in the same place (a common feature of working in remote settings) collected by a social worker from colleagues. We would suggest that the gathering of such narratives would form a useful basis for practitioner or post-graduate research and in the process make an impact on the recognition of rural social work practice in the UK. The importance of such stories lies in the idea of *practice wisdom* discussed in the opening chapter—a factor in social work not unique to the rural context, but the evidence in this book suggests that its value can be found in the narratives of its actors.

The second recurrent theme flows from mentions of the impact of **Digital Technology** and the **Digital Revolution**, the particular subject of Chap. 7. As Jane Pye's Chap. 7 points out, whilst perhaps inevitable, the trend was accelerated by COVID and has forced workers to use digital communication mediums such as Zoom, MS Teams and WhatsApp that were unfamiliar to many prior to March 2020. This was accompanied by forced working from home and a reduction in office use, again a trend that was in increasing evidence over the preceding decade and not always welcomed: a Guardian Newspaper and Social Work England survey in 2020 into work-life balance for social workers found that for many, stress levels had increased through the blurring of boundaries between work and family life and the absence of collegial and supervisory support (Guardian Online, 2020). For rural social workers, distance suddenly ceased to be the issue it had been: as Jane Pye suggests, this had obvious benefits, not least for time management. However, whilst the digital revolution has, for better or worse, introduced new ways of working, it has also brought changes in the communities in which we work. As Colin Turbett points out in Chap. 9, they have, to some extent, negated rural and urban differences. However, they have also increased risks to the vulnerable and these are explored in some detail in Sarah Nelson's Chap. 11 in relation to children. Whilst highlighting these risks, Sarah also locates possibilities for asset building, utilising the strengths within rural communities, which might mitigate them—useful suggestions applicable to other vulnerable groups within rural communities. We have to remind ourselves, as Heather Still does in Chap. 3, that new levels of disadvantage and inequality might occur through the fact that some cannot, and may never, use the new technologies—a matter to remain mindful of as we get caught up in the digital revolution.

The third recurrent theme throughout the book is that of **community**—a subject given prominence in the first chapter where we outlined *Community Social Work* as a model that addressed issues in a way that fitted with the multiple definitions and descriptions of rurality described. We believe that approaches to work that involve an understanding of community are central to practice for individual rural practitioners, the services they work within and those who determine policy at local and national levels. Some aspects of this such as 'rural proofing' are discussed in the opening chapter.

How can we approach the dual task of challenging the hegemony of individualisation in mainstream social work in the UK whilst raising awareness of how community social work offers something different? A realistic proposition here is that we have to find ways to work with the values and philosophy of community social work (CSW) *within* the individual casework model that dominates social work practice (Fenton, 2019). This is not to be defeatist about the possibility of changing the entire way social work is practised in the UK; it is instead to recognise we have to be realistic. It seems to us that the most obvious place to start disrupting the dominant narrative of casework is in social work education. Dominelli (2007, p. 35) calls for social work educators to be 'inspirational' within the context of what social work is now overwhelmingly framed to be. On a very basic level, social work qualifying programmes must cover rural social work and CSW to ensure that newly qualified social workers recognise the difference between working in rural and urban areas and how in rural settings practice must involve communities. Educators must ensure student social workers understand the macro picture of social work so that they can critically locate individuals, families and groups within the broader structural factors that are impacting their lives. This is courageous and complex but will result in ethical and effective practice. It could be that we also develop post qualifying programmes to support the understanding of this way of working for existing social work such as the post-graduate programme 'Social Work and Community Development Approaches' available in Northern Ireland (NISCC—Northern Ireland Social Care Council), 2020). One of the authors reflects often on a discussion with a manager in a local children's services setting in which the author privately acknowledged concerns about whether remaining focused on teaching aspirational social work was actually disadvantaging social work students because when they moved into qualified practice, they often found a culture of practice focused entirely on individuals and framed the problems these individuals faced as entirely their own. The response from the manager was remarkable; she passionately stated that once social work educators stop teaching from a perspective of what social work should be, we will experience complete capitulation towards a neoliberal, managerial and oppressive profession.

Those of us working in education or who have any kind of influence must support others to understand that an individualised casework or case management approach is not the only model of social work practice and all social workers must be educated to understand how this model is shaped and influenced by political ideology (Dominelli, 2007). Keeping CSW firmly on the agenda, even if in educational terms it is simply to serve to disrupt the hegemonic narrative around individualisation and pathologisation, is essential. Rural social workers are the natural leaders and experts in this area and should be invited into social work educational settings to share their knowledge, skills and expertise with students and social work researchers. Some suggest that it is the role of the academy to start the critical discussions that are needed when thinking through how we conceptualise social work (Higgins, 2015) and the impact of politics on what social work becomes. Clearly (2018) proposes that a community of concerned people must come together to act in response to this and we would argue here that it is essential that people with expertise and experience in community approaches are included. This will inevitably mean the inclusion of locally focused rural social workers.

Final Words

The various chapters in this book have offered proof that rural social work practice is alive and well and that beyond the urban settings that dominate in the UK, there are vibrant ideas and experiences to place it firmly on the map and take it forward in all four nations. However, to foster its growth, macro-changes are required to practice and education across social work generally. There can be no doubt that social work education in the UK is an obvious place to include awareness-raising about what community-orientated practice (including community social work), which is fundamental to rural social work, is and can be. However, there are thousands of social workers across the UK who are unlikely to have any firm connections to social work educational institutions. Student social workers all have to spend significant amounts of time in practice placement during their education and a much-heard comment from social work teams who are open to social work students joining them on placement is how students bring with them a freshness and new perspective into teams. Whilst not suggesting that students should be responsible for sharing and debating contemporary thinking about social work practice, teams could harness students' thoughts and invite comments and thus gain access to what students have been taught and their thoughts about social work.

Realistically, the workload and working conditions of many social workers mean that they have little opportunity and time for critical reflection about what social work actually is and could be. But, there are inspirational leaders and professional bodies in social work who can help us all as a profession to ask critical questions about the future of what ethical and effective practice looks like. There are also people within social work who can provide creative ideas for individuals who do feel dissatisfied with the direction of social work practice. For example, the work of Fenton (2019) provides ideas that are realistic and tangible for individuals to incorporate into their practice which enables them to work in a way that does acknowledge the wider issues in social work than just that of the individual: for example, focusing on building relationships, thinking critically and developing moral courage in practice (Fenton, 2019). As social workers we all know the value of positive team culture and solidarity. These principles have allowed this edited collection to be developed through the coming together of people with a passion for rural social work practice: we have shared a commitment to build relationships with each other, to think critically when writing our chapters and have the courage to put on paper our views and beliefs about social work in rural settings. Through this, we have demonstrated that it is possible to critically explore rural social work from a contemporary perspective and, in doing so, prompt thinking about social work practice generally within the UK. We very much hope that others will do the same.

References

Bleakely, A. (2005). Stories as Data, Data as Stories: Making Sense of Narrative Enquiry in Clinical Education. *Medical Education, 39,* 534–540.

Cheers, B. (1998). *Welfare Bushed – Social Care in Rural Australia.* Ashgate.

Clearly, T. (2018). Social Work Education and the Marketisation of UK Universities. *British Journal of Social Work, 48,* 2253–2271.

Daley, M. (2021). *Rural Social Work in the 21st Century – Serving Individuals, Families and Communities in the Countryside.* OUP.

Dominelli, L. (2007). Contemporary Challenges to Social Work Education in the United Kingdom. *Australian Social Work, 60*(1), 29–45.

Fenton, J. (2019). *Social Work for Lazy Radicals.* Bloomsbury.

Ginsberg, L. (Ed.). (1998). *Social Work in Rural Communities* (3rd ed.). CSWE.

Goodson, F., Loveless, A., & Stephens, D. (2012). *Explorations in Narrative Research.* Rotterdam.

Guardian Online (22nd September 2020). *'Nine at Night and My Laptop Is Still Open' – Social Work in a Pandemic.* Accessed December 2022, from https://www.theguardian.com/society/2020/sep/22/nine-at-night-laptop-still-open-social-work-pandemic

Higgins, M. (2015). The Struggle for the Soul of Social Work in England. *Social Work Education, 34*(1), 4–16.

Martinez-Brawley, E. (2000). *Close to Home – Human Services and the Small Community.* NASW Press.

Miller, M. & Barrie, K. (2022). *Setting the Bar.* Social Work Scotland. Accessed August 2022, from https://socialworkscotland.org/reports/settingthebar/

NISCC (Northern Ireland Social Care Council). (2020). *Professional in Practice Approved Programmes [Online].* Accessed August 30, 2022, from https://niscc.info/app/uploads/2020/12/PIP-Approved-Programmes.pdf

Pugh, R. (2000). Rural Social Work Russel House.

Pugh, R., & Cheers, B. (2010). *Rural Social Work: An International Perspective.* Policy Press.

Turbett, C. (2010). *Rural Social Work Practice in Scotland.* Venture Press.

Index

Printed by Printforce, United Kingdom